More Than Just a Game

One Hundred Years of Organized Sport in Prince Edward Island, 1850–1950

More Than Just a Game

One Hundred Years of Organized Sport in Prince Edward Island, 1850-1950

CHARLIE BALLEM

THE ACORN PRESS
Charlottetown
2004

More Than Just a Game:
One Hundred Years of Organized Sport in Prince Edward Island, 1850–1950

ISBN 1-894838-08-4

Editing: Ed MacDonald, Harry Baglole, Michael Hennessey, Laurie Brinklow
Manuscript preparation: Shirley Wheaton, Laura Lee Howard
Cover and Interior Design: Paul Vienneau, Goose Lane Editions
Printed in Canada by AGMV Marquis

This publication was made possible through the generous support of Millennium Bureau of Canada, Partnership Program; and the Department of Community and Cultural Affairs, Government of Prince Edward Island. The Acorn Press gratefully acknowledges the support of The Canada Council for the Arts' Emerging Publisher Program and the Institute of Island Studies at the University of Prince Edward Island.

All proceeds from the sale of this book go to KidSport™ Fund of PEI.

National Library of Canada Cataloguing in Publication

Ballem, H. Charles
More than just a game : one hundred years of organized sport in Prince Edward Island, 1850-1950 / Charles Ballem.

Includes index.
Co-published by: Sport PEI.
ISBN 1-894838-08-4

1. Sports—Prince Edward Island—History—19th century.
2. Sports—Prince Edward Island—History—20th century. I. Sport P.E.I. Inc. II. Title.

GV585.3.P75B34 2004 796'.09717 C2003-906648-7

A co-publication of

THE ACORN PRESS
PO Box 22024
Charlottetown, Prince Edward Island
Canada C1A 9J2
www.acornpresscanada.com

and

SPORT PEI
P.O. Box 302
Charlottetown, Prince Edward Island
Canada C1A 7K7
www.sportpei.pe.ca

To my five grandchildren:

Lilly (Ballem) Gillespie,
Jessie & Jonah Jay, &
Jackson & Malcolm Jay Walling

Table of Contents

Foreword

Prince Edward Island has as rich and diversified a sports history as most areas triple its size anywhere in the world. The "game" is part and parcel of Island people, and, whether they realize it or not, almost every effort to do anything has always had some element of competition to it. This segment of Island life has fostered a heritage of sporting competition that now ranges through the past three centuries of our history.

Capturing all the elements of Prince Edward Island's sporting past has been a challenge undertaken by a native son whose interest in the topic has previously led to the recovery, preservation, and publishing of segments of valuable information on historical Island athletic endeavours.

H. Charles "Charlie" Ballem has earned a lifetime record of participation, teaching, and leading by example in the field of recreation and athletics. A dedicated researcher with a reputation for seeking and preserving facts rather than hearsay, he was the logical individual to pursue the information leading to documenting the history of organized sport on Prince Edward Island. In 1986 Charlie published *Abegweit Dynasty, The Story of the Abegweit Amateur Athletic Association, 1899–1954*, a rich local story that is a factual base of sports information.

What Charlie Ballem has uncovered in this publication represents the early era of our sporting history that, now preserved, becomes the legacy of sportsmanship for today's Islanders and future generations to follow.

RON H. ATKINSON, Charlottetown
Sportsman and Author of *A Treasure Called Belvedere*

Acknowledgements

A research project that covers a century of our sport/social history, 1850 to 1950, requires the collective efforts, intellect, and resources of many people. Now, after four years of research, writing, and collaborating with athletes, coaches, academics, and sport buffs across the province, I am humbled by the magnitude of the undertaking and the willingness of so many to help make it happen. Without the wholehearted support and contribution of people across the Island, this project would not have succeeded.

And the story is not finished. Rather, it is my persistent expectation that others will pursue this research further, uncovering the rich sport and cultural history that still remains hidden.

It is now time to express thanks to a very large number of people who contributed in such meaningful ways to the project. First and foremost to Dave MacNeill who recognized the importance of a research project on the history of sport in our province and committed the administrative resource of Sport PEI to the effort. Without such a strong endorsement the project would have foundered on the proverbial rocks of good intentions.

Moral support and encouragement came from my wife, Joyce, whose creative energy was always forthcoming when needed most. And, to

Shirley Wheaton, my administrative assistant at Dalhousie University, whose expertise and enthusiasm for the project never wavered.

My experience with the "A-Team," that front-line group of researchers, was most gratifying, their initiative and eagerness to search out information and to piece together the bigger picture demonstrated an unselfish commitment to the project. They are Charlie Gillis, Ron Atkinson, Paul H. Schurman, Fran Sark, Cletus Dunn, Joe Coyle, Dick Carroll, Donna Collings, Barb Morgan, Chester Gillan, and Dick MacLean. Others who filled in the gaps with specific knowledge and information included Cathy Hennessey, Ron Legere, Kathy Meagher, Brian MacMillan, Renée (Grebbers) Arsenault, Perley Hardy, Kay Wood, Waldron Leard, Wilf McCluskey, Garth Vaughan, the late Reg MacAdam, George and Anne Morrison, Aquinas Ryan, Parker Lund, Dr. Bobby Lund, John Hughes, Fred "Fiddler" MacDonald, John Likely, Wendell Horton, Aquinas Ryan, Cecil MacPhail, Jennifer Ballem, Frank Zakem, Doug Cameron, Buster Dutney, Vince McIntyre, and numerous others who provided pictures, scrapbooks, and related sources that helped create images of our distant past.

Behind the scene there are people and organizations who brought resources to the task and greatly facilitated the process: The Millennium Bureau of Canada, Partnership Program; the School of Health and Human Performance, Dalhousie University; Marilyn Bell and the staff at the Public Archives and Records Office; the Department of Community and Cultural Affairs; the PEI Sports Hall of Fame; the New Brunswick Sports Hall of Fame; the Nova Scotia Sports Hall of Fame; the PEI School Athletic Association; and UPEI Athletics Department.

And, finally, there is that essential group, the editors, who so willingly gave of their expertise to refine, clarify, and interpret the manuscript. To Dr. Edward MacDonald, Laurie Brinklow, Michael Hennessey, and Harry Baglole, it was a tedious task, and I thank you for your forbearance.

Introduction

Embedded in the last two centuries of Prince Edward Island history are numerous episodes dealing with the development of organized sport, and the contribution sport has made to the social and cultural history of our province. The story is vibrant, revealing the achievements of Island athletes on the playing fields of the Island, to the ultimate athletic achievement in amateur sport: participation in the Olympic Games. The script is punctuated with accounts of athletic excellence, expressions of community pride, and the visionary leadership of men and women who recognized the value of sport as an integral component of community life. While history, at times, has a reluctance to reveal the past, the intruders who probe can gain insight into and an appreciation for a bygone era.

While it is acknowledged that the early inhabitants of the Island, First Nations people and European settlers, engaged in a variety of physical recreation activities and leisure pursuits — notably canoeing, horse racing, fishing, and ice skating — the focus of this book is on organized sport. Organized sport is characterized by several criteria that distinguish it from informal games, play, and recreational activities. These include rules to govern the activity, structure of competition, opportunity for participation by all levels of society, and the growth of organizations to organize competition and administer sport.

Upon applying the criteria to Prince Edward Island, only cricket and rifle shooting attained an identifiable level of organization during the mid-1880s. The Charlottetown Cricket Club formed in 1850 as the first urban sport club in the province, and the Provincial Rifle Association was organized in 1861.

Over the next several decades, sport gained a level of organization across the province that fostered inter-community rivalry, competition, and administrative leadership that constituted the elements of a sport delivery system. What transpired in the ensuing years is a story of athletic excellence by men and women who forged a sport legacy for Prince Edward Island that extends over 150 years.

CHARLIE BALLEM
Point Prim, Prince Edward Island

Part One

The advent of the "special train" on Prince Edward Island during the 1870s had a monumental impact on the development of organized sport across the province, and was a fascinating episode in the province's social and sporting history. (PARO 2320-28-2)

1

The Early Years

A Sense of Community

This story is about the development of organized sport on Prince Edward Island. From the rudimentary games and social activities of the early settlers to the highly structured, commercialized, and often contrived influences of modern day sport, the story is about athletic achievements, community pride, and perhaps the most significant, the contribution of sport as a catalyst for personal and community development. The story goes back to the early years of settlement on the "Île Saint-Jean" when opportunity for recreational activities were greatly inhibited by the frontier circumstances that existed. The pioneers faced many diverse problems during the early part of the 18th century as they struggled to establish new homes and a sense of community. Canoeing, fishing, and hunting undoubtedly brought moments of enjoyment to the participants; nevertheless, the primary purpose of such activity was utilitarian. And the folklore of the Mi'kmaq suggests a peaceful existence by their people prior to European settlers coming to the crescent-shaped Island. The lush vegetation, abundance of wildlife, and the bounty of the sea provided the inhabitants with the essential sustenance during their migratory lifestyle.

French explorer Jacques Cartier was the first European to visit the land of Abegweit, making land on the north side of the Island twice during the summer of 1534. The Island remained basically undisturbed for two hundred years, save for the visits of the Mi'kmaq and a few venturesome explorers. Permanent settlement took place on the Island after 1713, when, under the Treaty of Utrecht, mainland Acadia and most of Newfoundland were ceded to Great Britain, while Isle Royale and Île Saint-Jean remained under French jurisdiction. At the time of the first census in 1728, the population, all French, was listed at 326 people, dispersed over seven settlements. The largest gatherings were at St. Peters and at Port La Joye, which was located at the mouth of a natural harbour (Charlottetown) and the confluence of three rivers. The rivers, notably the East River, permitted easy access to the interior of the Island and facilitated the early settlement of Mt. Stewart and smaller communities along its banks. During the next twenty-five years, the Colony experienced a gradual population growth. By 1755, the census enumerated more than 4,400 persons, many of them refugees from the Expulsion of the Acadians on the mainland.

When war once again broke out between France and Britain in 1744, a period of political and social unrest developed in the region. For the inhabitants of Île Saint-Jean, the full impact of the war hit home in 1758 when the French fortress at Louisbourg fell to the British. Many of the Acadian settlers, anticipating the arrival of the British ships off Port La Joye, fled the Island for northern New Brunswick and Quebec; over 3,200 inhabitants, however, were rounded up by the British soldiers and deported to France. The one settlement to escape the deportation was Malpeque, inhabited by approximately 200 French settlers.[1]

The first domestic initiative taken by the British to colonize the Island was to carry out a detailed survey of the area to encourage land settlement and the fishery. The survey, conducted by Captain Samuel Holland in 1764–65, divided the Island into 67 townships and selected the sites for the three county capitals, including the future colonial capital, Charlottetown. Charles Morris, Chief Surveyor of Nova Scotia, drew up the plans for Charlottetown in 1768, and they were refined in 1771 by Governor Walter Patterson and his Surveyor General, Thomas Wright. The significance of the Wright/Patterson modification for sport and recreation was the addition to the plan of four green squares designated for play, recreation, and leisure pursuits. The squares still exist in Charlottetown, and undoubtedly represent the first land designated for sport and recreation on the Island.

The first half of the 19th century was one of rapid growth for the Colony, with a population increase from 2,000 in 1805 to over 80,000 by 1861. The main factor for growth was the steady stream of English,

Irish, and Scottish immigrants, and a few Loyalists who were displaced by the Revolutionary War in the United States. The new settlers, in effect, "filled up" the Island while remaining predominantly rural and dispersed. As the Colony took on the new "face" of settlement, institutions that characterize an emerging community appeared across the Island. Churches, schools, a mail service, banks, and other commercial entities collectively contributed to a sense of community. In this context, if certain spiritual, social, and commercial institutions comprised the prominent, visible appearance of a village or town, would it not be prudent to assert that other less conspicuous components of community life were equally essential to the cohesiveness and vitality of that community? Institutions referred to are those that constitute the intimate aspects of social life, cultural events, fraternal organizations, clan gatherings, recreation, and organized sport. Finley Martin raised such a query in his history of Montague, *A View from the Bridge,* when he mused, "It takes more than a few houses and stores to make up a community, but exactly what it does take is debatable."[2]

The emergence of sport as an integral part of Island society coincided with the rapid growth of the population from 1800 to 1865. Charlottetown was really the only urban centre, with the remainder of the population living in rural communities and small villages dispersed across the province. In this context it is reasonable to conclude that the initial recreational and sport activities of the people of the Island reflected a "transfer of culture," immigrants bringing to their new homes activities and sentimental attachments from a previous lifestyle. Skating, cricket, horse racing, rifle shooting, athletics, and clan gatherings, each significant in a former life, were now instituted as part of their new communities on Prince Edward Island.

Sport historians have basically agreed that sport developed in major urban centres in Canada during the mid-19th century, as a result of a cluster of factors, most notably urbanization, industrialization, and the "British influence." These factors are not disputable in the case of large cities; however, they do not account for a comparable development of sport in rural communities. In Prince Edward Island, where the population was mainly rural during the latter part of the century, sport emerged as a vital part of community life. S. F. Wise, in *Sport and Class Values in Old Ontario and Quebec*, concluded, "Sports and games have never been absent from Canadian life, not even from the small town — and were certainly not an exclusively urban preoccupation."[3]

By the middle of the 19th century, the societal/commercial conditions that existed on the Island fostered an interest in sport and recreation. Charlottetown was an urban centre with significant commercial activity in agricultural markets, shipbuilding, and lumber exports. It also supported a distinct social/occupational stratification — comprising an upper class of merchants, bankers, lawyers, physicians, and other citizens with political and military influence. A middle and working class also existed, although with less rigidity in their social mobility than in larger urban centres. This segment of the population eventually sought a meaningful involvement in recreation and leisure activities, and had a democratization effect on the profile of participants involved in organized sport. As an emerging community during the 1850s, Summerside reflected a different profile at this point in its transition from a rural to an urban community. During the shipbuilding and lumber export era, there was a disproportionately small upper class, due primarily to the nature of its workforce. Shipwrights, joiners, and carpenters attracted to the community by the "shipping" boom comprised a high percentage of the town's population, yet with little commitment to the development of the community.[4] Consequently, the period was not conducive to the development of sport and recreational activities for the permanent residents of the community.

When the shipbuilding boom sailed away during the late 1870s, Summerside became a market town and commercial centre for an expanding agricultural and fishery export market. Later, with a more stable demographic profile, organizations that promoted sport and recreational activities in the community appeared, notably the Young Men's Christian Association in 1874, the Reform Club as early as 1878, and the Summerside Amateur Athletic Association during the 1890s.

The first initiatives to organize recreational activities in Charlottetown came from the social elite of the community, who organized events primarily for their own pleasure. The Charlottetown Sleighing Club, later the Huntley and/or Tandem Sleighing Club, organized in Charlottetown in 1840 and was often the target of resentment from other citizens for its ostentatious rides through the streets of the city. The club would meet on Queen Square and consisted of some dozen sleighs "all handsomely furred and painted."

Led by His Excellency the Lieutenant-Governor, Sir Charles Fitzroy, "with his handsome, well-equipped and gaily caparisoned four in hand," the club drove through the city streets and "made the town quite lively with the tingling of the bells and the trampling of the steeds." *The Royal Gazette* commented in its December 15, 1840, issue

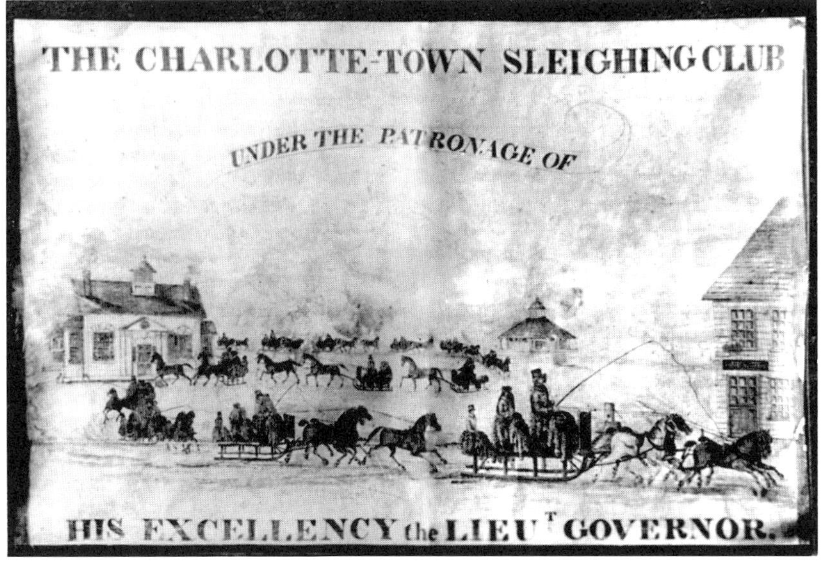

Horse sleighing was a popular recreation for the socially elite of Charlottetown during the 1830s and 1840s. The Charlottetown Club, later the Huntley and Tandem, regularly gathered on Queen Square to participate in sleigh rides through the city streets and adjoining countryside. (PARO HF78 72-6)

that "it becomes the Society of Charlottetown to meet in this way as it brings the inhabitants more frequently together, and produces a social and cordial feeling among them." This observation was not shared by all of the populace. The Opposition Club, representing a different level of society, soon made an appearance on the streets of Charlottetown. The club, which consisted of "young mechanics, gay, rollicking, devil-may-care sort of fellows," had ten or a dozen sleighs with horses not all of the highest breed; nevertheless, some were "showy bits of blood" and cantered in admirable spirit as if to show that the Huntley Club should not have all the sport their own way. On several occasions there were near collisions and confrontations between members of the two clubs as they engaged in their nightly rides. Such episodes reflected resentment towards the social elite of the city by members of the working class who sought the opportunity to participate in recreational activities and organized sport.

While social elitism as a criteria for participation in organized sport gradually diminished within Island society during the latter half of the 19th century, the urban sport club system remained the prominent administrative format. Sport clubs were organized around a specific sport with rules, fees, and membership policies designed to maximize the social and competitive benefits of the sport for its members. The first sport to formally organize on Prince Edward Island was cricket, duly organized as "The Charlottetown Cricket Club" (CCC) on April 9, 1850. That cricket was the first sport to organize in the province can be attributed to the popularity of the game in England at the time, and the British influence on the early development of sport in the province. The game was immensely popular during the reign of Queen Victoria, and was boastfully claimed to be the "best of all games." The organizational meeting of the CCC, held at the Masonic Hall, was attended by twenty-nine prominent "gentlemen" of the city who adopted a series of resolutions covering the election of officers, a limit of thirty-five members, an entrance fee of three shillings, an annual subscription fee of five shillings, and the adoption of the rules of the game as laid down by the Marylebone Cricket Club of London, England. The executive comprised the Honorable William Swabey as president; James D. Haszard, Esq., vice-president; Benjamin Desbrisay, secretary; and A. H. Yates, treasurer. Yates was directed to collect the fees as soon as possible, to purchase bats, balls, wickets, and gloves, and to procure a field for the use of the club during the ensuing summer. The organization of the Cricket Club was a significant first for sport on Prince Edward Island, as it provided an administrative model for other sports to emulate.

The decision by the Cricket Club to locate its activities on the Government House grounds was, in retrospect, a very prudent one for the development of sport in Charlottetown. At the time (1850), the area was considered the private estate of the Governor and was a working farm. The presence of regular sport activities in proximity to Government House undoubtedly required the consent of the Governor, and, with it, his implicit support for sport and recreation activities in the city. In 1873 the Provincial Legislature passed an Act to restore approximately forty acres of the area to the City of Charlottetown for "the use and benefit of all Her Majesty's subjects, as a park, promenade and pleasure ground." The park was named "Victoria," after the reigning monarch, and became the primary location for sport and recreation activities in the city. The legacy of Victoria Park as the premiere outdoor sport complex in the province extends over 150 years, and is resplendent with the achievements of Island athletes. Only in 1897, when the Charlottetown Amateur Athletic Association (CAAA) built the "CAAA Grounds" on Upper Prince Street, did the Park share its prominence as a mecca for sport. Following the Second World War, when Memorial Field was built in the Park and dedicated in memory of Island athletes killed in the conflicts in Europe, Victoria Park blossomed as the centre of a vibrant sport scene.

Cricket went through a period of consolidation during the 1850s, when the activities of the members consisted of intra-club matches and social events. Bankers vs. lawyers, married vs. single members, and left-handers vs. right-handers served to maintain a level of interest in the sport and to improve the level of skill of the members. Eventually, the club sought inter-colonial competition and ventured into a series of matches during the summer of 1864 against Pictou, Moncton, and the highly rated Thistle Club of Halifax. It was a courageous decision on the part of the Cricket Club to engage in "inter-provincial" play, lacking as it did any previous external competition in the sport. Was it only coincidence that September 1, 1864, marked the occasion of the first meeting of the Fathers of Confederation in Charlottetown to consider closer ties between the British North American colonies?

Perhaps it was the heightened spirit of the citizenry that inspired the Charlottetown cricketers as they engaged the experienced Thistle Club eleven in a match at Truro on September 16. The *Vindicator* newspaper suggested there was little expectation of victory for the Charlottetown club, but when news "conveying the pleasing intelligence that the Islanders were victorious — Charlottetown 160 runs and The Thistle Club 118 runs — it was greeted with most enthusiastic cheers" by the newsroom of the *Vindicator* newspaper. The next evening, when the SS *Heather Belle* approached the Pownal Wharf in Charlottetown carrying the victorious Islanders, "cheer on cheer rent the air." The spirited group paraded to the Pavilion Hotel where the team was fêted and honoured by the large gathering. Mr. A. MacNeill expressed the sentiment of many Islanders when he spoke eloquently about the pride and admiration held for the conquering heroes:

> (He was) proud to state that Islanders appear to be equal to every emergency, and when they go forth to contend either with the cricketer's bat or the volunteer's rifle they come off crowned with the laurels of victory. In the most serious pursuits of life too, on the field of battle, and in the paths of literature, not a few of them rise to distinction — may they ever proceed in their onward path until their fame extends to the uttermost ends of the earth.[5]

MacNeill's reference to the "volunteer rifle" undoubtedly related to the success of Island riflemen in inter-colonial competition against Nova Scotia and New Brunswick. Island marksmen, representing the Provincial Rifle Association, organized in 1861, won the first competition between the colonies in October of that year at Sussex Vale, New Brunswick. The success of the Island team, led by Patrick Hickey, prompted Island bard John LePage to commemorate the victory with the following verse:

Prince Edward Island fair and free
The Muse shall sound thy name
Now marching forward steadily
In honor's path to fame.
Let envious tongues no more assail
Thy noble-minded boys
They've won the cup at Sussex Vale
And carried home the prize
Success to Hickey, three times three,
The champion marksman hail —
That plucked the laurels from the tree
That grew in Sussex Vale.

Two years later the Island riflemen reclaimed the Championship at Truro, touching off "unbounded enthusiasm" across the Island. When the victory was announced in Charlottetown with a bonfire on Queen Square, the "occasion gave rise to much joy."

The spontaneous outpouring of admiration by citizens of the Island for their athletic heroes is an intriguing psychological behaviour that seems to characterize "Islanders." While the expression of pride in the success of "fellow citizens" is not unique to Islanders, there is often a heightened expression of the emotion when it is demonstrated within the geographic and sociological context of a place apart. In ways it served as an affirmation of their worthiness as a people of a small society. For Prince Edward Island it seems that for centuries the Northumberland Strait has given the Island its separate and distinct identity; it beckoned visitors and commerce during the summer. Yet, in winter, during the early years, it often brought hardship and adversity. The era of the ice boats and the first ice breaker, the *Northern Light*, speaks of the seasonal isolation imposed on the Island during this period of our history. From adversity comes fortitude; for athletes representing their native province, the conquest greatly outweighed the obstacles of geography and climate.

The prominence accorded athletes representing the Provincial Rifle Association and the Charlottetown Cricket Club generated considerable interest in competitive sport across the Island. The most visible evidence of this was the staging of the first annual Gathering of the Caledonia Club on August 17, 1864, when over 4,000 people thronged the grounds of Government House in Charlottetown. The program was impressive, with prizes for athletics, Gaelic poetry, Highland pipe music, and dancing. The significance of the event and the spontaneity of the participants were captured by the *Islander* newspaper in its August 19 issue: "The games, etc. commenced about 11 o'clock and were kept up with great spirit and animation till 6:00 p.m. This being the first attempt at anything of this kind in Prince Edward Island."

The first Highland Games on Prince Edward Island provided keen competition, with the athletes heartened by the festive atmosphere, an emotion many of those present had not felt since leaving their native Scotland. Frederick Horn was in "feats of strength a general favorite of the crowd," as he dominated the caber toss, heavy and light hammer, and heavy stone events. A. W. Fraser of East Point was also "much admired" for his graceful running and leaping. Fraser showed his competitive edge after he lost the footrace, when he challenged "any man on Prince Edward Island" to a match race. There was speculation that Fraser had competed at the Nova Scotia Highland Games in Pictou the previous year while he was a resident of Antigonish, hence giving him an edge in the competition.

The evolution of the Highland gatherings in Scotland is a long and storied tale, steeped in the culture and traditions of the Scottish people. That the gatherings would be staged in the Maritime provinces as part of a social and cultural celebration, where about 45 per cent of the population in 1864 had Scottish ancestry, is readily understood, as the Scottish immigrants attempted to retain such significant events from their previous lifestyle. The first Highland Gathering held in the Maritimes was in Halifax in 1862 only two years before the first Island Gathering. Three years later, the Games were held in Pictou County, and eventually Antigonish became the permanent site of the Highland Games in Nova Scotia. The ease of travel by steamer between Pictou and Antigonish to Georgetown and Charlottetown gave considerable impetus to the popularity of the Highland Games staged on Prince Edward Island.

The annual Gathering of the Clans became a much-anticipated sporting and cultural event in the province during the latter part of the 19th century, attracting visitors from Nova Scotia, New Brunswick, and even the United States. The 1878 Gathering, held on the Pope Grounds in Charlottetown, was patronized by Lieutenant-Governor Robert Hodgson, members of the clergy, politicians, and over 5,000 Islanders, who travelled to the city by steamer from Belfast and Mt. Stewart, while the eastern and western trains brought thousands from all parts, and hundreds more came into "the town in wagons and other vehicles." The names of victors MacLeod, Campbell, Nicholson, and Morrison, from places such as Valleyfield, Strathalbyn, Hazel Grove, and Breadalbane, reflected the Scottish composition of Island society and intricately linked the origin of athletics and cultural events to the celebration of the Caledonia Games.

The first sport club formed in Summerside was the Prince County Cricket Club, which officially organized in June 1869 only a decade or so after the town took shape on what had been Green's Shore. While the membership policy of the club was likely designed with good intentions, the executive leadership of the club, perhaps unwittingly, discouraged this from happening. All the original members of the club were from the business and professional class of Summerside society. Mr. R. McStavert, manager of the Summerside Bank, was the club's president; Dr. Fuller and barrister J. W. Howe were the executive members; Dr. C. J. Shreve; W. A. Brennan, publishing; Caleb Schurman, steamboat agent; John O'Connor, clerk; and Archibald McMillan, the son of a shipbuilder, comprised the original members. Although the club staged local matches and engaged the Phoenix Club of Charlottetown in inter-club competition, it remained on the periphery of sport interest in the community.

While the British influence remained a prominent factor in the evolution of sport in the province, other forces more indigenous to the climate and geography helped to dictate the recreation and sport activities pursued by the residents. Baseball, lacrosse, swimming, and athletic events staged at fraternal gatherings complemented the established sports of cricket, rifle shooting, and track and field in the summer. However, it was during the long harsh winters that residents of the Island demonstrated their best adaptation to the physical environment. Skating and snowshoeing provided much enjoyment for Island residents during a period of the year when there was extra time for leisure and recreation. Both activities originated in the countries of northern Europe and Switzerland, and were brought to Canada by the early immigrants. An excerpt from *A History of Alberton*, written by Alice Green, conveys the sheer pleasure of skating on the frozen waterways that intertwined across the countryside: "Before there were rinks, and indeed for many years afterwards, Alberton skaters had good times on ice covered fields and on the creek. Evening bonfires on the creek added to the merriment and when the weather was really cold it was good to skate up to the fire for warmth."[6] Similarly, residents of Souris and surrounding area enjoyed skating on Norris Pond, where a sheet of ice was usually frozen by late December. "A skate there (Norris Pond) on a moonlit night with a bonfire burning on the shore and the cities could keep all their closed-in rinks."[7] A similar story could be told of most Island communities.

The popularity of skating was not confined to Prince Edward Island. Don Morrow, noted Canadian sport historian, states that in the 1860s an ice-skating "mania" enveloped eastern Canada at all levels of society. When the Victoria Skating Rink was constructed in Montreal in 1863, it created widespread interest in various forms of skating: recreational, speed, and figure skating and special events, notably the fancy dress carnivals. Morrow notes that the elaborate design of the Victoria Rink was parallelled only by its social exclusiveness which required screening of prospective members in a "blackball" voting system.[8] The policy of social exclusiveness was characteristic of urban sport clubs during the era, and was the most notable difference to the more democratized development of organized sport in towns and rural communities.

With interest in skating rampant across the province, several communities constructed outdoor and indoor rinks. The first indoor rink in Charlottetown was opened on January 10, 1872. Located on the east side of Government Pond, the rink was generously patronized for several years; however, its round shape was conducive to neither marathon nor speed skating, both popular outdoor events. Within a few years, a second rink, the Citizens' Skating Rink, was built on the corner of Fitzroy and Prince Streets. The facility, owned by shareholders, provided the city with a rectangular ice surface that was well-suited for social and competitive skating. Mt. Stewart boasted a rink by 1878. It undoubtedly sparked the interest in marathon skating on the Hillsborough river, between the village and Charlottetown. There are vivid accounts of gruelling treks up and down the meandering waterway. The exploits of Jack Mills as a long-distance skater highlighted the imposing challenge. In 1892 Mills skated the 18 miles in 50 minutes, a record that remains un-

Norris Pond, Souris, often referred to as Lovers Lake, was a favourite skating spot for residents of the Souris area, long before indoor rinks were built in the community. Skating on the frozen rivers and ponds was a popular recreational activity for the early settlers. (PARO HERITAGE FOUNDATION COLLECTION, 3466 HF74.285.217)

challenged. Mills honed his skill as a speed skater and hockey player on the ice of Government Pond, and was a member of the West End Rangers hockey team of the early 1900s. Similar tales are told of skating from Summerside up the Wilmot River and of skating parties on the leeward side of Park Island in Summerside Harbour. While skating with vigour on the natural ice surfaces of creeks, ponds, and rivers would remain a popular recreational pursuit, the "Rink" became the centre of social and recreational activities during winter months. The rink was, in a way, a symbol of community progress. William A. Brennan, editor of *The Summerside Journal and Western Pioneer*, chided civic leaders on several occasions when he advocated a rink for the community: "Mount Stewart has a skating rink, when is Summerside to have one?" Residents of the town agitated for the facility as early as 1877, when a committee representing community interests was formed to consider the project. After two years of deliberations, the committee recommended the conversion of the Militia Drill Shed for use as a temporary site for the rink. The much-anticipated "opening" occurred on February 9, 1880, when a "large and enthusiastic" crowd of skaters and spectators displayed their approval of the renovated facility. The Drill Shed facility served the community well, hosting carnivals and skating events until 1886, when the Crystal Rink was opened to the public.

The resourcefulness of a community to provide recreational opportunities for residents was not restricted to Charlottetown, Mt. Stewart, or Summerside. Alberton had an open-air rink in operation by 1883. It was located behind the "old school" where the Court House is presently situated. Sinclair Wells was the rink manager. Victoria evidently had a rink as early as 1884, the year the first of many successful fancy dress carnivals was held in the community. The rink, located on Nelson Street, apparently collapsed and was replaced by a second rink in a building at the corner of Bardin and Russell Streets. It was 1921 before a permanent facility was constructed on Brien's wharf. This rink would later launch the era of the famous Victoria Unions hockey team. By the mid-1880s, Georgetown, Souris, and Kensington also had open-air rinks in their respective communities, thus forming a network of skating rinks across the province that has been perpetuated to the present day.

The positive impact of a rink on the morale of a community was praised by editors of both the *Charlottetown Examiner* and the *Journal Pioneer*. During the winter of 1878, the *Examiner* made frequent references to the "enjoyment" of skating, and urged the Directors of the Citizens' Rink to reduce admission prices to suit the "hard times." *The Journal* commended the rink as "a great source of enjoyment" for citizens, and reported that hundreds were in attendance at the Grand Carnival of January 18, 1883. After the skating, the merriment was continued at the Clifton Hotel where a midnight meal was consumed, followed by dancing.

The Fancy Dress Skating Carnival, as a social/recreation event, was immensely popular across the province during the decade of the 1880s. Charlottetown held its first in 1877, and continued to stage elaborate events for more than a decade. The Carnival of 1890, held in the Hillsborough Rink, was considered to be one of the best in Eastern Canada. Summerside, Victoria, Georgetown, Alberton, Kensington, and Souris each staged carnivals throughout the 1880s, thereby providing a meaningful recreation activity for the citizens of the community.

The advent of the PEI Railway in 1875, linking communities from Tignish to Souris and Georgetown, had a dramatic effect on the development of organized sport in the province. Communities that were virtually isolated from each other during the winter, and accessible primarily by steamer in the summer, were now connected and able to extend sport and recreational activities beyond a local culture. From a sport perspective, the initial beneficiaries of the new mode of travel were the annual Caledonia Games, the Winter Carnivals, and sports such as cricket, speed skating, harness racing, and tennis. The long-term impact was of much greater dimension, fostering fan visitation and team rivalries that were both cordial and competitive. Banquets frequently followed the "game," and it was common for the host to bid their competitors "safe journey" at the train station in the wee hours of the morning. The era of the "special trains" is an intriguing chapter in Island sport history, one that symbolizes intense inter-community rivalry throughout the early years of the 20th century.

While the train provided the speed and comfort of travel and facilitated inter-community contact, conversely it exposed the culture and lifestyle of local communities to the influence of larger urban centres. As the cradle of organized sport in Canada, Montreal had a significant impact on the development of sport in eastern Canada during the 19th century. Halifax, Saint John, Moncton, and Charlottetown, in turn, had a similar influence on smaller communities throughout the Maritime provinces. The process of metropolitanism was gradual on Prince Edward Island, initially encompassing Summerside, and, eventually, villages and rural communities. To illustrate, although the Phoenix Cricket Club, formerly the Charlottetown Cricket Club, had maintained an active presence in the capital city for more than twenty-five years, including matches with Halifax, Pictou, and Moncton, it had never played the Prince County Cricket Club of Summerside. On July 1, 1878, three years after the railroad had connected the two communities, the situation was permanently altered. The event was described in the July 22, 1878, issue of the *Examiner*:

> An eleven Blue-Stockings of the Phoenix Club went up to Summerside in the early train Friday morning, to play a friendly game with the Summerside eleven. — Had the batting of the Summerside eleven been equal to their bowling they would have given the Blue-Stockings a hard shake for it — they (Summerside) are all a nice lot of fellows anyway.

The outcome of the game was of lesser significance in this case than the mode of travel.

Lacrosse and baseball enthusiasts both made attempts to establish their sport in the province as early as 1877. Lacrosse advocates organized the Charlottetown Lacrosse Club on May 31, 1877, naming prominent businessmen H. C. Brownell as president, and H. Haszard as vice-president. Thirty-six members joined the club at the organizational meeting. Within days, twenty members played a "spirited" game, and club secretary Daniel Davis suggested that the club challenge a Montreal club to a "friendly" game. While the aspirations of the club were prematurely high, the members were committed to their sport for several years, and conducted regular practices, club meetings, and intra-club games. With no other lacrosse teams in the province, and little opportunity for inter-provincial competition, interest in the sport dwindled, and within a decade the game of lacrosse had disappeared from the sport scene in Charlottetown. Brian Flood chronicles a similar story, albeit a decade later, in the port city of Saint John, where a lack of organized competition and the defection of players to the game of baseball contributed to the demise of lacrosse in the New Brunswick city.[9]

Baseball came to the Maritime provinces during the decades of 1860s and 1870s. And while fraught with debate and controversy as to its origin, the game has experienced longevity and popularity ever since. Two versions of the game's evolution have received extensive discussion over the years, the English version that maintained a direct link with the games of rounders and cricket, and the American claim that the "real" game of baseball originated with the formation of the New York Knickerbockers on September 13, 1845. While the proponents of each maintain their posture, elements of each version undoubtedly reside within the game.

Baseball caused a flurry of activity across Prince Edward Island when the game made its debut during the summer of 1877. The game was already established in Halifax and Saint John, where direct exposure to the American game created considerable interest. Two teams were playing in Halifax in 1867, and six teams were organized in Saint John under the Saint John Baseball Association. Sport historian Don Morrow described baseball in its early years as a "working-man's sport that caught on quickly in villages and rural communities."[10] The pattern remained true on Prince Edward Island, where the game prospered throughout rural communities. Noted Island sports "buff" Waldron Leard of Kingsboro relates the story of early baseball in Souris, when American fishermen visiting the port to replenish supplies, or seek refuge from storms, played baseball on the Town Square. It is conceivable that such occasions represent the earliest form of baseball to be played in eastern King's County. The Prince Edward team organized in Summerside almost at the same time as the St. Lawrence Club formed in Charlottetown. Quick off the mark, the Prince Edward team challenged the St. Lawrence squad to a match game on July 2, 1877. The teams were unable to agree on the age limit of players, however; and, consequently, the game was apparently not played. The situation was indicative of a problem that plagued baseball during the early years of the game: the lack of a co-ordinating body at the time the sport was emerging as a significant activity in both rural and urban communities.

The following summer, the impact of the game was felt across the province. A second team, the Centennials, organized in Summerside and engaged the established Prince Edward squad in the first official game in the town on July 20, 1878. The game was played on Greens Square, and resulted in a 65–15 win for the Prince Edwards. In Charlottetown "clubs were springing up all over the city," with four senior teams and two juvenile teams active. The first organized game in Charlottetown was between the St. Lawrence Club and Prince of Wales College, played on June 28, 1878. The St. Lawrence team won the first game, but lost to the college "boys" in a return match a week later. A few days after the inaugural game, teams representing Pownal Square and Rochford Square — areas of the city designated for recreation and sport a century earlier — engaged in a friendly match. The Rochford team won the game 60–20. The high scores recorded during the era were not unusual, as gloves for fielders, chest protectors for catchers, and a backstop were not considered part of the game. Catchers would frequently take up a position fifty feet behind the batter for fast pitches, and move closer to the plate for slower pitches and third strikes. Major changes were made to the rules, primarily for the safety of the players, in the 1890s.

The appeal of baseball to young, middle- and working-class men spread during the 1880s. Fort Augustus was the first rural community to field a team, organizing during the summer of 1879. After several practices, the team issued a challenge to the Rochford Square team for a game during the Saint Patrick's Day picnic in their community. The more experienced Rochford Square team won the game by 34 runs. Of greater significance to the development of sport, however, was the composition of the two teams: rural vs. urban in a sport contest. In retrospect, it seems appropriate that baseball, with its strong rural underpinnings, would be the game that diminished the urban, elitist connotation associated with participation in sport.

The Fort Augustus team was the forerunner of baseball in rural Prince Edward Island. Within a few years, a team formed in Tryon, "started by several young men recently returned from the States," and new teams organized in both Summerside and Charlottetown. While several factors worked in favour of baseball gaining prominence in the province — notably its wide participation base — other factors deterred its progress. The organizational leadership implicit in the sport club system, i.e., cricket, rifle shooting, lacrosse, and lawn tennis, was absent from the mass participation sports of track and field and baseball. Consequently, games tended to be played as challenge matches at picnics or on holidays, with as few as three or four exhibition games constituting a season. Nevertheless, baseball persisted and can claim over 125 years of continued activity in the province.

Likely unbeknownst to the early participants in baseball on Prince Edward Island were the adventures of one Henry Oxley of Covehead. Oxley was born in 1858, the son of blacksmith Alexander Oxley and his wife Mary (Stead). Shortly after Henry was born, the Oxleys moved to East Boston, where Henry learned the rudiments of the game of baseball on the vacant lots and crowded streets of the city. Even as the game was catching on across Prince Edward Island, Henry Havelock Oxley became the first native Islander to play baseball at the professional level.[11]

The Island's "early years" of sport were characterized by several significant trends that ever so perceptively moved sport into an organized state. Initially, "cultural transfer" played a significant role across the colony, as harness racing (both summer and winter), rifle shooting, snowshoeing, skating, and related physical recreation constituted much of the leisure activities of the early immigrants. While time for recreation was limited, notably during the busy summer seasons, out of the social milieu of the first half of the 19th century a detectable form of a sport system emerged, with the formation of fraternal organizations, urban sport clubs, and the staging of clan gatherings.

Underlying the social and technological advances during the era was the increased opportunity for participation in sport by all members of society. What had until then been the preserve of the social and political elite was becoming accessible to a growing number of middle- and working-class members of Island society. The process of democratization in Island sport was observable in track and field, competitive skating, and baseball.

Undoubtedly the most significant technological advance during the latter half of the 19th century was the advent of the railway. For sport the impact was enormous, as the ribbons of rail linked communities across the Island and fostered inter-community visitations, competition, and rivalry in sport.

While significant progress was already achieved, the era of 1880 to early 1900 would prove a period of major development for sport in Prince Edward Island. Complementing the existing sports, new games such as lawn tennis, cycling, rugby, hockey, clay-target shooting, sailing regattas, yachting, curling, boxing, basketball, and golf were all poised to make an unprecedented sortie into Islanders' lives.

2 "Sport for All (Almost)"

The most observable characteristic of organized sport in Canada during the 1880s and 1890s was the entry into sport of large numbers of middle- and working-class athletes. This "democratization of sport" provided the opportunity for participation in sport based on the interest and ability of the athletes rather than on their ethnic, social, or occupational status. Until that time, only those members of society with the leisure time, financial resources, and organizational skills were able to gain entry to meaningful recreation activities and sport competitions.

The main impetus for the widespread interest in sport during the era came from the major urban centres of eastern Canada, where strong social and industrial forces were influencing the direction of organized sport. The most observable social agitation came from an expanded middle class, who demanded access to sport competition. The access was, in turn, made feasible by a more regulated work environment and improved methods of travel and technology. Montreal, at the time Canada's largest city, and considered the cradle of organized sport in the country, provided the ethnic, social, and cultural diversification needed for sport to thrive.

The initial organizational structure for sport in Montreal was the urban sport club, whose membership comprised the social elite of the city. The first such club to form was the Montreal Curling Club in 1807, with membership consisting of "twenty elite citizens of Montreal, all of them Scottish." Other clubs followed, notably the Montreal Cricket Club and the Montreal Snow Shoe Club (MSCC), both in 1843. Sport historian Don Morrow credits the Snow Shoe Club with "providing a significant incentive to organized sport in Montreal." Initially, the MSSC conducted regular cross-country tramps in the vicinity of Montreal, and introduced competitive racing with standardized format and events during the 1860s. By 1870, there were twenty active snowshoe clubs in Montreal.

The most consequential outcome of the evolving sport system in Montreal came in 1881, when the Montreal Amateur Athletic Association (MAAA) was formed. It constituted the first multi-sport club in Canada. The Association consisted of the influential Snow Shoe Club, the Lacrosse Club, and the newly formed Montreal Bicycle Club. The organizational structure of the MAAA was pyramidal, with mass recreation at the base and an ascending hierarchy of teams and individual sports. From an initial base of 600 members in 1881, the membership of the multi-sport association grew to 2,600 by 1899. Although organized primarily as a Montreal-based association, the MAAA became the most powerful sport organization in the country, with its members occupying strategic administrative positions in regional and national sport-governing bodies. In effect, the MAAA permeated every level of organized sport in Canada, and served as the administrative model for amateur sport for over half a century.

Maritime Canada quickly followed Montreal's lead. The Halifax Wanderers Amateur Athletic Club, formed in 1882, was the first multi-sport association to organize in the Maritime provinces, while the Maritime Provinces Amateur Athletic Association (MPAAA), organized in 1888, was the first regulatory body for amateur sport competition. The distinction between the two groups was that the Wanderers Club was an athlete-centred organization that sponsored athletes in provincial, national, and international competition. The MPAAA, in turn, was responsible for regulating eligibility and sanctioning amateur sport competition throughout the Maritimes. Prince Edward Island was invited to send a representative to the organizational meeting of the MPAAA in 1888, but declined the invitation due to the lack of an organizing body for amateur sport in the province. At the time, those who participated in sport in the province did so through the urban sport club model, i.e., cricket, lawn tennis, and Gun Club, or at the initiative of individual players/teams in rugby, cycling, and baseball. There was no overall administrative or co-ordinating body.

The situation on Prince Edward Island during the era contained many of the same social/commercial elements evident at the regional and national level, although not at a comparative magnitude or intensity. That there was an increasing social/leisure agitation for greater access to organized sport at all levels of Island society during the 1880s is indisputable. Ascribing to the logic that social agitation precedes leadership initiatives, the critical deficiency in the evolving scene in the province was not a lack of interest in competitive sport; rather, it was the absence of leadership at the community level. Editorials in several Island newspapers advocated the formation of an athletic association to bring a semblance of order to the situation. In its March 21, 1887, issue, *The Daily Patriot* extolled the benefits of physical recreation and sport:

> The question of organizing an athletic association in this city is again being reviewed, and we understand that the Abegweits and their friends will meet at an early date to talk matters over. — The idea is a good one if an association could be formed like the Wanderers of Halifax, including as members [*sic*] proficient in all sports, and charging a moderate membership fee, the result, no doubt, would be a great benefit to our young men. — There are scores of young men in our city, who would surely take an interest in the association and be enabled to gain that exercise and pleasure which in moderation is indispensable, and which tends to keep a healthy mind in a sound body.

Several months later, in June 1887, the *Summerside Journal* and *Western Pioneer* urged the formation of a similar club for that town, albeit a less structured organization than the one envisaged for Charlottetown. "It is a matter of regret that the young men of Summerside have not yet organized a good baseball, cricket, or football club." What the *Summerside Journal and Western Pioneer* editorial overlooked in its advocacy was that a cricket club, baseball teams, and a lawn tennis club had previously existed in the town; however, they had not become permanently established in the community that was re-energizing its social, cultural, and fraternal institutions. It fell to the YMCA, the Reform Club, and, later, the Summerside Amateur Athletic Association to demonstrate a social consciousness and provide leadership for the emerging sport scene in the community. Both the YMCA and Reform Club conducted recreational programs with their limited resources, the Reform Club in bowling and billiards, and the Y with gymnastics, physical exercises, and a reading room. The situation was similar to the agitation that had existed in Charlottetown and other Maritime urban centres a decade earlier; a growing interest in sport and physical recreation that evoked a leadership response from the community.

The introduction of lawn tennis to the sport fraternity in Charlottetown in the late 1870s provided a significant impetus to the evolving sport scene in the capital city. The sport followed the organizational format of the successful Charlottetown Cricket Club, and, while both clubs restricted membership to the professional and social elite, the addition of a second stable sport entity in the city elevated organized sport to a level of considerable prominence.

Tennis as we know it today was invented by a British Army Officer, Major Walter C. Wingfield, in 1873. Wingfield derived his new game from the ancient game of court tennis that had been played indoors for centuries by monarchs and aristocrats of France and England. When the popularity of court tennis declined throughout the British Isles in the mid-1800s, Wingfield unveiled his outdoor game at a garden party in Wales. The game had two features that contributed to its popularity with the garden party "social" set: it engaged participants and spectators in the excitement of the game, not practical with court tennis, and it encouraged play by both women and men. What was surprising, even for Wingfield, was the instant acceptance of the game. Within months it spread to Bermuda via a military gentleman who was present at the unveiling in Wales, then to Boston by Mary Ewing Outerbridge, who pioneered the game in the United States. Within two years the game spread to Canada, when the Toronto Lawn Tennis Club was organized in 1876.[12]

The first lawn tennis activity in Charlottetown occurred during the summer of 1878 when a group of novice players gathered at Victoria Park to experiment with the new game. While the identity of the group members remains elusive, there is reason to conclude they eventually formed the nucleus of the Fitzroy Lawn Tennis Club, the first lawn tennis club to organize in the province.[13] When Summerside organized the Summerside Lawn Tennis Club in 1881 at a meeting in the Clifton Hotel, there was "much interest," and over forty members signified their intention to join. The meeting appointed Mr. and Mrs. Francis H. Arnaud, Richard Hunt, and several junior members to oversee the administrative details and to secure a suitable location for courts. Even

Lawn tennis was fashionable with both men and women during the early 1880s, with a court on the front lawn at Beaconsfield. (PARO 2301-51)

with the apparent support from the community, the initial effort to organize lawn tennis in Summerside was abbreviated. Apart from a social/competitive visit from Charlottetown players in August 1882, the club slipped into inactivity. Several factors contributed to the situation. Richard Hunt, a prominent merchant at the time, was involved in other sport initiatives in the community, including his role as chairman of the Rink Committee, a group of a high-profile citizens who were actively seeking a suitable skating facility for the community. Also significant was the transfer by the Bank of Nova Scotia of Mr. and Mrs. Arnaud from Summerside to Charlottetown in 1883, which deprived the Summerside Club of much-needed leadership. The Arnauds became active members of the Fitzroy Tennis Club following their move, and remained involved in the sport for over a decade.

The organization of the Micmac Lawn Tennis Club in Charlottetown on May 2, 1883, established a solid base for the growth of lawn tennis in the city. The inaugural meeting was held at the residence of Dr. John T. Jenkins. It elected Alexander B. Warburton as president and Alice Jenkins as secretary. The presence of a second club in the city proved beneficial for the sport, as inter-club competition became feasible, while skilled players from each club combined for competition with visiting naval ships and inter-provincial play.

Two aspects of the game of lawn tennis that were prominent features in its popularity in the British Isles had significant social implications for the two clubs in Charlottetown. The game was confined to the social elite of the community, and, more significantly, women were actively involved in both the administrative and competitive aspects of the game. While elitism in sport was evident to the citizens of the city via the cricket club, active participation in sport by women was new. It was a significant step, taken during an era when the prevailing social attitude considered it "inappropriate" for women to participate in strenuous sport and physical exercise. While the inclusion of women as active participants in lawn tennis was readily accepted by the sport fraternity in Charlottetown, it was several decades before they gained a significant involvement in other sports in the province.

The occasion of the Royal Visit to Charlottetown in June 1884 by His Royal Highness Prince George, second son of the Prince of Wales, provided an excellent opportunity for Charlottetown to showcase sport as an integral part of community life, as both cricket and lawn tennis were given prominent places in the Royal itinerary. The twenty-year-old Prince, obviously athletically inclined, participated in several tennis matches with members of the Fitzroy and Micmac clubs and later joined his fellow officers from HMS *Canada* in a match against the Park Cricket Club. The spirited match was won by the officers 119–108. The established cricket club provided both a competitive and a social atmosphere for the large crowd of spectators, with lunch served at the end of the first inning and a photo session in front of the clubhouse by professional photographer C. Lewis. The Royal visit, occurring as it did in the month of June, when the Island was at its summer best, was an auspicious occasion, capped off by a Grand Ball at Government House in honour of Prince George and officers of HMS *Canada*. The *Daily Examiner* deemed it a "brilliant and enjoyable affair."

The prominence accorded sport during the Royal visit gave considerable impetus to both cricket and lawn tennis and undoubtedly exposed the virtues of organized sport competition to a broad cross-section of Island society. Loyalty and respect for the British monarchy remained high among Islanders during the era, and such emotions were enthusiastically demonstrated on the occasion of royal visits and subsequent calls by ships of Her Majesty's Navy. The Cricket Club, which was in a "lingering" situation prior to the visit of Prince George,

Members of the Fitzroy and Micmac Lawn Tennis Clubs gather at Victoria Park during the visit of His Royal Highness, Prince George, in June 1884. The Prince arrived in Charlottetown aboard HMS Canada *and actively participated in lawn tennis and cricket as part of his itinerary. Visits of ships of Her Majesty's navy were a much-anticipated sport and social event during the era.* (PARO HERITAGE FOUNDATION COLLECTION, 3466/HF72.18.10)

was energized, and staged a series of inter-provincial matches with Pictou, Stellarton, and Moncton. However, the most popular competitions for both players and spectators were those against the officers of HMS *Bellerophon*, HMS *Pylades,* and HMS *Canada,* which visited Charlottetown on a frequent basis during the late 1880s and early 1890s. During the visit of the flagship *Bellerophon* in 1891, sport competition constituted much of the activity for men and officers of the ship. Games were contested in cricket, lawn tennis, and rugby football, and the public schools were closed to permit students the opportunity to view a full-fledged naval review "exercise" at Victoria Park, staged by 250 men and officers of the ship. The naval review coincided with a Grand Athletic Exhibition staged at the Citizens Rink by the Charlottetown Athletic Association and the YMCA, in what was undoubtedly the first public display of formal gymnastics in the province.

Lawn tennis also benefited from the heightened profile of sport, due in part to the Royal visits, but also to the social and competitive amenities afforded members of the Fitzroy and Micmac Clubs. The clubs carried out an active competitive program that included the first inter-provincial matches against Pictou in 1888. The visit to Pictou included a combination of competitive events, won by Charlottetown, and social activities, which included a reception at the Revere Hotel (Pictou), and

A group of cricket players assemble at their Club House at Victoria Park on the occasion of the visit of His Royal Highness, Prince George, to Charlottetown aboard HMS Canada, *in June 1884. The established cricket club provided both a social and competitive atmosphere for an enthusiastic crowd of spectators. The officers aboard Her Majesty's ships, which visited Charlottetown frequently during the late 1880s, provided much enjoyed competition for the Park Cricket Club. Prince George is in front on the right side of the picture: grey hat, black tie, cigarette in hand. Park Club players include Harrison Carvell, R. V. Longworth, George LePage, Dr. Jas. Warburton, D. C. Hobkirk, R. R. Hodgson (umpire), Sidney Grey, W. A. Weeks, J. A. Longworth, J. A. LePage, R. R. Fitzgerald.*
(PARO CHARLOTTETOWN CAMERA CLUB COLLECTION, 2320/83-1)

dinner and a ball at the Masonic Hall. The names of participants in the sport reflected the professional and political elite of the city: Miss Amy Brecken, May (or Maude) DesBrisay, Tilly Ball and Messers D. B. Stewart, Leith Brecken, H. J. Palmer, and Mr. and Mrs. A. A. Bartlett. The competent leadership from such a group was undoubtedly a major factor in the success of the sport.

That there was interest in tennis beyond the confines of the two established clubs was demonstrated by the formation of the Rochford Lawn Tennis Club, and other recreational play by members of two city churches, St. Paul's Anglican and Zion Presbyterian, during the late 1880s. While play was sustained by both groups for several years at the recreational level, it would be several decades before competitive lawn tennis in Charlottetown extended beyond the boundary of the well-established Fitzroy and Micmac Clubs. In 1889 the two clubs amalgamated to form the Charlottetown Lawn Tennis Club (CLTC), which has maintained continuity in the sport to the present day. Whether the new CLTC absorbed the tennis "interest" evident in the general community at the time, or remained aloof, is difficult to ascertain. It is clear only that lawn tennis prospered under the new administrative format.

Both cricket and lawn tennis projected an elitist membership policy in their respective sports during the early years of sport development in the province. Nevertheless, each made a substantial contribution towards administrative efficiency and leadership that moved sport towards an organized state and its recognition as an integral part of the social and cultural life of the community.

The game of rugby, first played on the sport fields of Rugby School in Warwickshire, England, in 1823, also had a profound effect on the development of sport on Prince Edward Island. The game was the first to attract large numbers of participants (mass participation) within an organized framework, and the first to achieve a following of loyal fans. The appeal of the game, with its "rough and tumble" style of play, was strong, permitting players to exhibit aggressive behaviour within a socially accepted context. Observers of the sport considered rugby to be "a hooligans' game played by gentlemen," while soccer, an equally popular game in Britain, was conversely considered to be "a gentlemen's game played by hooligans."

A distinctive aspect of the development of rugby throughout England was that it was played primarily within the educational system, rather than following the usual pattern of involvement by military personnel and urban sport clubs. When the game was exported to Canada, it became established at McGill University in Montreal, and Trinity College in Toronto. Parents of British descent, who were wealthy enough, often sent their sons to England to receive their primary and secondary education. They undoubtedly played rugby there, and it seems these students brought the game back to Canada with them. What is considered to be the first authentic account of a rugby game in Canada occurred in 1865 in Montreal between officers of the British regiment and a civilian team composed mainly of students from McGill. From Montreal the game spread east to Halifax, where it was firmly established by the 1880s, with teams representing the Wanderers Club, Officers of the British Garrison, Dalhousie College, and Acadia College engaged in competitive games.

As interest in rugby grew across the Maritimes, a group of young men gathered at Victoria Park in Charlottetown during the spring of 1884 to form a rugby football club. It was a pivotal event, for not only was the group destined to become one of the best rugby teams in the Maritimes, during the late 1880s and the decade of the 1890s, it marked the inception of the "Abegweits," a name that became synonymous with athletic excellence and administrative efficiency in Prince Edward Island and throughout eastern Canada. The group included six players who had previous experience at colleges and universities. A. Ernest Ings had learned to play at Cheltenham College in England; George Robinson, Albert MacNeill, Kenneth Martin, and F. J. Stewart had played at Dalhousie University; while W. A. Weeks, Jr., had played half-back at McGill. It is likely that Dan Cameron of Little Sands had played at Queen's, where he was an outstanding half-back and a star in track and field. His untimely death would cut short a brilliant athletic career in rugby and track and field. The remaining members of the group, Hooper Robinson, Aeneas MacDonald, Daniel J. MacDonald, P. Macdonald, J. F. Whear, Charles Leigh, Jr., T. W. L. Moore, J. H. Shaw, George Gordon, and Charles Kennedy, were novices at the sport.

The team practised for two years before engaging in inter-provincial competition, all the while honing their skills and tactics at the new game. The team's first challenge came in Pictou on May 24, 1886, when the Abegweits defeated the home team 4–0 in an impressive win. Even the Pictou squad acknowledged themselves "fairly defeated." The victory by Island athletes, playing under the Abegweit banner established a precedent for excellence in sport that extended over half a century. The Abegweits were cheered on by about 250 fans who travelled with the team on the SS *Princess of Wales*. The opportunity for fans to accompany athletes/teams on holiday excursions was a significant social activity during an era when leisure options were limited. While the sport competition was the main attraction, other social amenities — i.e., banquets, bands, socializing, and, on occasion, dances — were also part of an "Abegweit excursion."

The presence of the Abegweit rugby team in Charlottetown contributed to the interest in the game at both Prince of Wales College (PWC) and St. Dunstan's College (SDC), the local collegiate institutions. The

The original Abegweit rugby team of 1886 was a major factor in creating a social environment for mass participation in sport on Prince Edward Island. By 1890, upwards of twenty rugby teams were competing in organized leagues in Charlottetown, including St. Dunstan's College, Prince of Wales College, and the YMCA. Back, l-r: F. J. Stewart, C. Leigh, T. W. L. Moore, Dan Cameron, D. J. Macdonald, A. McNeill, C. Gordon; Centre: J. F. Whear, P. Macdonald, G. E. Robinson, W. A. Weeks, A. MacDonald; Front: C. Kennedy, D. H. Robinson, J. H. Shaw; Missing: A. E. Ings, K. Martin. (PARO CAMERA CLUB COLLECTION, 2320/81-1)

two academic rivals met for the first time in a sport contest when they squared off in rugby on May 15, 1886, at Victoria Park. Several members of the PWC team had been training with the Abegweits prior to the historic contest, while only two of the approximately hundred students enrolled at SDC had previous experience at the game. Prince of Wales won the initial game 14–0, "the emoluments of the struggle to consist of the honor and glory of victory." While the Abegweits played most of their initial games against Nova Scotian opponents, the formation of teams at PWC and SDC established rugby on a solid competitive basis in Charlottetown. Why the game did not become established in other Island communities, notably Summerside, at this point is a matter for conjecture. The absence of post-secondary educational institutions to form competitive teams was undoubtedly a contributing factor, as was the lack of players with previous experience in the sport.

By 1890, rugby was well-established in Charlottetown, with the Abegweits playing New Glasgow, Pictou, Halifax Wanderers, and Dalhousie University. The team, led by H. D. "Harry" Johnson, was considered to be the strongest in the Maritimes. The 1890 Abegweit Rugby Team embodied skill and sportsmanship. Back, l-r: Dr. J. A. Johnstone, J. F. Whear, T. W. L. Moore, C. Leigh, H. T. Macdonald, J. J. Macdonald, R. H. Macdonald; Centre: A. McNeill, D. H. Robinson, A. E. Ings, G. E. Robinson, J. Sullivan, — Matheson; Front: J. Rundle, Dr. H. D. Johnson. (PARO CAMERA CLUB COLLECTION)

The Abegweits returned to Pictou in the fall of 1886 to face their first major test, participation in a five-team tournament against the Halifax Wanderers, Dalhousie University, Pictou, and New Glasgow. After three days of competition, the Abegweits were declared the superior team of the tournament, having played the Wanderers and Dalhousie to ties, and defeated Pictou.

During the next several years, the Abegweits remained undefeated and their reputation grew. On its annual visit to Pictou in 1890, the team demonstrated its superiority by defeating Pictou 12–0. The New Glasgow *Enterprise* concluded, "the verdict of disinterested spectators was that Pictou was overmatched, for the Abegweits were undoubtedly the best team in the Maritime Provinces." When the Abegweits travelled to Halifax in November 1890, they defeated the Wanderers 4–0 in what was described as an "easy win." The following day, the Abegweits battled Dalhousie University to a scoreless tie. The *Halifax Morning Star* cited the skill and conduct of the players:

> The Abegweits have some splendid men — Dr. Johnson winning the admiration of everybody not only for his exceptional good playing, but quite as much on account of the genial smile that never left his face. Indeed the whole team played with the keenest, heartiest good humour, never displaying even a shade of ill feeling, and the same can be said for the Dalhousie boys.

What the Abegweit rugby team accomplished on the field of play was equalled by their immense impact on sport in Charlottetown. Coinciding with the team's popularity, hundreds of boys and young men began playing rugby in what was the first age-classified sport program in the province. At least nineteen rugby teams were organized at the juvenile, junior, intermediate, and senior levels, and began competition during the fall and spring of 1890–1891. The best organized clubs at the juvenile level were the Thistles, Brighton Heroes, Hillsborough Stars, Warriors, Village Boys, Hercules, and Anchors. The YMCA, Prince Edwards, Victorias, Crescents, and second teams from the Abegweits, SDC, and PWC played at the intermediate level, while a senior league consisted of PWC, SDC, the Crescents, and Abegweits. Members of the Abegweit Club coached, officiated, and strengthened other senior teams with their own players. It was a bustling scene, with games played across the city, at Victoria Park, Prince Street School, and on the network of open squares located throughout the city.

Several reasons can be postulated for the surge of interest in rugby in the city. The sport was the first to organize that had mass appeal to boys and young men, and the game was aggressive, exhibiting many of the skills and emotional intensity displayed in normal play behaviour. Further, many civic leaders viewed sport as an antidote to deviant social activities and lauded fraternal organizations (YMCA), educational institutions (SDC and PWC), and sport groups (Abegweits), for their efforts to encourage young men of the city to engage in sport. Perhaps the most obvious and compelling influence was imitation; boys and young men tended to mimic their athletic role models. Athletes wearing the colours of the Abegweits, St. Dunstan's, and Prince of Wales were experiencing notable success in their respective rugby competitions, which in turn attracted boys and young men to play the game.

Placed in the context of a fledging sport system during the 1880s, where cricket and lawn tennis were well-established and horse racing claimed the interest of "thousands," the contribution of the Abegweit rugby team to the development of sport on Prince Edward Island can hardly be overstated. In its first five years of play, the team consolidated several key conditions necessary for sport to thrive and become a stable entity within the community.

The era marked the realization that participation in organized sport was a right shared by all Islanders according to their inclination, regardless of their social, occupational, or ethnic status. The reality of the situation was, however, that not all sports became immediately accessible, nor have they become so in our present era. Those sports that organized as urban sport clubs remained essentially exclusive. Nevertheless, the influx of participants in a wide variety of recreational and competitive games extended across the Island, and brought a new awareness of the role of sport as a catalyst for community identity.

3 Post-Time, Gentlemen

The Derby race, as described by John Rowan, in his book, *The Emigrant and Sportsman in Canada*, perhaps best describes the fascination that horse racing held for the early settlers to Prince Edward Island. For the race found expression in both winter and summer and helped sustain the spirit of the settlers during the early years of settlement in the Colony.

> The Derby [race] is held in mid-winter. A circular mile course is laid off on the ice and marked out with spruce bushes. The races are trotted in mile heats. — They are off is the cry. The jockeys yell hideously at their flying steeds, 100 sleighs follow in their tracks, 500 bells jingle. Men on foot and boys on skates crowd towards the winning post in indescribable confusion. — How the winner is ultimately decided upon is a mystery, nor does it matter much, for the stakes are small, and as for the honour and glory they are equally divided.[14]

The deep affection for horses that was acquired over many years by the Scottish people was noted in correspondence written to a fellow "Scot" in 1831 by Bishop Angus MacEachern when he wrote, "Our people are extravagant in tea drinking, dress, grog, and horse racing." The first

Bishop of Charlottetown displayed a profound insight into the habits and lifestyles of the Highlanders to whom he ministered.

During the term of Lieutenant-Governor General John Ready, from 1824 to 1831, significant educational, commercial, and social progress occurred in the colony. He encouraged agriculture and the fishery, improved breeding stock for farm animals, stressed education, and built roads and bridges to improve transportation and travel. He was also keenly interested in recreation and sport, especially horse racing, and his direct involvement in the "Charlottetown Races" gave the sport considerable status. In 1824 Ready imported a thoroughbred stallion, Roncesvalles, and a mare, Roulette, from England to improve breeding stock, and the results were remarkable. The *P.E.I. Register* noted in its October 7, 1828, edition that "great expectations are formed of fine running next year, from various matches already made amongst the proprietors of the stock of Roncesvalles, the valuable horse imported from England by His Excellency in 1824, and unmatched for strength, bone and beauty." The Roncesvalles Product Stakes were held in October 1829, with patronage from a cross-section of Island society. While the political and professional members of Island society possessed both the time and financial resources to fully participate in the sport, settlers, many of whom had developed a love of horses in their homeland, were equally attracted to the races to enjoy one of their favourite leisure pastimes.

Following Governor Ready's departure in 1831, difficult travel conditions across the colony prevailed from the 1830s through the 1870s, and the horse racing industry took on a localized character, with priorities directed towards the improvement of breeding lines and the development of a commercial market for Island horses with neighbouring provinces and the state of Maine. The O'Brien family of Alberton and William A. Brennan of Summerside were considered to be the leading breeders of standardbred horses at the time. Standardbred horses, trotters, and pacers were considered to be more versatile than the thoroughbreds in meeting the needs of Island farmers/horsemen, adaptable as they were to both work and recreation.[15]

While organized races at the provincial level were not held during the pre-railroad era, impromptu races against neighbour horses were held at every opportunity. Folklore of the era tells of such races on country roads or on the frozen inlets and rivers that encroached on the Island coastline. Donald MacKenzie, a horse owner, driver, and official from Belfast, reflected that a favourite time for such challenges seemed to be following church on Sunday mornings, when horse owners and family were decked out in their "Sunday best." It was a natural outgrowth of Islanders' legendary love of horses, an appetite for speed, and the reality that people either walked, rode, or drove horses wherever they went. Following Sunday service was one time when a group of people would be driving light carriages or sleighs at the same time. This was a natural opportunity to race.

The early years of horse racing in the Maritimes were turbulent ones, notably in Halifax where the sport endured a long period of social and political denouncement. In the early 1800s, Nova Scotia Governor Campbell actually banned the sport due primarily to the attraction the sport held for the most "undesirable characters." Gambling, intoxication, and rowdyism were readily observable at most of the early races staged on the Halifax Commons. In an effort to overcome such an undesirable — and some thought undeserved — reputation, the Halifax Turf Club, comprising prominent citizens and military officers, formed in 1825. The Club had two primary objectives. The most imperative was to improve the administration and crowd control at race events by employing competent judges, starters, and stewards. The second, more long-term objective, was to improve the breed of horses across the province. Within this context the sport gradually gained a level of respectability, and, by 1860, horse racing experienced a renewed interest and popularity in Halifax. Ice races were held annually on the Bedford Basin; challenge races were staged and the sport of horse racing returned to the Halifax Commons during the late 1860s.

In Saint John, the sport was closely linked to the militia, with races conducted on the sand flats of Courtenay Bay as early as the 1790s. When the tides of the Bay of Fundy rolled out, horsemen used the firm, smooth surface of the flats to stage their races. While horse racing was immensely popular in the port city, the sport was not without deviant social behaviour and rowdyism by spectators. Brian Flood, in his book, *Saint John, A Sporting Tradition*, vividly describes occasions of "rioting," feuds and drunkenness associated with the sport during the 1850s. When the Torryburn track opened September 26, 1865 (later replaced by The Moosepath oval on August 23, 1871), it provided horse owners and race fans with a relatively permanent racing facility that marked a new era of respectability for the sport in Saint John.

The sport of harness racing on Prince Edward Island was not inflicted with the same level of social disruptions and rowdyism during the early years of its development. While there were fights and excess in the use of alcohol at racing events, by and large, the crowds were well-behaved. Local newspapers regularly reported three aspects of a horse race: the winning horse(s), the size and demeanour of the crowd, and the number of fights. Factors that contributed to the relatively smooth development of horse racing in the province were undoubtedly the rural underpinning of the sport and the late development of regular racing events, in contrast to previous races in Nova Scotia and New Brunswick.

While the sport of harness racing during the mid-1800s lacked organization, it did not lack enthusiasm, and during this period the foundation was laid for one of the most pervasive sport and recreation activities in which Islanders indulged.

By the late 1870s there was an increased interest in staging race events during both winter and summer, facilitated undoubtedly by the improvement in travel options provided by the railway. During the winter of 1878, the *Summerside Journal* made several references to horse racing on the harbour ice, "from the want of any other amusement." Organized races during the summer of 1878 at the Summerside Driving Park attracted large crowds, over a thousand for a September date, as did the opening of the Kensington Driving Park on October 16, 1879. The ripple of activity generated by winter racing, the appearance of new tracks, and the staging of highly publicized match races combined to expand public interest during the 1880s.

One event that aroused considerable excitement came during the summer of 1888, when the owners of two celebrated stallions became embroiled in a public debate over the merits of their respective horses. W. W. MacLeod of Summerside, owner of Hernando, issued a challenge to Benjamin Dockendorff of Charlottetown, owner of Black Pilot, to "put up or shut up" for a best of three heats with a side wager of $200. The race was originally scheduled for the Upton track in North River; however, it was moved to the newly renovated Summerside Driving Park due to the widespread interest generated for the event. On the day of the race, special trains from all points of the Island, carrying thousands of race fans, converged on Summerside. *The P.E.I. Agriculturist* captured the mood of the day:

> Thursday last had long been anxiously looked forward to by thousands, and all were glad when it dawned bright and clear — From early dawn streams of carriages poured into Summerside from every road, the morning express, two heavy specials from

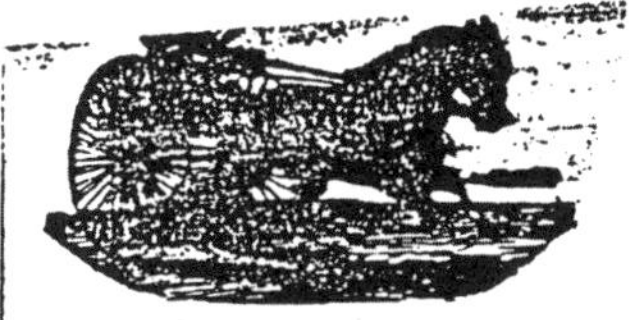

THE GREAT

Match Race

BETWEEN the popular and fast Stallions HERNANDO, 2891, by Almont, 33, and BLACK PILOT, by All Right, 5817, will take place on the

SUMMERSIDE

Driving Park,

—ON—

THURSDAY, Aug. 30th inst.

Special Trains will be run from Georgetown, Souris and Charlottetown to Summerside. Passengers from Tignish and intermediate stations will come by regular train, and return by regular in the evening, which will be detained at Summerside until 5.30 p. m., local time, at reduced rates.

The Track is located in the Town limits, only thirty chains from the Court House, convenient for parties coming by train. It will be the fastest race ever trotted in the province. The best of order will be maintained, and the race being between two of the fastest stallions in the Maritime Provinces, it will be very exciting and interesting, as a very close contest is predicted.

No other horses allowed on the track or in the enclosure during the contest.

Refreshments provided on the grounds. Only temperate drinks will be permitted to be sold. No "exhilarating fluids" can be procured, therefore a good time may be expected.

Entrance Fee 25c. at the Gate.

Ladies Having Escort, Free.

Race to take place between one and two o'clock, p. m.

GREEN BROS.,

An advertisement for "The Great Match Race."

the east, and the regular train from Tignish, were all packed with a living freight, and by one o'clock, the biggest gathering of people ever seen in this town was surging into the new Summerside Driving Park. It is certain that about six thousand people were on the park during the progress of the contest.

The result of the match race was anticlimactic, however, as Black Pilot won three of the four heats in convincing fashion. "Pilot's beautiful trotting in winning the last three heats was the subject of much favorable comment." Time: 2 minutes, 32 ¾ seconds.

The era prior to the First World War witnessed a phenomenal growth in the horse-racing industry across Prince Edward Island. People flocked to the race tracks scattered across the Island to watch faster horses, keener competition, and a higher level of decorum in the management of the sport. A measure of the passion for horse racing is the significant drop in race times during the era. When Black Pilot won the "Great Match Race" against Hernando in 1888, he trotted the mile in 2:32 ¾, and was considered to be the fastest horse on the Island. Several weeks later he won a free-for-all trot at Halifax in 2:30 ¼, thereby staking his claim to being one of the fastest horses in the Maritimes. Ten years later, over the same

Halifax track, W. S. McKie of Charlottetown drove his prized stallion Provider to victory in 2:21 ¾ over a slow track. Then, in 1912, Thoughtful, owned and driven by Hammond Kelly of Southport, established a new track record at Summerside in a time of 2:19 flat. In August of the same year, Iona Girl, owned and driven by Dan MacKinnon, made a new record at the Halifax Races, when "she sprang a surprise in the talent by outclassing her field and winning easy in three straight heats." Iona Girls' time was a fresh 2:20 ¼ in the 2:30 Trot and Pace classification. Two weeks later, MacKinnon had his prized mare in stride when she won, in a faster class, in 2:19 ¼ "remarkably fast." It goes without saying that the names of Kelly and MacKinnon became synonymous with the horse-racing game on Prince Edward Island, contributing leadership and devotion to the sport over many years.

The proliferation of race tracks across the province was perhaps the most visible sign of the popularity of the sport during the era. The Summerside Raceway and tracks at Kensington and Travellers Rest were the earliest to operate in the province, tracing back to the late 1870s. Alberton boasted a trotting track by 1889, as did Central Park in Hope River. The *P.E.I. Agriculturist* of August 2, 1888, conveyed the story:

> The horsemen of Alberton are about constructing a half-mile trotting track, for which tenders have been called. The track will be in a beautifully situated field belonging to Mr. R. B. Reid, a few steps from the business part of town.

The opening of the Alberton Trotting Park occurred on August 22, 1889, with James E. Birch taking the role of secretary. A special train, carrying several of the finest horses in the province and hundreds of fans, arrived from Charlottetown for the "Grand Opening."

The official opening of the Charlottetown Driving Park (CDP) on October 2, 1889, provided an impetus to the sport that had provincial ramifications. Under the direction of a competent and influential board of directors, the CDP received a charter from the Provincial Legislature to construct a race track and facilities for the Provincial Exhibition. Exhibiting farm animals, produce, fruit, flowers, and other finery at county exhibitions was an established tradition on the Island, and it appeared mutually beneficial to combine the two major attractions. The first races were held at the CDP on October 2 and 3, 1889, with Winnie C. winning the historic race in a time of 2:39. The following year, the

The Provincial Exhibition Building, erected in 1890, was destroyed by a spectacular fire on April 6, 1945. The impressive building symbolized the close working relationship between the Provincial Exhibition Association and the Charlottetown Driving Park. (PARO 2320-19A-5)

Provincial Exhibition moved from its location at the Drill Shed, adjacent to Government Pond, to the Kensington Road site, where the first combined CDP/Exhibition races were staged on September 2, 1890. The prominence of the CDP and Provincial Exhibition remain to the present time a significant cultural component of Island life.

A similar process evolved at Georgetown when the Kings County Exhibition Association took the initiative to construct a "trotting course on the western square at Georgetown in 1890." The June 30, 1891, issue of *The Guardian* reported that "Everybody's coming" to the Georgetown Driving Park to witness "the finest trotting one could wish." In light of the association with the Kings County Exhibition, it is likely that agricultural produce and farm animals were also exhibited, as in Charlottetown.

The Souris Driving Park Association was also active in bringing horse racing to their community. Under the leadership of James J. Hughes, a prominent Souris merchant/entrepreneur/politician, a track was constructed on the Flannigan farm adjacent to the Souris River, which afforded "a wonderful view of the surrounding country and was conveniently close to the railway." The opening races were held in late September of 1891 when "six cars of a special train from Charlottetown were filled to capacity when they arrived for the opening."[16]

An innovation that attracted many spectators of the new race track

THE

Provincial Exhibition and Races,

WILL BE HELD AT CHARLOTTETOWN

On Tuesday, Wednesday, Thursday & Friday,

SEPTEMBER 24th, 25th, 26th & 27th, 1895.

All Animals and Articles for Exhibition must be entered at the office of the Secretary, Cameron Block, Charlottetown, on or before Saturday, 21st September.

NOTE—Section 4 of Classes 8, 9 and 10, which reads "Bull Calf (1894)" should read "Bull Calf (1895)."

First Day: Tuesday, 24th Sept., 1895.

BICYCLE RACES.

(1) One Mile Race; (2) Three Mile Race; (3) Five Mile Race, for Cup and Championship of P. E. Island.

Entrance fee, each race, $1.00. Entrance money in One and Three Mile Races to be applied in purchase of a Medal or other trophy for winner. Entrance money in Five Mile Race to be applied to purchase of medal or other trophy for second man. Entries close 11th September.

Second Day: Wednesday, 25th Sept., 1895.

Horse Races Premiums, $1,300

THREE MINUTE CLASS .... Purse $150
TWO YEAR OLD (Futurity). Entries closed .... " 150
FREE FOR ALL (open to Canada and the United States)... " 300
RUNNING RACE .... " 150

Third Day: Thursday, 26th Sept., 1895.

THREE YEAR OLD CLASS .... Purse $150
2:28 CLASS .... " 250
2:35 CLASS .... " 150

Entries close 11th September. No horse barred by record made after 1st of August, 1895. For further particulars see Prize List; to be had on application to Secretary.

Special Attraction

Arrangements have been made for **Grand Balloon Ascensions** on second and third days, with parachute descent each day, aeronaut dropping to the ground a distance of 2,000 feet or more.

All communications to be addressed to the Secretary.

Benj. Rogers, President. **A. B. Warburton,** Secretary.

Charlottetown, August 31, 1895.—71

An advertisement for "The Provincial Exhibition and Races," 1895.

TETOWN GUARDIAN

MORNING Daily—Catches All Morning Mails.

PRINCE EDWARD ISLAND

ADA, FRIDAY MORNING, AUGUST 16, 1912 "FIRST OF ALL."

J. MCKINNON REELECTED SECY

rs Elected For Ensuing Year

pecial to The Guardian)

OTH, N. S., Aug. 15—The odge of the I. O. O. F. re- session this afternoon with usiness. The evening mass n the Curling Rink was ad- y prominent members of the dge. At the morning ses- rts of special committees, ection of officers took place, as follows

laster—Dr. Dougald Stew- ewater.

Grand Master—C. A. Cruick- w Glasgow.

arden—H. E. Codner, St.

ecretary—J. J. McKinnon, own.

s.—J. H. Balcom, Halifax.

presentative—W. S. Hoop- ton.

RETALIATION BY THE POWERS

In the Case of Panama Canal Toll

(Canadian Press.)

LONDON, Aug. 15—Melbourne Telegrams indicate that strong feelings have been aroused in Australia over the Panama canal bill and that Premier Fisher of the Labor Ministry of the Commonwealth has made representations to the Imperial government especially concerning the proposal to grant free tolls to America coasting vessels.

It is feared that the international and inter Imperial complications may arise from the action of the United States Senate on the matter.

(Canadian Press.)

LONDON, Aug. 15—The Evening News points out that there are many ways in which England and other powers could retaliate if the Panama canal bill, procured for discriminating rates, should become law, for instance they could boycott the San Francisco Exposition ...

2500 SPECTATORS AT TUNNEL TRACK

EXTENSION OF TIME FOR TENDERS FOR CAR FERRY

(Special to The Guardian)

OTTAWA, Aug. 15—The Railway Department has extended for a month the time for receiving the tenders for the P. E. I. car ferry which were to have been in today.

Several British and American firms are figuring on the work.

J. D. McArthur has secured the contract for building the second section of the Hudson Bay Railway, 68 miles long.

The price is $1,825,000.

Record Attendance—Record Racing—Record Time—Record Order

The weather man favored the genial and obliging proprietor of Tunnel track yesterday.

The day was an ideal one for horse racing and the rain on the previous night put the track in good shape.

The day's racing was no exception to the rule and, as on previous occasions, proved one of the fastest and most exciting of the season.

The attendance numbered in the vicinity of 2500 people.

As predicted, the bait that Mr. Irving hung out brought to the four of the fastest trotters in the Mari-

Horse racing at the Tunnel Park Track at Cape Traverse makes headlines in The Charlottetown Guardian, *Aug. 16, 1912.*

at New Annan in 1910 was introduced by Mr. James "Big Jim" Pendergast and his partners, James J. McKinnon (Jockey Jack) and Jim MacDonald. In addition to providing a full race card, the proprietors interspersed other forms of entertainment, consisting of fiddle music, step dancing, gymnastics, temperate drinks, and later, boxing matches. Seating arrangements in the new grandstand could accommodate a thousand people. In effect, the New Annan Driving Park provided entertainment for families and spectators other than the "die hard" race fans, and was the forerunner of entertainment features during race cards that later were adopted by other communities in the Province, the most notable example Old Home Week at the CDP.

The race card that perhaps best typified the pervasiveness and popularity of harness horse racing across the Province during the First World War era was one held at Tunnel Park at Cape Traverse on August 15, 1912. The track name, in and of itself, suggests an insightful promoter in Mr. J. P. Irving, who presented a race program that attracted "lovers of good horse racing from all sections of the Province." *The Charlottetown Guardian* carried front-page headlines of the event:

2500 SPECTATORS AT TUNNEL TRACK

Record Attendance – Record Racing – Record Time – Record Order

(See previous page for an image of the actual article.)

The event had a gala atmosphere with special trains carrying spectators from Souris, Charlottetown, and Tignish, and many other stops along the way. Meals were served on the grounds, ice cream was available, as were "Refreshment Saloons." It was a time for travel, excitement, and socializing. The results of the races convey the pervasiveness of the sport during the era, with horses coming from such geographically dispersed communities as Souris, Cape Traverse, Elmsdale, Summerside, Charlottetown, North Tryon, and Tignish.

In essence, horse racing on Prince Edward Island was much more than a contest between two horses, for the sport embodied a relationship between horse and owner/spectator that exceeded casual interest or even entertainment. It was, in fact, an emotion deeply embedded in the expression and culture of the immigrants who made the province their home. The British people brought the kinship with them, and others acquired it on Prince Edward Island in an environment that was expressly rural.

4 Towards an Organized Sport System

Islanders engaged in sport with eagerness during the latter years of the nineteenth century, spurred on by new games, new competition, and new leadership. Even though residents had participated in a variety of sports and physical recreation in the post-Confederation era, it took until the period between 1880 and 1899 before sport achieved recognition as an integral part of community life. These years are considered to be the most prolific period of sport development in the history of the province.[17] To substantiate such a claim one needs only to contemplate the thousands of athletes and fans who were attracted to sport, and the proliferation of new games and sport organizations that evolved during the period. In effect, sport evolved to a new level of administration and organizational complexity, with an increased emphasis on mass participation, competition, and winning.

While horse racing, cricket, rifle shooting, skating, bowling, fox hunting, billiards, yachting, rowing, and snowshoeing remained viable sports and recreational activities from earlier years, the games that are now the foundation of organized sport in the province had their origin during the 1880s and 1890s. The sports of rugby, track and field, lawn tennis, baseball, speed skating, clay-target shooting, cycling, curling, and hockey became established and contributed to the development of a cohesive sport system. Other sports followed in the early years of the new century. Golf, boxing, basketball, and fancy skating (a forerunner of figure skating) combined with a variety of physical recreation activities, reflecting a province-wide interest in sport participation. Taken in the context of a community dynamic, the development of amateur sport to an organized state on Prince Edward Island during the latter years of the nineteenth century constituted a social/cultural expression of considerable significance.

While the success of rugby was still reverberating in the community, cycling rose rapidly in popularity, due to both social trends and its appeal as a competitive sport. Within a few years of the formation of the Montreal Bicycle Club in 1878, there was interest in the sport on Prince Edward Island. Cyclists were training in Charlottetown as early as May 1886. It was the invention of the "safety" bicycle during the late 1880s, with its pneumatic tires and two wheels of equal size propelled by a chain to the back wheel, that created wide appeal for the bicycle for sport competition, social excursions, and new commercial enterprises.

As a means of transportation the bicycle extended the boundaries of one's community, permitting trips and outings for both personal and public reasons. It also created subtle changes in women's fashions. Women cyclists, of which there was an ever-increasing number, found that long skirts became entangled in the chain and back wheel of the bicycle, so they adapted the length of their skirts to accommodate the new leisure activity. Commercially, the popularity of the bicycle created new enterprises. In 1892–1993 the Timothy Eaton's store produced catalogues focused specifically on bicycles, and by 1899 the CCM company was producing upwards of 40,000 of the vehicle annually.

The impact of the bicycle on sport on Prince Edward Island was of considerable magnitude. Cycling races created the first sustained inter-community rivalry, which then carried over to track and field, hockey, and baseball (rugby was established as an inter-provincial sport with a strong competitive base in Charlottetown and Nova Scotia). The sport elevated athletes to the status of role models and heroes, as adoring fans, numbering in the thousands, thronged the sport venues where cycling races were held. The popularity of the sport also provided the first indication of commercial exploitation of athletes for the promotion and marketing of sport products. The bicycle was one such product. On July 2, 1895, *The Daily Examiner* carried an illustrated advertisement for the Stearns bicycle, which inferred that popular racer Lorne Unsworth's victory in the cycling races the previous day at Summerside came because he rode a Stearns bicycle.

An advertisement for Stearns bicycles.

Due to the lack of a facility specifically designed for bicycle racing — even the public roads were unsuitable for most of the year — cyclists were drawn to the horse-racing tracks that were scattered across the province. By the mid-1890s, major cycling and track and field events were an annual feature at both the Summerside Raceway and the Charlottetown Driving Park. The first organized competition in the sport between Summerside and Charlottetown occurred on July 1, 1895, at the Dominion Day Races at the Summerside Driving Park, where over 2,000 people witnessed a combined program of horse and cycle races. As the *Examiner* observed, "The bicycle races were sandwiched in between the heats of the horse races."

While the combined horse/bicycle races remained a feature for several years, it was not a satisfactory arrangement for either sport. Horsemen saw the bicycle competition as a distraction from their races, causing long interruptions in the program; while cyclists found the track rough due to hoof divots and manure on the track surface. Nevertheless, the arrangement, albeit a brief one, provided the cyclists with a

Frank Cannon of St. Eleanor's was one of the first high-performance athletes to hail from Prince County. He excelled in bicycle racing and speed skating. During the late 1880s and early 1890s he competed against the top cyclists in the Maritimes. His main rivals on the Island were Lorne "Whitey" Unsworth in cycling and Art Gaudet in speed skating.
(EARLE CANNON COLLECTION)

much-needed facility for training and competition during the early stages of the sport's development.

The strength of the sport of cycling was its capacity to organize and promote its own development. In Summerside, the Park Cycle Club, first organized in 1893 and reorganized in 1895 as the Park Bicycle Club, provided competent leadership for the sport. The Club named John E. Lefurgey, a prominent ship-builder in the community, as honorary president, and elected Thomas B. Grady as captain and Frank Cannon of St. Eleanor's as first lieutenant. Both Grady and Cannon were accomplished racers. In Charlottetown there was a flurry of activity as several clubs initially formed, including the Victorias, the YMCA, and the Charlottetown Amateur Cycling Club. Within a year, however, an amalgamation occurred when the Charlottetown Cycle Club assumed jurisdiction over the sport. Colonel Ernest Ings, who was actively involved in several sport initiatives in the city, was elected the Club's president, and subsequently became the consul for the Canadian Wheelman Association (CWA) for Prince Edward Island. The authority of the CWA, and its intention to regulate the sport, was evident during the summer of 1895 when the national body cautioned Unsworth, B. C. Prowse, and Cannon about competing in unsanctioned

A. Ernest Ings was a prominent leader in the development of organized sport on Prince Edward Island during the 1890s. While he was an athlete of note, his main contribution came as an organizer/administrator in cycling, rugby, golf, and the Charlottetown Amateur Athletic Association.
(RON ATKINSON COLLECTION)

meets. Athletes tended to take every opportunity to compete regardless of when and where the competition was held, and so the intervention of the CWA was a positive action, an effort to elevate the administration and conduct of cycling across the country. By the summer of 1896, cycling was a well-organized, highly competitive, and popular sport on the Island. Provincial championships were staged at both Summerside and Charlottetown under CWA rules, and Frank Cannon, Lorne Unsworth, and B. C. Prowse emerged among the most recognizable athletes in the province due to their successes in Maritime competition.

The reaction of fans to the success and popularity of cyclists was unprecedented in Island sport in terms of its exuberance and intensity. Sport fans had previously demonstrated pleasure and admiration for members of cricket and rifle teams in their conquest of mainland opponents during the 1860s, and loyal fans of the Abegweit rugby team, often numbering in the hundreds, travelled with the team on its excursions against Nova Scotia opponents throughout the late 1880s and 1890s. What was different with cycling fans was their unabashed spontaneity of expression. They often spilled onto the track to embrace a winner of a cycling event. A sense of belonging and identification with a social group — in this case, sport's team — beyond one's immediate

Lorne Unsworth was an outstanding Abegweit athlete during the 1890s, and became a favourite with the thousands of fans who came to the venues to watch him perform. While he excelled in hockey, rugby, and speed skating, his reputation was gained in cycling where his burst of speed to the finish line popularized the sport and created one of the Island's truly great athletic heroes.
(AUTHOR COLLECTION)

kinship unit is often the underlying factor in such an expression. The phenomenon reached feverish proportions in subsequent decades when strong inter-community rivalries developed in hockey, and special trains carrying avid fans regularly crisscrossed the Island.

Perhaps no athlete of the era received greater adoration from fans than Lorne "Whitey" Unsworth. Unsworth was a talented, charismatic athlete who competed in cycling, rugby, speed skating, and hockey. His greatest achievements, however, came in cycling. Fans related to Unsworth for the excitement he generated, invariably winning races with a burst of speed in the homestretch. He was also doggedly determined. While competing in a half-mile race at Moncton in the summer of 1896, during a downpour of rain his bike slipped fifteen yards from the wire, as did the bike of his teammate Prowse. Both were thrown headlong from their wheels. Not to be denied, "Unsworth grabbed his wheel and running with it under the wire secured second place."

Earlier in the summer after a victorious competition in Halifax, Unsworth and William Cook were given a rousing welcome upon their arrival home on the SS *St. Lawrence*. The *Charlottetown Guardian* was lavish in its description of the arrival in its August 3, 1896, issue:

> The elections are over. Politicians have come and gone and their arrival here aroused much enthusiasm. But the recognition given Messers Unsworth and Cook on their arrival home from the Halifax Races Saturday equaled, if not eclipsed, that accorded any of the political leaders. — The entire wharf was covered with enthusiastic admirers of Charlottetown's two victorious wheelmen. — It was one of those crowds that defy estimation. — They were carried on the shoulders of the people.

By the 1897 season, cycling had reached its pinnacle in Island sport, with elite racers, leadership in both Summerside and Charlottetown, participants from both urban and rural communities, and avid fans who fuelled public support and involvement. During the latter years of the decade, the sport was considered to be a model of organizational efficiency and athletic prowess. At the time only rugby and horse racing offered a similar level of competency in the administration and promotion of their respective sports. Lawn tennis was considered an efficient sport club; it, however, had self-imposed limits on membership and expansion policies.

While the earlier arrangement between the horse-racing fraternity and cycling officials for the use of race tracks for training and competition of cyclists was not satisfactory, a compatible arrangement was forthcoming between track and field and cycling. Both sports required quarter-mile tracks with competitors in close proximity to spectators. Consequentially, combined meets proved popular, and became the format for competition for both sports over the next several summers.

Track and field (athletics) evolved from a modest beginning on Prince Edward Island, dating back to the first Caledonia Games on August 17, 1864. The stated objective of the Caledonia Club was "the preserving and perpetuation in Prince Edward Island of the national dress, music and athletic games of the people of Scotland." The games were well-established by 1877, when over 5,000 people thronged the grounds of Government House in Charlottetown. The track and field competition was the main attraction.

With no governing body to regulate track and field until 1888, when the Maritime Provinces Amateur Athletic Association (MPAAA) was formed, Island athletes competed in the Caledonia Games on Prince Edward Island and similar Scottish competitions at Pictou, New Glasgow, and Antigonish. The Gathering was the social highlight of the year for many Scottish people, as the event brought many visitors, as

James A. MacEachern began his athletic career in 1882 at the age of sixteen. He trained seriously for the pole vault event and consistently vaulted over 10 feet, using a bamboo pole. He won the pole vault event at the first MPAAA Track and Field Championships, held at Pictou in 1888. His son "Wacky" was a star hockey player with the Abegweit team of the early 1920s.

(PRINCE EDWARD ISLAND CHAMPION ATHLETES AND FIREMEN'S TOURNAMENT TEAMS — JAMES COYLE)

well as athletes, to the province to celebrate their heritage in music, dance, and athletic contests.

Even though equipment and facilities were often makeshift in comparison with modern-day standards, performances were exceptionally high. Benjamin F. Stewart and D. A. Stewart, both of Brudenell, Dan Cameron of White Sands, Daniel "Big Dan" MacDonald, and James MacEachern of Charlottetown were all consistently the top point-getters at the annual Games. It is noteworthy that Benjamin Stewart, upon leaving the Island, was equally successful as an all-round athlete in various Scottish Games held in the New England States. Dan Cameron in turn, while attending Queen's University, consistently won the "best athlete" award in track and field, and played a pivotal role with the university's rugby team.

The level of performance achieved by athletes of a bygone era with those of recent times is often the subject of considerable conjecture. Such comparisons are often viewed with some skepticism, the assumption being that time tends to embellish performance. Nevertheless, a cursory comparison of selected events extending over a seventy-five-year period reveals a remarkably high standard of athletic performance by our athletes of bygone days.

Comparison of Selected Track and Field Events

	YEAR/LOCATION/PERFORMANCE			
	Caledonia Games Charlottetown 1888	**Caledonia Games Charlottetown 1905**	**MPAAA Ch'ships, Hfx. 1909**	**Senior (<20 yrs) Provincial Inter-scholastic Records to 1965**
Hop, Step & Jump	45' 9" B.F. Stewart Montague	38' 8" J.L. Beer Montague	40' 9" Cameron Pictou	40' 3" Lyall Huggan PWC (1964)
Running long Jump (leap)	20' 1" Dan Cameron White Sands	20' 5" John MacPherson Montague	18' 6" Cameron Pictou	20' 4¾" John Poirier Summerside (1963)
Pole Vault	10' 4" James MacEachern & Marcus Henderson	9' 8½" Charles MacGregor Montague	10' 4" Harry Harley Charlottetown	10' 6" George Cheverie Tignish (1965) Robert Waugh PCV (1964)
Running High Jump (Leap)	1877 – 5' 3" not reported 1888	5' 4" D.P. MacPherson Montague	5' 9" Evans Sydney	5' 7" Dave Bernard Summerside (1960)

Note: Events that were measured by tape were taken as likely more reliable results than timing events. Description of weight equipment inconsistent, i.e., light stone, hammer with handle, etc. (RESULT TAKEN FROM WEEKLY EXAMINER NEWSPAPER.)

The question of professionalism was often raised when athletes competed in the Caledonia Games. It was the usual practice of the Caledonia Club to award small amounts of money to the athlete who finished first ($5.00), second ($3.00), or third ($1.00) in an event. In addition, a gold medal was usually awarded to the best all-round athlete for the meet. While the acceptance of such prizes by an athlete would conceivably categorize him as a professional, there was no ready alternative to the situation during the early years. Not only were competitive opportunities few for the athletes, but it was difficult for the meet managers to acquire suitable prizes. The gold medal was a highly prized (and priced) award. In 1889, when D. A. Stewart of Brudenell won the all-round award at the Scottish Games, *The Weekly Examiner* carried a detailed description of the medal, and recommended it be placed on display for public viewing. Later in the evolution of track and field, with regional and national governing bodies in place, the distinction between professional and amateur status was more clearly defined.

Apart from the superb athletes who carried on the traditions of their Scottish homeland, the evolution of track and field was sporadic on Prince Edward Island from 1864 until the mid-1890s. Essentially, it was thirty years, 1864–1895, before a sustained effort was made by sport leaders to establish athletics as part of the growing sport scene across the province. In addition to the Caledonia Games, track and field meets were held sporadically at Souris, Dundas, St. Peters, Summerside, and Georgetown during the era. The meet at Georgetown on July 8, 1892, attracted over 1,400 people and was noted in *The Weekly Examiner* as a "Great Day at Georgetown. Athletic sports a great success." Georgetown was active in promoting summer sport during the period, with horse racing, the annual boat races for the Hodgson Cup, track and field, baseball, and, later, hockey and boxing. Its direct connection, via steamer, with northern Nova Scotia communities placed the town in a favourable geographic position for inter-provincial sport competition. Summerside in turn staged its first major track and field meet at the Summerside Driving Park on August 6, 1896. Over 1,000 spectators crowded the facility to witness keen competition among athletes from Saint John, Moncton, Charlottetown, and the host community. The *Summerside Journal* commended the Summerside Amateur Athletic Association and its president, Alfred Lefurgey, for staging the meet "in a manner highly creditable to a new organization like the S.A.A.A."

With interest and participation in track and field widespread in Nova Scotia and New Brunswick, sport officials on the Island took decisive action to energize the sport across the province. When the ninth annual Track and Field Championships of the MPAAA took place in Moncton in September 1896, about fifty observers from the Island were in attendance. The delegation included members from the reorganized Charlottetown AAA and the Summerside AAA. While the group was undoubtedly interested in the performance of cyclist Lorne Unsworth, the only Island athlete to compete, their main reason for the visit was to

Dr. H. D. "Harry" Johnson was a pioneer in the development of amateur sport on Prince Edward Island. His influence as an athlete, sport advocate, and administrator was felt across Canada. In 1913 he was elected President of the Amateur Athletic Union of Canada, at the time the most influential sport administration body in Canada. (PARO 2320-103-1)

observe the protocol for staging a major track and field/cycling event. Whether it was a matter of civic pride or an acknowledgement of the deficiency in summer sport facilities in the province, the visit to Moncton prompted decisive action: a clearly defined mandate "to construct a facility for track and field, baseball, rugby, cycling, and other summer sports." The project was realized on September 7, 1897, with the official opening of the Charlottetown AAA Grounds at the north end of Upper Prince Street.

The opening of Charlottetown's first outdoor athletic complex was a landmark event in the evolution of sport on Prince Edward Island, and it was accomplished with great fanfare. The Board of Directors of the CAAA was comprised of several of the most influential men in the community, people such as Dr. H. D. "Harry" Johnson, A. Ernest Ings, J. B. Dawson, B. C. Prowse, George T. Rogers and George A. Dixon, and they made every effort to showcase the new facility. The Maritime Cycling Championships were staged on the new track, with track and field events interspersed over a two-day program. Over 2,000 people crowded the site in an atmosphere of excitement and anticipation, for Olympian Ellery Clarke of Boston, a double gold-medal winner in the long jump (20' 10") and the high jump (5'11¼") at Athens the previous summer, was present, as was the Canadian champion in the quarter-mile cycling race, H. A. Courissarat of Montreal. Lorne Unsworth surprised Courissarat on the first day of competition by winning the quarter-mile in a fast time of 35 seconds. Unsworth also won the ½-mile and 1- mile events, further enhancing his reputation as one of the top racers in Canada. Courissarat won a measure of revenge by defeating Unsworth in a match race on the following day.

The importance of the CAAA Grounds to the development of sport in the province cannot be over-emphasized. By the standards of the era, the Grounds were impressive, providing facilities for track and field, cycling, rugby, baseball, and later tennis, plus a grandstand and clubhouse. From an athletic perspective, the new facility created widespread interest in competitive sport, fostering interscholastic and junior development programs and enabled senior athletes to train and compete on an equal basis with athletes from Halifax, Moncton, Saint John, and other Maritime communities. In retrospect, the Grounds were comparable to such significant sport landmarks as the Charlottetown Driving Park (1889), the Charlottetown Forum (1930), Memorial Field (1948), and the Summerside Recreation Centre, Queen Elizabeth Park (1951–1952).

As it turned out, the immediate beneficiaries of the facility were track and field, rugby, and baseball, rather than cycling. Track and field gradually replaced cycling as the predominant summer sport while rugby retained its popularity during the spring and fall seasons. A contributing factor in the decline of cycling was the retirement of its brightest star, Lorne Unsworth. In one of his last races, at the MPAAA track and field championships in Charlottetown, September 8, 1898, he won in typical Unsworth fashion. *The Daily Examiner* extolled his achievements:

> Unsworth won the race by a plucky and very fast quarter coming down the home stretch at a terrific rate amid the most vociferous cheering of the day. Crowds rushed on the track and carried him bodily into the dressing rooms so glad were they to see the Champion of other years again wearing the laurel leaf of victory.

Even as cycling relinquished its position as a popular summer sport to track and field, the sport retained a group of loyal athletes and fans. During the years leading up to the First World War, cycling events were staged in conjunction with track and field meets and long-distance races were held on Island roads. Following the war, veteran George Walker and a young Ed Hornby created renewed interest in the sport.

The excitement generated by track and field across the province following the opening of the CAAA Grounds was truly amazing. It was akin to the exuberance displayed for rugby in the late 1880s and for hockey during the 1890s. Within weeks of the opening of the Grounds, St. Dunstan's and Prince of Wales held a joint field day, Queen Square and West Kent schools organized track and field meets, the YMCA staged an indoor meet at the Hillsborough Rink, Summerside held a series of track meets on successive Dominion Days, and the Caledonia Club traversed the province with its annual Highland Games. Taken in the context of the era, sport became one of the most substantial social/cultural activities in the province, generating immense excitement and contributing to community pride and boosterism through the excellence of our athletes.

When the MPAAA Championships were held in Charlottetown on September 8, 1898, so widespread was the interest that the City of Moncton decided to keep stores open on Labour Day and to close them on the day of the Track and Field Championships in Charlottetown. The practice of closing commercial businesses to avoid conflict with major sport events was mutually agreed to by many communities at the turn of the century. The attitude of community leaders was evidently based more on the intrinsic exhilaration generated by participation in sport than on any commercial/economic benefits derived.

When the first Electric Light Sports were held at the new facility (August 11, 1898), several thousand fans thronged the Grounds. The *Daily Examiner* reported that the illumination of the CAAA Grounds by the Prince Edward Island Electric Light Company was "strikingly beautiful" and that everything was in readiness for the big event.[18] In anticipation of the large crowd, the CAAA placed instructions for walking and parking in *The Examiner*. They read in part: "A limited number of horses and carriages will be admitted to the grounds, but the horses must be tied so as not to interfere with the spectators." Seldom had the citizens of Charlottetown been so caught up in the excitement of a community event. While the running of the Gold Cup and Saucer race at the Charlottetown Driving Park in the present era is undoubtedly more lavish and appeals to the very heart of the Islanders' love of horses, in the context of the era, track and field competitions were capable of attracting immense interest across Maritime communities.

While rugby, track and field, cycling, lawn tennis, hockey, and horse racing were experiencing strong public support and increased participation during the latter years of the 19th century, a group of lower-profile sports were asserting their position as part of the evolving sport scene across the province. Baseball, clay target shooting, curling, rifle shooting, and later golf, basketball, and boxing collectively broadened the scope of organized sport.[19] It is noteworthy that several of the new clubs, notably gun club, curling, and golf, were organized initially as a result of the leadership initiative of a group of city gentlemen who exerted considerable influence over the formation of the above-noted sport clubs.[20] While their motives were undoubtedly sincere and consistent with the development of these sports in other urban centres in eastern Canada, the external impression was one of private clubs with exclusionary membership policies. It would be several decades before a more open policy would be adopted, thus facilitating the expansion of rifle shooting, yachting, curling, and golf to a significant presence in the sport delivery system of the province.

After its abbreviated start during the late 1870s, baseball maintained a low profile during the decade of the 1880s. Play was confined primarily to a recreational level during family picnics, usually on Sunday afternoons, and fraternal gatherings. Don Morrow[21] maintains that baseball developed as a working-man's game that caught on quickly in the rural villages and small towns of Southern Ontario during the mid-1800s. The assertion remains valid for Prince Edward Island, as the early development of the sport reflects a strong rural affinity that encompasses both social and occupational factors. A more practical explanation for the rural affinity of the game across the Island resides in the fact that a slight modification of the rules would permit fewer than nine players per team, and less experienced participants could be assigned positions that were not critical to the outcomes of the contest. As the game evolved to a more complex form of play, the availability of skilled players became an issue. In Charlottetown, meanwhile, baseball had to compete for participants and spectator interest with several well-established sports, notably cricket, rugby, cycling, and track and field. This was not the situation in rural communities; consequently, baseball spread as the game of choice throughout Queen's and King's Counties during the decade of the 1890s and early 1900s.

The difference between the rudimentary state of baseball in the province during the late 1870s, and the renewal of interest in the game two decades later, is readily detectable. Previously the sport lacked leader-

Souris West Baseball Team, 1911. The player sixth from the left is playing coach W. J. "Billie Archie" MacDonald. Others are unidentified. MacDonald became an outstanding athlete, coach, and educator while a teacher at Souris West School, and a professor at Prince of Wales College. He served as president of the Abegweit AAA in 1925–1926. He was appointed Lieutenant-Governor of Prince Edward Island in 1963. (LEARD COLLECTION)

ship and competition, but in the decade of the 1880s there was sufficient commitment by players and interest from spectators to sustain baseball as a viable part of the sport scene in the province. At the turn of the century, there were at least twenty baseball teams organized and playing exhibition and challenge games in rural King's County and Charlottetown. The activity was the forerunner of the King's County Baseball League, which remains a success story to the present time.[22] There were several attempts by the Summerside AAA to expand the game westward, but, with the exception of O'Leary where two teams formed in 1889, it would be the early years of the new century before the game became established in the western part of the province.

By 1891, the Pisquid Baseball Club was well-organized, and that summer its talented members issued a challenge in the *Daily Examiner* to any team in the province: "Baseball challenge. The Pisquid Baseball Club intends holding a picnic on their grounds near Pisquid Station on Thursday, July 23 [1891], on which day they are prepared to meet and play any other nine on Prince Edward Island." While there was likely a response to the Pisquid challenge, the outcome is unknown.

Evidence of the improved skill level of the players was reflected in the low scores in games and the increased emphasis placed on pitching. In a well-played game on August 18, 1894, Peakes Station won over Baldwins Road by an 11–10 score. *The Examiner* carried the following account:

> A very hotly contested game of baseball was played on the grounds of Mr. Edward Gay, Peake's [*sic*] Station on Saturday, August 18th, 1894. The coveted laurels remained suspended, and temptingly invited the more skilled nine to seize the prize; but when darkness drew her veil over the campus the Peake's Station boys had one more run to their credit. . . The game was witnessed by a large number of spectators, and all declared that excellent playing was done on both sides.

The Peakes team consisted of eight McDonalds; only George Hume, the catcher, was able to break into the family-based Peakes line-up. During the 1896 season, Pisquid and Charlottetown played off for the "Championship of the province," Charlottetown winning 26–17. It was a dubious claim to a provincial title; nevertheless, it demonstrated the desire of the various teams to elevate the status of the sport to a higher competitive level.

Perhaps the following account in the *Examiner,* September 8, 1897, of a baseball game played between the Northside baseball team and West St. Peters best describes the elements of the game as it was played more than a century ago. The elements reflect rural communities: teachers as leaders, picnic lunches, a pasture field for a diamond, the excellence of the players, and a slight bias towards the home team:

> A match game between the Northside Baseball Team which was a picked team made up of players from The City Tignish, [sic] Trachadie, [*sic*] and Point De Roche, and the West St. Peters Team was pulled off on Saturday the 4th inst. in the beautiful field of Mr. John L. McAdam, West St. Peters. The Northside Team played nine innings and made 15 scores. The West St. Peters Team played eight innings making 43 scores, with the ninth or last inning to their credit not played. R. L. Macdonald, teacher of West St. Peters was captain of the home team, and J. J. Macdonald, teacher of Blooming Point was captain of the Northside team. Mr. James MacDonald Jr. of West St. Peters umpired the

game to the entire satisfaction of both teams. All of the players of the home team played splendidly, but the playing of the catcher Mr. George Hume deserves a special mention. About 200 spectators witnessed the game. This is the third victory for the west side baseball team this season, having beaten the Northside baseball team twice, and the Mt. Stewart team once.

A breakthrough for baseball occurred in 1903, when the Abegweit AAA leased the CAAA Grounds and lent its considerable support and prestige to the advancement of the game. The Club added a baseball diamond and two lawn tennis courts to the impressive list of facilities at the "Abegweit Grounds." By the middle of the decade, baseball play was extensive in Charlottetown, with teams representing the Abegweits, Victorias, Mohawks, Sundowners, Local Nines, Unions, and St. Dunstan's College playing at the senior level. New teams also organized in rural Queen's and Prince Counties, expanding the game ever westward, with a game between Darnley and Malpeque on July 25, 1905, attracting over 300 spectators.

The formation of a baseball team in Summerside was critical to the development of the game, and while attempts to organize a provincial league were apparently premature, several exhibition games were played between existing teams. What can be described as the first game of baseball between Summerside and Charlottetown occurred on August 2, 1906, notwithstanding that an attempt to play such a titled game between the Prince Edwards of Summerside and the St. Lawrence Club of Charlottetown occurred thirty years earlier.

When the Diamond Baseball Club formed in Summerside in 1910, it established a basis for the development of the sport in the town. W. W. Muttart was elected the Club's president, with Frank Johnston and Fred MacLeod as members of the executive. The Club acquired the Weatherbie plot in the east end of town for practice and intra-squad games. While the Diamonds did not establish any baseball legacy in its own right, it did contribute to the formation of the Summerside Baseball League in 1912. The league was organized as a town league by J. A. "Archie" McMurdo and Joseph McCullough, and consisted of three teams: the Pioneers, Red Sox, and Independents. Alberton also formed a team as early as 1912, when they played a home-and-home series with Kensington. The first game, won by Alberton 12–7, attracted a large crowd of curious spectators, and, in effect, brought baseball to western Prince County. With a broadly based interest in baseball across the province, one would expect a provincial league and inter-provincial play to become established. However, with King's County apparently content to play at the County level, and Summerside and western Prince without any previous tradition in the game, Charlottetown became the hub of baseball activity in the years prior to the First World War.

The growth of baseball in Charlottetown in 1912 was reflected in the formation of three leagues: the Abbies, Vics, and YMCA in the senior league, four teams in an intermediate loop, and three teams at the junior level. While the improved level of play attracted a large number of spectators, it did not translate into a willingness to pay a price for the entertainment. For an Abbies vs. Vics game at the Abegweit Grounds, June 5, 1912, the gate receipts totalled $5.18. Later in the summer, when the Halifax Pirates came to Charlottetown to play the Vics and Abbies, a "good" brand of baseball was played. While the Pirates won both games, 14–8 over the Vics and 9–8 over the Abbies, it was the pitching of "Lou" Campbell that sent a buzz through the crowd. Campbell struck out twelve batters in his impressive debut in inter-provincial play. Campbell started his athletic career while a student at West Kent School and became one of the Abegweits' most versatile athletes, starring in baseball, hockey, track and field, and rugby. In 1973 he was named the Island's "athlete of the century" by the PEI Sports Hall of Fame. While baseball experienced considerable growth during the years leading up to the First World War, it remained in the shadow of track and field, rugby, and distance road-running as a major summer/fall sport attraction in the province.

Even as the mass participation sports of baseball, rugby, harness racing, track and field, and hockey were experiencing sustained growth and popularity with athletes and spectators at the turn of the 20th century, a significant segment of the population sought their sport experiences, competitive and social, through the semi-private and private sport club system that was evolving across the province. Cricket, rifle shooting, and lawn tennis were the early proponents of the system, and, with the addition of clay-target shooting, yachting, curling, and golf enthusiasts, formed an influential sector within the sport system. While the two systems functioned with minimal tensions, there were instances of class, gender, and ethnic discrimination. Gender and ethnic discrimination has all but disappeared in the present era, but social and economic factors still represent a deterrent to full access to sport participation.

The Belvidere Gun Club was a private club in the true sense of the word, admitting to membership only sixteen of the most prominent

Newstead Gun Club, May 1909. A group of shooting enthusiasts met at the farm of Jim Morris to prepare for a field trip to hunt the elusive grouse. Shown above are Col. John Longworth, Louis Haszard, John Hyndman, Ernest Peake, and Harry Morris. (PARO 2320-78-17)

professional and businessmen of Charlottetown who had a strong personal interest in hunting. The first formal meeting of the Club was held on June 18, 1884, at the residence of Dr. Edward Blanchard, the Superintendent of the Provincial Insane Asylum at Falconwood. The inaugural meeting elected city magistrate Rowan R. Fitzgerald as president, the Honourable Frederick Peters, a future premier, as vice-president, and Dr. Blanchard as secretary-treasurer.

While the stated objective of the Club was clay-target shooting, the underlying motive for participation was undoubtedly to enhance the shooting instincts of the members. Prince Edward Island was a mecca for hunting migratory water fowl, notably Canada geese and a variety of ducks, as they moved along the eastern flyway on their annual flight to and from their nesting habitat in eastern Quebec and Newfoundland and Labrador.

While the Club experienced moderate success, its membership policy eventually contributed to the Club's demise. In his book, *Pull*, Ron

Atkinson characterized the Club's members as the elite of Charlottetown society, who had a vested interest in keeping the membership exclusive. While there were good years with camaraderie and keen competition, the formal function of the Belvidere Gun Club basically dissolved in 1892. It was seventeen years later (1909) that a modification of the sport was revived under the direction of a new group of shooting enthusiasts, members of the Newstead Gun Club.

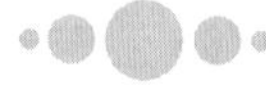

> Today I saw a band of Scotchmen, who were throwing large balls of iron like tea-kettles on the ice, after which they cried 'Soop! Soop!', and then laughed like fools. I really believe they ARE fools.[23]

The Scottish "influence" was instrumental in establishing the game of curling in Canada in 1807, when twenty elite citizens of Montreal, all of them Scottish, formed the Montreal Curling Club. While the group was initially more interested in socializing than curling in the frigid outdoors of a Montreal winter, the meeting at Gillis's Tavern on January 27, 1807, nevertheless provided Canada with one of its most enduring winter sports. While the game was established in Halifax in 1824 when the Halifax Curling Club organized, and later in Pictou and New Glasgow, it was more than fifty years before the sport became organized in Charlottetown.

Even so, the "roarin'" usually associated with the game of curling was somewhat subdued during the early years of the sport's development in Charlottetown. For the first twenty-five years of its existence, the sport was hampered by a small membership, the lack of an appropriate ice surface, infrequent inter-club competition, and an elitist membership reputation. In spite of the apparent obstacles, a small group of men persisted, and, on February 3, 1887, they organized the Charlottetown Curling Club (CCC). It was a low-key initiative with the stated intention "to promote the game of curling in the City." The meeting elected George MacLeod as the Club's first president, John J. Davis as vice-president, A. A. Bartlett as secretary-treasurer, and Reverend J. Carruthers as chaplain.

From an initial membership, listed at ten, the Club gradually increased its numbers to the low twenties, sufficient to stage intra-club competition. One of the first competitive matches played was in February 1888 at the Excelsior Rink, when the Rev. J. C. Jones rink won the Curling Club medal over the Dr. Alexander Warburton rink, 18–4.

The Excelsior and the Hillsborough Rinks, both indoor natural ice facilities, were the main ice surfaces used during the early years of the sport's development in the city. When the Excelsior burned down in 1910, the Club resorted to the open spaces; patches of ice on the frozen harbour and on Government Pond, much as the forerunners of the sport did in Montreal more than 100 years previously. While the open air was no doubt exhilarating, it was not conducive to the finer points of the game, i.e., finding one's weight or reading the natural ice. Confronted with the problem of finding suitable ice, the CCC became inactive from 1911 to 1913.

The turning point for the sport in Charlottetown occurred in 1913–1914 when a new curling rink was constructed at 32–36 Grafton St., providing for the first time a facility specifically designed for the game. In its January 20, 1914, issue, the *Charlottetown Guardian* commented on the occasion of the gala opening:

> The new curling rink was opened with much enthusiasm last night; President James B. Paton and vice-president Col. H. M. Davison throwing the first stones and also skipping the first game. — All were delighted with the new rink with its appointments, and especially delighted with the rollicking enthusiasm with which the players entered into the spirit of the roarin' game. The ice was in splendid shape and will be even better tonight.

Within weeks of the opening, competition was arranged with Summerside and Pictou, and, while Summerside did not have an organized club, a rink skipped by C. Hensley defeated the Charlottetown rink of Col. Davison 10–6. Hensley apparently derived considerable physical and spiritual support from his teammates: Dr. Sinclair, lead, Rev. Taylor, second, and Rev. J. M. Rice, mate. While there is an accepted association between bankers and curling on PEI (i.e., curling clubs follow bankers to a given community), the involvement of the clergy is not as evident, except perhaps that the "men of the cloth" were not expected to be good at "throwing stones."

After a quarter-century of commitment to curling by prominent business and professional men of the city, the game could claim a permanent place in the sport system of the province by 1914. Following the Great War of 1914–1918, the sport would gain momentum, expanding to include a club in Summerside in 1923, one in Montague in 1926, and later in Alberton in 1937.

The lure of the game of golf has often been misunderstood with taunts of "chasing a little white ball" or "a good walk spoiled" directed at the participants. In his Foreword to the book, *St. Andrew's Golf Club, 1888–1963, Westchester County, New York*, Alexander B. Halliday put the game in perspective, claiming that it answered "Man's need for a sport that would take him into the open, would be a test of his skill, and would offer an opportunity to pass his leisure pleasantly." It is apparent that the people who pioneered golf on Prince Edward Island were imbued with much the same spirit.

The Charlottetown Golf Club was from the beginning a success story. Once again, the leadership initiative for the promotion of the new game can be attributed to a select group of professional and businessmen of the community, several of whom were previously involved in the organization of tennis, clay-target shooting, and curling. Interest in bringing golf to Charlottetown was sparked by the rapid growth of the game throughout North America and the Maritime Provinces. The first golf club to organize in the Maritimes was apparently the Algonquin Club in St. Andrews, New Brunswick, in 1895. The first initiative to organize the game in Charlottetown came during the summer of 1902, after several businessmen of the city viewed play at the Saint John course. The activity led to a general meeting in Charlottetown of prospective members who adopted "the Charlottetown Golf Club" (CGC) as the official name of the new venture. Critical decisions were made at the initial meeting held on October 24, 1902, when several committees were appointed to activate the game. Two of the committees were charged with responsibilities that held major ramifications for the future direction of the Club, namely, recommending a location for a golf course, and a membership dues policy structure. Ron Atkinson, in his book, *A*

Treasure Called Belvedere, alludes to the deal the "Group of Six" presented to the Club's Annual Meeting in the spring of 1903. They recommended a location in the Belvidere Woods as the permanent location for the new golf course. What was questionable about the deal was that during the previous winter, unbeknownst to the general membership, a group headed by Dr. Blanchard had acquired a lease/purchase agreement for the tract of land under consideration. Disregarding the apparent conflict of interest by the six members, the general meeting accepted the recommendation, and a major step towards the realization of a golf course was achieved. The first nine holes opened for play during the summer of 1903, and the first club competition, play for the Standard Cup, was won by William A. Weeks.

Two other controversial policies were adopted at the outset: the black ball system for accepting/rejecting prospective members, and the exclusion of women from serving on the Board of Directors, despite the fact that in 1905 women members outnumbered men 62 to 56. Both policies were exclusionist. While the CGC was undoubtedly influenced by the policies of other golf clubs in the region, a similar attitude, closer to home, existed within the Belvidere Gun Club and the Charlottetown Curling Club. With the number of semi-private sport clubs increasing in the province, only lawn tennis extended full membership privileges to all its senior members. This is not to deny that some restrictions were likely placed on the number of individuals gaining membership in the tennis club.

The success of the Charlottetown Golf Club continued unabated during its first decade of operation, with a steadily increasing membership and intra-club and inter-provincial competitions that stimulated interest amongst the members. Only the Great War, that great watershed in Island history, which placed a strain on the energy of members and the financial operation of the Club, interrupted the progress. While the early policies of the Club had the potential for inherent tensions, the long-term impact was positive, and the efforts of the early pioneers of the game resulted in the province's first golf course with one of the most picturesque layouts in the region.

When the Charlottetown Yacht Club was formally organized in 1937 and incorporated in 1938, it could call upon a long history of rowing, yachting, and regattas that had existed on Island waters for over half a century. Newspaper notations, old trophies, pictures, and scrapbooks convey the pleasure and exclusiveness enjoyed by a few members

Early activity at the Hillsborough Boat Club, ca. 1900. (PARO 2320/85-5)

of Island society. In reporting on the Annual General Meeting of the South End Boating Club, the May 14, 1889, issue of the *Weekly Examiner*, carried the following comment:

> With such advantages as we have for boating — no more health giving recreation can be conceived, and none more pleasant when once experienced than to launch off morning or evening in the summer months, and be relieved of the smoke and dust of the city for an hour or two.

While details are obscure regarding the early history of rowing, yachting, and regattas, it is apparent that rowing enjoyed a measure of popularity as early as the 1870s, when William Dean, with his brother Frank, Daniel Davies, and Dr. Robins competed against the "best the Maritime Provinces could produce." A keen local (Charlottetown) rivalry also existed over many years between Dean and John A. Hales for the harbour championship, and, while Hales was considered to be as

ADVANTAGES FOR YACHTING

In Charlottetown Are Unsurpassed and Many Fine Yachts and Boats Are Daily to be Seen on the Beautiful Harbour.

GEORGE J. ROGERS
Commodore of Charlottetown Yachting Club.

While the early leadership of yachting/rowing is somewhat inconsistent, it is apparent that George J. Rogers played a leading role in promoting the sport as early as 1905. Rogers also served as Commodore of the Charlottetown Yacht Club for a number of years, and raced his cruising yacht, Charlotte, *at local and interprovincial regattas.* (PARO: GUARDIAN, JULY 13, 1908)

good an opponent "as ever feathered an oar," he was unable to defeat Dean in their annual competition.

The first organization actively to promote the sports was the South End Boating Club, which conducted regular meetings and staged competitions as early as the 1880s. John Joy, Thomas Lourie, and William Hughes comprised the executive of the Club, and Frank Collins was the trainer. Later, the Club became known as the Hillsborough Boat Club and located its activities at the foot of Pownal Street. It is evident that yacht clubs were active in Souris and Summerside at the turn of the century, as were annual boat races at Georgetown and Borden.

George J. Rogers is noted as the Commodore of the Charlottetown Yachting Club in the July 13, 1908, issue of the *Charlottetown Guardian*, where he alludes to the "Advantage for Yachting" in the waters that surround the province. Rogers owned and raced his cruising yacht, *Charlotte*, a "handsome sloop" slightly under forty feet in length. Other sloops owned by Charlottetown yachtmen included the *Dreadnaught*, *Hawatha*, *Wanderer,* and *Micmac* — "all of which are to be reckoned on in a race."

The energy generated by competitive sport and related social activities created widespread community involvement across the Island at the turn of the 20th century. It was a period of sustained growth for

Sailboat winners of the HBC Challenge Cup, 1903. L-r: Lawrence Gaudet, Gus Aylward, James Currie, and John Currie. (PARO HF 87-29-2)

amateur sport as new games, rivalries, and leadership heightened the awareness of the value of sport as a physical/social endeavour. While the established sports of harness racing, rifle shooting, cricket, lawn tennis, and a host of physical recreation activities provided a receptive milieu for sport to thrive, it was clusters of new games that collectively captured the support and enthusiasm of Island sport fans. And while rugby, track and field, baseball, cycling, curling, and a host of sport clubs generated immense excitement, nothing perhaps took fiercer hold of Islanders' sporting loyalties than hockey.

5 Hockey
Winter's Favourite Pastime

The game of hockey had its beginning on Prince Edward Island during a period of unprecedented growth in amateur sport. During the last decade of the 19th century, the game spawned "hockey fever" across the province, engulfing community life in an otherwise bleak winter season. The relative inactivity of winter months allowed Islanders the leisure time to participate in sport, and soon natural ice rinks, outdoor and indoor, dotted the Island landscape. Hockey became a passion for thousands of people, whether they skated on the frozen ponds and rivers that filled the countryside, played shinny, or scrimmaged in "pick-up" games that became the foundation of the sport in the province. While horse racing was a year-round sport, and rugby, cycling, and track and field dominated the summer sport scene, the decade of the 1890s saw hockey become winter's favourite pastime.

The evolution of ice hockey occurred over many years. The English game of bandy and the Scottish game of shinny/shinty, both played on ice, resemble hockey. Neither game, however, developed to a highly structured form. It was the game of hurley (hurling), an Irish field game played with sticks (hurleys) and a ball, which, when adapted to ice, developed into the game of hockey. Hurley is considered to be an aggressive game played with speed, skill, and tactics, similar in many ways to hockey.

The game evolved slowly during the latter half of the 19th century, gaining momentum only during the late 1880s and 1890s. Two factors that contributed to the slow development were the difficulty in winter travel, which tended to "localize" the game, and the different sets of rules that existed in different regions of the country. Once travel conditions improved, and inter-community competition became viable, standardizing the rules for the game became imperative. It was the early 1880s when an official set of rules was adopted, consisting of a mix of the Halifax Rules and the Montreal Rules. For instance, the Halifax Rules permitted the forward pass while the Montreal Rules did not; as well, Montreal Rules used goalposts parallel to the end of the ice surface, where previous rules had the goalposts perpendicular to the end boards. Both sets of rules contributed to the eventual standardization of the game and furthered the development of ice hockey across Canada. The first organized league in the Maritimes was formed in Halifax in 1888 with six teams comprising the league, including the Halifax Wanderers and Dartmouth Chebuctos. Both teams became durable entities in the sport and provided strong competition for Island teams, notably the Abegweits, Victorias, and Summerside Crystals.

Meanwhile, interest in hockey was aroused in both Saint John and Charlottetown. Undoubtedly, there was sufficient awareness of the popularity of the sport in Halifax to entice both cities to promote the game. The first game in Saint John was played during the winter of 1892 at the Singer Rink, "before a large crowd of spectators who apparently were very much taken with the sport."

The first hockey game in Charlottetown, on February 7, 1890, was actually a low-key event. The announcement of the game was contained in the "News of Local Interest" column in local newspapers and merely stated, "A hockey match will be played at the Hillsborough Rink on Friday evening next at 8 o'clock. Band in attendance." There was no mention that it was the first hockey game to be played in the province and that the new Hillsborough rink, built in 1888, was an excellent facility for the inaugural game. The game, which was played as an intra-squad competition of the Hillsborough Hockey Club, ended in an 8–8 tie and actually attracted considerable public attention. In reporting the event, the *Charlottetown Patriot* described the new sport as "a very interesting and exciting game both for spectators and players."

One year later, on February 6, 1891, *The Daily Examiner* carried a report of an intra-squad game of the Hillsborough Hockey Club, be-

The Victoria Hockey Club, established in 1893, was the second hockey club to organize in Charlottetown. The Hillsborough Club, formed in 1890, was the first. Front, l-r: D. S. Robinson, L. B. McMillan; First Row: C. J. C. Stewart, D. MacIsaac, J. A. Miller (Captain), J. A. Collings (President), W. M. Brehaut, F. Haszard; Second Row: H. Mabon, W. W. Moore (Secretary- Treasurer), J. F. MacKie, W. P. Pickard, W. S. Hobkirk, J. A. Webster, A. F. Miller; Third Row: J. H. B. Stumble, P. S. Hogan, L. R. Unsworth, W. H. MacKie (Vice-President). (PARO HERITAGE FOUNDATION COLLECTION)

tween the westenders and eastenders, which indicated the positive reception the sport was receiving in Charlottetown:

> Dr. Johnson secured the ball out of a lively scrimmage near the northern goal and by a well directed shot scored the first goal of the evening for the west, amid great applause... The spectators were delighted with the game and liberally applauded the several fine plays made...

When the Victoria Hockey Club organized in Charlottetown in January of 1893 under the presidency of E. J. Higgs, it provided a natural rivalry in the community and heightened public interest. Following a series of intra-club games, the Vics declared themselves ready to meet the established Hillsborough Club for the City of Charlottetown Championship. Played on February 7, 1894, before a large and vocal crowd at the Hillsborough Rink, the historic game was won by the Hillsborough Club 3–1.

During the early 1890s, the sport of hockey was about development, introducing the game to communities across the Island. The first reference to hockey in Summerside was in early March 1891, when the Hillsborough Hockey Club journeyed to the western town to demonstrate the intricacies of the game. Friends and fans accompanied the team, travelling by special train.

The 1895 season was one of rapid growth for the sport, both as a competitive game and for the camaraderie the sport evoked. When the Summerside Stars played the Charlottetown Victorias in March of 1895, they were lavishly entertained at the Davies Hotel by the Charlottetown team: "70 gentlemen (were) seated around the Board" with speeches, toasts, and song led by chairman J. B. Dawson. John E. Lefurgey, president of the Summerside Club, and Alfred Saunders, team captain, responded. "The special train left on return to Summerside about half-past two this morning, amidst the cheers of Charlottetown and their friends who escorted the visitors to the station." Meanwhile, in Summerside, *The Journal* declared, "Hockey-instant popularity," as the entertainment value and excitement generated by the sport attracted public involvement. In March of 1896 the Summerside Hockey Club, led by Alfred C. Saunders, Alfred A. Lefurgey, Harry T. Holman, and Creelman McArthur, embarked on a trip to Moncton, Saint John, and Amherst. The trip marked the first inter-provincial play for an Island hockey team. In losing to Moncton and Saint John, and winning 3–2 over Amherst, the team acquitted itself well, and placed the standard of hockey in the province on a par with neighbouring cities.

Hockey came to Eastern King's in a "flurry." In her book, *Ten Farms Become A Town*, Adele Townshend recounts the visit of the Charlottetown Victorias to Souris in 1893 to showcase the game. So positive was the response that Souris immediately organized two teams and formed a hockey club. James McInnis was the Club's first president and Wallace Coffin the secretary-treasurer.

From Souris the game spread to Georgetown. Harry McLean, himself a skilled player, related many years later the details of one difficult journey:

> Fifteen players planned to take two sleighs to Georgetown, but one (sleigh) backed out at the last minute. As the load was too much for one horse, the players walked at least half the distance.

They arrived late but were able to put on a game. They returned home the next day.

Souris made a significant contribution to the early development of hockey in the province, with its spirited efforts against the Victoria Club and Prince of Wales College of Charlottetown, and its rivalry with Georgetown. What was undoubtedly the first game played between the two King's County communities occurred on March 20, 1896, when Souris defeated Georgetown 9–3 in the Souris rink. Renamed the Stars, the Souris team was "hard to beat" in their home rink, cheered on by their exuberant fans.

The much-anticipated entry of the Abegweits into hockey occurred in 1896. The team comprised a nucleus of the Club's rugby players, plus members of the defunct Hillsborough Club. Together, the two groups represented a formidable group of athletes, and the combination experienced immediate success under the Abegweit banner. When Dan MacKinnon, secretary of the Abegweit Rugby Club, issued a challenge to St. Dunstan's College for a game of hockey, February 1896, it extended a rivalry that existed in rugby into the game of hockey.

St. Dunstan's declined the initial challenge, stating their lack of experience with the game. The "Saints" did, however, engage Prince of Wales in a match on February 7, 1896, the first game in the sport for both teams. The game, won by SDC 7–3, was highlighted by the skillful play of P. Duffy who tallied three goals for the Saints. When St. Dunstan's constructed a rink on its Malpeque Road campus in the fall of 1897, it greatly accelerated the involvement of the college in intermediate and city league hockey.

The rapid development of hockey across Prince Edward Island during the decade of the 1890s is an amazing story. Faced with a patchwork of small rinks, many open air facilities, and adverse winter travel conditions, the sport thrived in an atmosphere of inter-community competition and social interaction. In a matter of six years, hockey grew from the single intra-squad game of the Hillsborough Hockey Club on February 7, 1890, to an organized sport that encompassed the entire province. During the developmental years there was a camaraderie of sorts, even between opposing teams; bouncing the referee, "three cheers" and entertainment customarily followed the game, with expression of thanks in the newspapers for the hospitality bestowed.

When the Abegweits, Victorias, and Summerside agreed to play off for the Island Senior Championship in 1897, it raised the intensity of

The Abegweit Hockey team, 1897, were the First Provincial Senior Hockey Champions. Note that this was only a seven-man team. Back, l-r: W. Carbonell, W. E. Flood, T. Howatt, D. M. Sullivan; Front: L. B. McMillan, Smiler (Mascot), H. L. Bethune, L. R. Unsworth. (AUTHOR COLLECTION)

play, and there was a greater emphasis placed on winning by team officials, players, and fans. Community pride and the prestige of victory dictated such expectations. An advertisement in the *Summerside Journal*, promoting the first league game with the Abegweit on January 27, 1897, declared that the game "promises to be one of the greatest sporting events that has ever taken place in Summerside." In a later game between Summerside and the Vics, won by Summerside 10–2, the referee was replaced midway through the game after protests from both teams. When the first provincial senior championship came down to a deciding game between Summerside and the Abegweits on March 31, 1897, the importance of victory was underscored when the two teams could not agree on a local referee. An agreement was reached only when a certain Mr. Pyke, an experienced referee from Halifax, was brought in to handle the crucial game. The game had all the elements of playoff hockey: exciting play, a capacity crowd, and good sportsmanship. The Abegweits proved victorious, 4–3.

The formation of the Crystals Hockey Club on October 27, 1899,

The Summerside Crystals became the first team to defeat the Abegweits in Island senior hockey league play when they won the league championship during the 1899-1900 season. The Crystals, organized on October 27, 1899, replaced the Summerside Hockey Club as the town's representative in the Island Senior Hockey League. Back, l-r: W. J. Green, H. H. Grady, L. B. Hunt (Patron), H. Baker, L. Sharp. Front, l-r: F. Compton, A. C. Saunders (Capt.), C. McArthur. (PARO 2890, 15.1)

was a momentous event in the annals of Island hockey, for it marked the advent of what would be one of the Island's most successful hockey franchises. The new Club supplanted the Summerside Hockey Club as Summerside's representative in senior hockey, and relegated the Stars to an intermediate classification. As if to presage its distinguished future, the Crystals inflicted defeat on the Abegweits in their first encounter, and went on to win its first Island championship during the 1899–1900 season. The victory "gave cause for great rejoicing in Summerside." While the Crystals won the deciding game over the Abegweits 5–3, gaining possession of the coveted trophy was another matter. The Abegweits demanded a bond be posted by the Crystals before relinquishing the trophy that they (Abegweits) had held for the previous three seasons.

The Island Hockey League was highly competitive during the early years of its existence, with game results reported as front page news in Island newspapers. The Victorias etched their name on the trophy for the first time during the 1900–1901 season, defeating the Abegweits 4–3 in the semi-final, and the defending champion Crystals 5–4 in the final. The Charlottetown *Guardian* proclaimed the victory: "Vics win Championship 5–4 over Crystals, White and Blue and Trophy Too," the latter a reference undoubtedly to the tug-of-war over the trophy between the Abegweits and Crystals the previous season.

Island Senior Hockey Champions – 1897-1914

1897 – Abegweits, *First Island Champions*	1906 – Crystals
1898 – Abegweits	1907 – Abegweits
1899 – Abegweits	1908 – Victorias
1900 – Crystals	1909 – Crystals
1901 – Victorias	1910 – Victorias
1902 – Abegweits	1911 – Victorias
1903 – Abegweits	1912 – Victorias
1904 – Abegweits	1913 – Victorias
	1914 – Crystals
1905 – Controversy over playoffs *no league champion declared*	1915 – League play suspended *First World War*

With the competitive aspect of the season relegated to the record books, the Victorias and Abegweits came together in a congenial atmosphere for a lavish banquet at the Davis Hotel in Charlottetown. The "feast," hosted by the management of the Hillsborough Rink, featured such appetizing menu items as raw oysters, mock turtle, boiled bass, fillet of beef, ox tongue, cabinet pudding, and strawberries — a meal fit for champions.

In light of the hockey buzz in Charlottetown at the turn of the century, it was unfortunate that the West End Rangers were unable to find a competitive niche for their considerable hockey talent. The team was composed of residents from "The Bog," a social/cultural enclave in the west end of Charlottetown that was home to most of the Island's black

The West End Rangers, ca. 1900. The Rangers Hockey Team was organized in 1899 by Tommy Mills, and used the wide expanse of Government Pond for its practices and games. Known for their lightning rushes, the team played games against the Abegweits, Truro, New Glasgow, and the Halifax Seasides. In 1920 the team claimed the Maritime Coloured Championship. The team members were Tommy Mills, as coach and manager; his sons Jack, Albert, Lemuel, and George; and Harry MacNeil, Al Ryan, and Edmund Byers.

(BLACK ISLANDERS, JIM HORNBY, INSTITUTE OF ISLAND STUDIES, 1990)

population. The team was formed in 1899 by Tommy Mills, and used the wide expanses of Government Pond (a lost recreational treasure) for their hockey practices and games. The Pond was well-suited to the style of hockey played by the Rangers, who were known for their "lightning rushes," which on occasion carried all the way out to the Charlottetown Harbour. When the Rangers played the vaunted Abegweits in 1900, losing 5–3½ [*sic*], their reputation as hockey players grew.[24] Unable to arrange a return match with the Abegweits, the Rangers turned to Truro and Halifax for exhibition games against other teams of black players. In their first encounter with the Truro Victorias, the Rangers won 20–0. Later the team played against the Halifax Seasides, losing 3–2. The Seasides were members of a special league for black players, called the Coloured League, which operated in Halifax at the turn of the century.

The exploits of the West End Rangers hockey team were considerable in view of the adverse social environment faced by members of Charlottetown's black community. It is reasonable to assume that several of the Rangers players were skilled enough to play with either the Abegweits or Victorias at the senior level, or to play as a team in an intermediate league; however, neither objective was achieved. Jim Hornby in his book, *Black Islanders*, comments that the Rangers' short life span was due in part to the breakdown of the Bog community, coming around 1900, when residents dispersed to other parts of Charlottetown and to rural communities. While racism undoubtedly was a contributing factor in "denying access" to organized sport in the community, it should be pointed out that, less than a decade later, the Abegweit AAA welcomed Michael Thomas of Lennox Island and Michael Paul of Rocky Point, both Mi'kmaq, as members of its track and field team. It appears that the athletic talents of Thomas and Paul, at least for the instant, superceded any racial concerns held by members of the AAA. In the ensuing years, Michael "Mick" Thomas became one of the Abegweits' most successful and highly publicized athletes.

Women were also quick to become involved in hockey. The first reference to a game appeared in the *Daily Examiner* on March 6, 1893. The match pitted the single and married ladies in Charlottetown:

> For beginners, the ladies should be congratulated on the manner in which they handled their hockeys, and the ease with which they avoided the onslaught of their respective opponents. We hope to see more of our young ladies join in this invigorating and exciting game. It develops speed, coolness in danger and a graceful carriage.

A ladies' hockey team was organized in Souris as early as 1903, which suggests that exhibition games may have been played earlier. As games between the Souris men's team and Charlottetown Vics were played as early as 1895, it is reasonable to assume that the women's team also played competitive hockey against Charlottetown teams during the late 1890s.

The Souris Ladies Hockey Team, ca. 1903, was likely the first women's hockey team to organize in the province, with exhibition games against Charlottetown teams played as early as 1903. Back, l-r: Laura Cox, Nellie Clarke, Rena McLean, Ella Matthew; Centre: Adele Sterns, Maude Morrow; Front: Ella Morrow, Maizie Duff. (MRS. G. A. LEARD COLLECTION)

The claim for "the first female game in Prince Edward Island hockey" was made following a match between the Summerside Alphas and Charlottetown Micmacs on February 4, 1905. The Alphas won the game 4–2 after two periods of overtime. In a special report to the *Guardian,* every detail of the game was described: team yells, injuries, lifting the puck, goals; and a comparison was made with the men's version of the sport. The commentary on the uniform concluded, "Skirts seemed an awkward dress sometimes but they were convenient for stopping the puck." No organized competition developed from the initial activity in women's hockey in the province. However, during the late 1920s and early 1930s, the sport would achieve a significant level of credibility across the province with the Summerside Crystal Sisters vying for national honours.

It was the usual practice for the Island senior men's league to complete its season and playoffs by early March, thereby releasing teams from local commitments to play against mainland teams. With the Island title won by mid-February 1902, and the local season thus prematurely ended, the Abegweits enticed the Halifax Wanderers to come

The Alpha Hockey Team, Summerside, 1905, were victorious over Charlottetown Micmacs on February 3, 1905, in one of the first women's hockey games played on Prince Edward Island. In addition to Summerside and Charlottetown, Souris had an organized women's team by 1903. L-r: Mamie Stewart (centre), Blanche Grady (rover), Cassie Matheson (right wing), Eleonore Alward (goal), Hope Massey (left wing), Gladys Holman (cover point), Nana Rogers (point). (AUTHOR COLLECTION)

to the Island for games against the Crystals and the Abegweits. The Island teams proved inhospitable hosts, with the Abegweits winning 7–4 and 8–5, and the Crystals 6–3.

In the wake of their defeat, the Wanderers groused about the small ice surface and the gas lighting in the Hillsborough Rink, a persistent complaint by visiting teams, which eventually led to the construction of the Charlottetown Arena in 1907. Nevertheless, the performance of the Crystals and Abegweits against the highly rated Wanderers established a significant degree of credibility for Island senior hockey. Amherst was, at the time, in possession of the Starr Trophy, a challenge trophy presented by the Starr Manufacturing Company of Dartmouth. The Company was renowned the world over for its innovations in the design and production of skates. Winners of the various senior leagues in the Maritimes were eligible to challenge the holder of the trophy, and, if successful, lay claim to the Maritime senior hockey championship. Following the completion of the 1904 season, the Abegweits tried to arrange a series with the Amherst Ramblers, the reigning Maritime Champions. When the Ramblers appeared reluctant, the Abegweits sent a terse tele-

The 1905 Abegweit Hockey Team was the first Island team to challenge for the Starr Trophy, emblematic of Maritime Senior Hockey supremacy. The team lost 12–4 and 12–5 in its bid to wrest the challenge trophy from Amherst. Back, l-r: J. R. Darke, J. Mahar, D. Sullivan, C. Moran, G. Hughes, R. Holman, L. B. McMillan; Front: J. Gormley, J. Lightizer, J. Mcmillan, S. Doyle, J. Cushing. (AUTHOR COLLECTION)

gram expressing the team frustration: "You are too cheap. We will give you double the sum if you come here. Roads are bad, potatoes low — can't go." The following season, 1905, the Abegweits did play the Ramblers in the first challenge by an Island team for the coveted Starr Trophy, losing 12–4 and 12–5 in a two-game series. Once again, a difficult crossing of the Northumberland Strait en route to Amherst exacted a toll on the travel-weary Abegweits.

While extended winter travel during the early years of the century, whether by train, ice boat, or steamer, was expected to be hazardous, not even the most hardy Islander would be prepared for the ordeal experienced by the Abegweit hockey team of 1907. The Abegweits embarked on the grueling trip on March 7, destined for St. John's, Newfoundland, arriving five days later, Tuesday, March 12. After playing a three-game series, extending over a one-week period, won by the Abegweits 12–2, 0–3, 16–3, the team began the trek back to Prince Edward Island. The first leg of the journey, St. John's to Pictou, was uneventful. There the team boarded the SS *Stanley* bound for Georgetown. Lurk-

Crossing the Northumberland Strait during the ice boat era (ca. 1752 to early 1900) was a hazardous journey, often exacting energy and creating stress for Island athletes and fellow travellers. Male passengers were expected to help haul the boat over the treacherous ice floes in return for a "reduced fare, from $5 to $2." (AUTHOR COLLECTION)

ing in the wrath of winter weather was wind, snow, and the treacherous ice floes of the Northumberland Strait, which gradually entrapped the *Stanley* in the shifting ice.

Wireless messages received in Charlottetown suggested that the *Stanley* was in danger of being crushed and would sink. With rumours rampant concerning the safety of the hockey team, and the sixty other passengers on board, families and friends maintained long vigils at the Wireless Office in the city. After several anxious days, fears were allayed as passengers adjusted to their confinement and the Abegweits provided entertainment by playing pick-up hockey on the massive ice-pans.

When it became apparent that the *Stanley* would be unable to break through the ice until a major shift in the weather occurred, the Abbies trekked across the ice to the shelter of Pictou Island, taking several passengers with them. The residents extended hospitality and shelter for four days before the group was able to walk back to Caribou on the Nova Scotia mainland. There they boarded a train for Cape Tormentine, New Brunswick, only to encounter another winter storm that delayed their crossing of the Northumberland Strait. Following a hazardous crossing to Cape Traverse by ice boats, the beleaguered group travelled to Charlottetown by horse and sleigh and train, arriving on March 8, thirty-two days after they had left their homes and jobs for a friendly hockey series.

After fifteen years of rapid growth, fan support, and exciting hockey across the province, disturbing trends surfaced in Island senior hockey. The Vics created turmoil during the 1909 season when the team embarked on an extended tour of New Brunswick at mid-season. When officials of the Island League insisted the team return to Charlottetown to fulfill league commitments, the team ignored the edict. The Vics further complicated the situation when they added three ineligible players from Fredericton for a game against Saint John. After two weeks of negotiating with the Vics, who were still on tour, the Island League suspended the team for the remainder of the season. The Vics claimed foul, but the League persisted, and following a playoff between the Crystals and Abegweits, declared the Crystals Island Champions. The Crystals, apparently, had an easier time defeating the Abbies than they did in gaining possession of the Championship trophies. The Vics, the *Examiner* reported, "won't give them up."

The challenge to league authority was not the only concern for Island hockey officials; the increase in the incidence of rough play and the intrusion of commercial/professional hockey were others. "Rough house" play was noted in the Island Senior League as early as 1904, and in 1907 the Abegweits withdrew their team from the ice during a game against the Crystals in Summerside, citing "rough play" as the reason. However, this style of hockey was not prevalent in the leagues, senior or intermediate. It was during the 1914 season that the first "fight" occurred between Ches Campbell of the Abbies and Charlie Burns of the Vics. The incident drew strong condemnation from the local press. It is entirely likely that such aggressive behaviour was incited by avid fans, and that fights in the stands preceded fights on the ice. Doug MacLean, in a personal interview with Ernie MacQuarrie, stellar player of the Summerside Crystals prior to the First World War, relates that "fans frequently became involved in 'brawls' in the stands, so reckless was their enthusiasm in support of their hockey team."

When the Maritime Professional Hockey League formed in 1910, consisting of Truro, New Glasgow, Halifax Crescents, and North Sydney Victorias, it changed the dynamics of hockey in the Maritimes. While the League was poorly organized, it nevertheless attracted new teams, Moncton and Dartmouth, in 1911, and a large following of fans. In one of the early games, 4,500 fans saw the Halifax Crescents defeat New Glasgow, 8–4. The number represented about a tenth of the population of Halifax at the time.

The presence of professional hockey in the Maritimes had an adverse effect on senior amateur hockey. The Island league was less affected than other senior leagues; nevertheless, the loop lost several of its top players to New Glasgow. Hockey officials on Prince Edward Island, notably Dr. H. D. "Harry" Johnson and L. B. "Lou" McMillan, were outspoken opponents of the move towards professionalism. The trend, however, seemed inevitable in light of the expansion of professional hockey across Canada. When the Stanley Cup was first presented in 1893, it was awarded to the amateur champions of Canada. The Montreal Amateur Athletic Association was the first winner. When professional hockey became established in the early 1900s, the provisions for winning the Stanley Cup were altered "to be presented to the team winning the professional hockey championship of the world."

When the Moncton Victorias won the Starr Trophy in 1909, emblematic of Maritime amateur hockey supremacy, the team gained permanent possession of the award, having won the coveted trophy for three successive years. With the Starr Trophy out of circulation, and Moncton declared professional champion in 1911, the Starr Company donated a new award in the form of a large shield, on which the team names of the yearly winners of the Maritime amateur hockey championships were inscribed. Enter the Charlottetown Victorias! The Vics, winners of the Island Senior league, were a strong hockey aggregation that included "Cyclone" Charlie Burns, Arnold Rattenbury, and Percy Rodd. The team challenged successfully, and defended, the Starr Shield for three successive years, 1911, 1912, and 1913. In a two-game total-goal series against Sydney in 1911, the Vics were so dominant that McAskill, their goaltender, spent part of the game sitting on the promenade. The following year the Charlottetown squad defended their claim to the Starr against the Halifax Orioles, and again over Amherst in 1913. It should be noted that both Halifax and Amherst had professional teams at the time, which undoubtedly affected the strength of their amateur squads. Whether the Vics' claim to the Starr Shield was ever duly recognized is now difficult to determine, as the Starr Trophy resurfaced in Sydney in 1913 and the Shield was lost in a fire in 1947. Regardless of the ambiguity surrounding the level of hockey played by the Vics hockey team prior to the First World War, their prowess in Maritime senior amateur hockey was of considerable magnitude.

If there was a beneficiary on Prince Edward Island from the turmoil in senior hockey during those years, it was the intermediate classification of hockey. Heretofore, only the senior Crystals, Abbies, and Vics had organized intermediate teams (often referred to as second teams) that played for a provincial championship. With numerous intermedi-

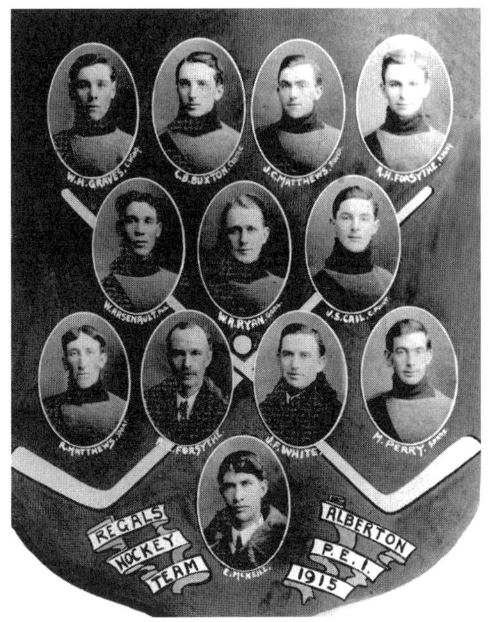

Alberton Regals Hockey Team, 1915. Hockey was played in Alberton as early as 1912 and became well-organized by 1915. Billie Arsenault, who previously played hockey in Summerside, helped organize the Regals team. Top, l-r: W. H. Graves, C. B. Buxton, J. C. Matthews, R. H. Forsythe; Centre: Billie Arsenault, W. A. Ryan, J. S. Cail, R. Matthews, A. E. Forsythe, J. F. White, M. Perry; Front: E. McNeill.

(ALBERTON MUSEUM, EILEEN OULTON COLLECTION, 986-12-245)

ate and junior teams playing in Charlottetown and Summerside, and in several rural communities, there was widespread interest in organizing provincial intermediate hockey across the province. That interest came from Montague, Cape Traverse, Victoria/Crapaud Unions, the Connaughts AAA, Wellington, and Souris. Later, Georgetown, Cardigan, and Alberton also iced teams at the intermediate level. The entry of the Montague Imperials added an important dimension to the intermediate league, as it brought the region of southeast King's County full-blown into the hockey competition. Previously, Souris and Georgetown were the main contributors to the development of hockey in the region.

Organized hockey experienced immense success during its first twenty years in the province. Played during a season that provided leisure time even as it limited travel opportunities, the game captivated the populace and evoked an intense emotional response. While ominous trends were evident in senior hockey, the sport nevertheless generated incredible competitive and social impact. The momentum would extend into the 1920s when senior hockey would regain its lustre, and intermediate, intercollegiate, junior, juvenile, and school teams would join the momentum created by the game of winter.

The Montague Primroses, Montague's first men's hockey team, organized in 1921. The played their initial games against Georgetown and Souris. Back, l-r: Ernest Parkman, George MacIntyre, Herb Campbell, Ed Annear; Centre: Jim MacIntyre, Alfie MacKinnon (Coach); Front: Bert Mellish, Harry Lemon.
(PARO 2320-93-1)

6 Leadership and Athletic Excellence

Circle the date April 18, 1899, as a red letter day in the development of amateur sport on Prince Edward Island, for the date represents an event of paramount importance: the formation of the Abegweit-Crescent Athletic Club as the province's first multi-sport organization. Similar in organizational structure to the original Montreal Amateur Athletic Association, the new sport body was an amalgamation of existing clubs operating in Charlottetown. The incorporation included the senior Abegweits, the intermediate Crescents, and the junior Anchors. Together they represented a formidable athletic organization. Initially called the Abegweit-Crescent AC, within several years the Club assumed its previous identity and became known affectionately as the Abegweits Amateur Athletic Association (AAAA).

The inaugural meeting, held on April 18, 1899, was enthusiastic, electing as president prominent Abegweit athlete and public civil servant, L. B. "Lou" McMillan.[25] McMillan's election established an important trend for the Association, the retention of athletes in key administrative positions. While McMillan was an accomplished athlete in hockey, track and field, and rugby, it was in his executive leadership of the Club that he made his greatest contribution. Following his term as president, McMillan remained active as an official, coach, and administrator for over forty years. He was followed by a succession of former athletes that included Lorne Unsworth, Dan MacKinnon, J. Walter Jones, James "Toby" Mcmillan, Sammy Doyle, and H. L. "Hamm" Bethune.

The combination of competent leadership and the provision of facilities at the CAAA Grounds occurred at an opportune time for Island athletes, as amateur sport at the regional and national level was in its ascendancy. Within months of its formation as a multi-sport club, the Abegweit-Crescents met their first real challenge when they engaged the highly touted Wanderers in Halifax on October 19, 1899, for the Maritime Rugby Championship. The Halifax press carried the news of a hard-found, 6–5 Abegweit victory and heaped praise on the team's performance:

> The Abegweits of Prince Edward Island, yesterday defeated the Wanderers of Halifax, thus winning the Maritime championship — it (game) was considered by the 4,000 spectators who witnessed it the fastest and most furious ever played here. — The Abbies deserve all the praise that can be bestowed on them. Not only did they face the veterans of a hundred matches but men who had played against and won from the champions of the world. — The spectators were wild with excitement when the Abbies would make brilliant play.

The next season (1900), the Wanderers paid a return visit to Charlottetown, ready to do battle with their arch rivals. When the SS *Princess* came up to the wharf, carrying the Halifax players, they set off a fireworks display and entered into a friendly banter with the Abegweits, who were on hand to greet them. The game generated extensive press coverage and spectator interest in Charlottetown as both *The Guardian* and *The Examiner* provided front-page stories about the Wanderers, referring to the team as the "top-notches of the Football World."[26] Unfortunately, the weather on the day of the important game, November 10, 1900, was unkind, as hurricane-like winds blew across the CAAA Grounds, making play for both teams difficult and discouraging many spectators from attending. The game, won by the Wanderers 5–0, was not without controversy as the referee, a Mr. Archibald from Truro, called several long lateral passes, made by Abegweit quarterback "Lou" McMillan to his half-backs Bethune and Ritchie, off-side. The ruling by the referee caused considerable "astonishment on the grandstand."

The keen rivalry that existed in rugby between the Wanderers and the Abegweits for fifteen years diminished after the 1900 season as both

The 1898 Abegweit Rugby Team. Much the same lineup claimed the first Maritime Championship in 1899 when the Abbies defeated the Halifax Wanderers 6–5 in Halifax. Front, l-r: W. Jones, H. L. Bethune, L. B. McMillan, W. McLeod, D. A. MacKinnon, H. Ritchie, F. H. Blake, Smiler (Mascot); Back: A. Gaudet, F. McConnell, J. Murnaghan, J. Donahoe, C. E. McQuillan, J. Darke, W. McKie, T. B. Foley. The 1899 team also included James Mcmillan, and B. McQuillan. (AUTHOR COLLECTION)

clubs shifted their focus to provincial competition. The turn of the century was an exciting era for rugby on Prince Edward Island as local rivalries developed and fan interest grew. In the fall of 1901 the PEI Football (rugby) Union was formed, providing administrative stability to the sport. The Union sanctioned league play at the senior and intermediate levels, and declared provincial champions. The emergence of St. Dunstan's College as a legitimate contender to the Abegweits, and later the formation of a rugby team by the Victorias AAA, contributed to local interest in the sport.

Battling the highly rated Halifax Wanderers for Maritime rugby supremacy in 1899 and 1900 was a major sport achievement for the Abegweits, greeted by front-page headlines in Charlottetown newspapers. What it accomplished, over and above a victory for a sport team, was to elevate the collective psyche of Islanders to a level that recognized that excellence in sport, or any other endeavour, was achievable. During the pre-Great War era Island athletes would demonstrate, over and over again, that such victories over "foreign" teams were not only attainable, but, in time, came to be expected.

Cyrus McMillan, Dan MacKinnon, and Lou McMillan. Abegweit stalwarts from a distant past, who, along with Lorne Unsworth, represented the Island at the Electric Light sports in Halifax in August 1897. The team scored 27 points against their Halifax rivals and by 1900 were the "heart" of the Abegweit first Maritime Track and Field Championship team.
(PEI SPORTS HALL OF FAME)

The importance placed on "winning" at this particular time of sport development in the province was underlined by *The Daily Examiner* in its editorial of August 25, 1900. The Abegweit-Crescents were about to embark for Halifax in their quest for a Maritime Championship in track and field when *The Daily Examiner* appealed to the public sense of provincial pride:

> It is three years since Charlottetown made its first showing at the Maritime Championships. — Last year at Moncton, the Island boys chased the Haligonians even harder, but a half point separating them from the coveted emblem of athletic superiority. This year a determined effort must be made if they are to win. Halifax, St. John, Moncton and other Maritime cities are vieing [sic] with each other, and no expense will be spared by these cities in order to send a team qualified to carry off the wreath of victory. Let Charlottetonians who take pride in athletic development awake to this fact and help in every way the sending of a team (Abegweits-Crescents) that will show to America that Prince Edward Island brawn and muscle can hold its own with the best Canadian athleticism.

Abegweit-Crescent Athletic Club Track Team, 1900. Led by the inspirational effort of Dan MacKinnon, the Abegweit club won its first of many Maritime track and field championships in 1900. The meet was staged at the Wanderers Grounds in front of more than 3,000 spectators. Back, l-r: A. Cameron, C. J. McMillan, W. H. Ritchie, T. Ronaghan (trainor), P. McPherson, L. Adams, J. R. Drake; Middle: W. Jones, D. A. MacKinnon (Capt.), L. B. McMillan (Pres.), L. F. Munsey (Sec.), R. A. Donahoe; Front: B. Brown, J. Dewey Payne (Mascot), P. A. Duffy. (AUTHOR COLLECTION)

Three thousand spectators witnessed a spirited competition between the best track and field athletes in the Maritime Provinces. The Island team, inspired by the heroic effort of Dan MacKinnon against Murphy of the Wanderers in the one-mile run, was not to be denied its first Maritime track and field championship. Noting that MacKinnon was competing under some difficulty due to a knee injury, and the effects of a rough crossing of the Northumberland Strait en route to Halifax, the *Halifax Herald* continued:

> "MacKinnon made a great effort to secure the lead here but his legs could not hold it out and he almost fell. Murphy staggered over the tape and had to be carried from the track. Time very fast — 4:38 3/5."

While MacKinnon finished second to Murphy, the determination of both runners drew an appreciative response from the large crowd of spectators at the Wanderers Grounds.

Dan MacKinnon, attired in his many awards, is a legendary sport figure on Prince Edward Island. As an athlete, a war hero, and a lover of horses, he demonstrated a quality of influence across many sectors of Island life. (PEI SPORTS HALL OF FAME)

Arthur Cameron of Montague began a brilliant cycling career in 1898, winning the two-mile novice race at the Caledonia Games in Souris. He later joined the Abegweit Crescents Athletic Club and became one of the elite bicycle racers in the Maritimes, holding Maritime Championship/records in several middle distance events.

Robert Donahoe of Roseneath, an outstanding sprinter and jumper with the Abegweit track and field team during the early years of the 1900s. He later became McGill University's top track and field athlete for four successive years. (PARO CAMERA CLUB COLLECTION, 2820/98-1)

The Abegweit-Crescents' victory, 54–45, over the second-place Wanderers, marked the first time that the Halifax Club had not won the MPAAA sanctioned meet, first held in 1888. It was an occasion for great celebration in Charlottetown. "The Wanderers are now the Wonderers," crowed *The Daily Examiner*. The new century had spawned a new dynasty in Maritime track and field; incredibly, it would extend over three decades.

The Abegweits not only won track and field meets during their initial years as MPAAA champions, they set new standards of performance. During a two-year period, 1902 to 1904, the team literally rewrote the record book. Walter Jones established new records in the 16-lb. hammer throw in three consecutive Maritime Championship meets, raising the mark to 128' 2" in 1904. Bob Donahoe and "Toby" Mcmillan each equalled the Maritime record of 10 seconds flat in the 100-yard dash, and Dan MacKinnon broke the indoor mark in the half-mile in a race at Charlottetown. Bill Halpenny in turn broke a record in the pole vault almost every time he competed, establishing a Canadian indoor record at 10' 9½" in the fall of 1903 at the Hillsborough Rink in Charlottetown, and a Canadian outdoor mark of 11' 5¼" in 1904 at Summerside. Halpenny's spectacular performance attracted national atten-

The 1904 Abegweit Track and Field team was one of the strongest ever assembled in Maritime competition. The team included one Canadian and four Maritime record holders, Bill Halpenny, Walter Jones, "Toby" Mcmillan, and Bob Donahoe. Front, l-r: H. Harley, William Halpenny. Middle: R.A. Donahoe, F. Hennessey, Fred Jenkins, James "Toby" Mcmillan, J. W. Jones, J. Howe, L. L. McIntyre; Back: N. McNair, J. Coyle, M. J. Murphy, R. Ronaghan, G. Hughes, H. L. Bethune. (AUTHOR COLLECTION)

tion. Consequently, the Abegweit Club decided to enter its young protégé in the 1904 Olympic Games at St. Louis, Missouri. Unfortunately, the St. Louis Games were an administrative disaster, plagued by incompetent organizers and officials. The pole vault event was itself marred by indecision on the part of officials. In fact, two vaulting events were held on separate days to appease various factions. In the confusion, it was difficult to determine Halpenny's final standing. Nevertheless, when Halpenny, the Island's first Olympian, and officials of the Abegweit Club arrived home, they were given a hero's reception. The *Morning Guardian* gave the event front-page coverage:

> A monster crowd with torches and the League of the Cross Band, greeted Wm. Halpenny, L. B. McMillan, Jas Darke and R. Nicholson at the station last night on [their] return from St. Louis. The procession marched to the Labor Hall, Kent St. where speeches were given by the returning ones.

William "Bill" Halpenny, Prince Edward Island's first Olympian, was one of the province's finest athletes. In September 25, 1911, he tried for a world record in the pole vault at the Canadian Track and Field Championship in Montreal. Twice Halpenny represented the Island and Canada at Olympic Games, St. Louis in 1904 and at Stockholm in 1912. (MONTREAL DAILY STAR)

Halpenny returned from the Olympic Games in time to help the Abegweits win the MPAAA Championship in Halifax in September 1904. The *Halifax Herald* commented that the young athlete was "in a class by himself." The same accolade could have been accorded the entire 1904 Abegweit team, one of the strongest ever assembled in the Maritime Provinces. The team included four Maritime record holders — Halpenny, Jones, "Toby" Mcmillan, and Bob Donahoe. In winning the 1904 Championships, the team placed either first or second in every event.

During his trip to the Olympics, Halpenny met several athletes from the Montreal Amateur Athletic Association. He and Frank Lukeman, the MAAA's outstanding sprinter, became close friends, and, within a year, Halpenny moved to Montreal to gain employment and join the Association's track and field team. As a member of the MAAA, Halpenny became one of the outstanding pole vaulters in the world, win-

1912 Stockholm C: 24, N: 11, D: 7.11. WR: 4.02, 13-2¼ (Marcus Wright)

		M	FT.-IN.	
1. Harry Babcock	USA	3.95	12-11½	OR
2. Frank Nelson	USA	3.85	12-7½	
3. Marcus Wright	USA	3.85	12-7½	
4. William Happenny	CAN	3.80	12-5½	
4. Frank Murphy	USA	3.80	12-5½	
4. Bertil Uggla	SWE	3.80	12-5½	
7. Samuel Bellah	USA	3.75	12-3½	
8. Frank Coyle (USA), Gordon Dukes (USA), Bill Fritz (USA)		3.65	11-11¾	

The official results of the pole vault event at the Stockholm Olympics, 1912, list Bill Happenny [sic] in a four-way tie for fourth place. After clearing the bar at 12'5½", Halpenny sustained a serious rib injury when he landed in the pit, forcing him to withdraw from the competition. Halpenny defeated Badcock in a competition held in the United States several months after the Olympic Games. (THE COMPLETE BOOK OF THE OLYMPICS, DAVID WALLECHINSKY, 1988)

ning numerous Canadian Championships, establishing indoor records in the United States, and representing Canada at the 1912 Olympic Games in Stockholm, Sweden.

Halpenny's second trip to the Olympics climaxed his extraordinary athletic career. The Stockholm Olympics were a model of organizational efficiency, and attracted the best amateur athletes in the world. Twenty-one vaulters started the pole vault competition. With only seven remaining, and the bar set higher than the existing Olympic record, Halpenny sustained a serious rib injury that forced him out of the competition.[27] In recognition of his outstanding effort, the International Olympic Committee awarded Halpenny a special bronze medal.

The success of the Abegweits as Maritime Champions in rugby and track and field created immense interest in sport across the Island. Whether as an Abegweit fan or a supporter of the Summerside Crystals, Victorias, or college teams, it became fashionable to identify with a sport organization. Beyond the competition there was a social whirl that ranged from afternoon teas at the Lawn Tennis Club and the Golf Club to hosting visiting teams, excursions on special trains, year-end banquets, and annual meetings, that on occasion were formal affairs. And there was perhaps the strongest bond of all, the vicarious participation in a sport club/organization.

A predictable outcome of the high profile of sport was an increase in participation and involvement by community institutions. Previously, as with rugby and hockey, age class teams were informally organized, often with no direct affiliation with a senior sport organization or community group. Consequently, the life span of impromptu teams tended to be short. At the turn of the century, the situation was much different than it was even a decade earlier. Direct involvement came from the public school system and community organizations that included the League of the Cross and the YMCA. The promotion of sport within the school system marked the emergence of interscholastic sport as a significant part of the sport delivery system in the province. Prince Street School was involved in hockey as early as 1896, while Queen Square and West Kent Schools developed a rivalry in hockey, track and field, and rugby. The competition in track and field was especially keen, with the first inter-school meet between the two schools held September 16, 1900, at the CAAA Grounds. The historic meet was won by Queen Square 98–65, with H. Bowden of QSS and Harry Toombs of WKS winning individual aggregate points for their respective schools. The *Charlottetown Guardian* provided front-page coverage of the event, and lauded the school principals and teachers for such a "praiseworthy initiative." The Cadet Corps of the two schools paraded to the CAAA Grounds for inspection by local militia officers and other dignitaries, followed by the athletic competition. On occasion as many as seven hundred students, representing the entire enrollment of the two schools, would be involved in the parade, corps inspection, and sporting events. The annual track and field competition between Queen Square and West Kent marked the beginning of inter-school sport in the province. Within a few years, Summerside Academy staged "field days," and Montague and West Kent Schools engaged in exhibition hockey. Gradually, other schools became involved, even the small one- and two-room schools that dotted the Island landscape.

The involvement of public schools in organized sport created a new social/sport environment, compatible with educational objectives. The pursuit of excellence, whether academic or athletic, was recognized as a worthy objective of the educational system.

With the Abegweit AAA riding a crest of popularity in the community, and the resultant high profile of sport, the Victorias Hockey Club decided to form a multi-sport club, similar to the Abegweit AAA. The decision was apropos as it added a competitive entity to the local sport scene that greatly enhanced fan interest and provided the opportunity for aspiring junior stars to play at the senior level. At its inaugural meeting on March 23, 1903, the Victoria Amateur Athletic Association elected B. McQuillan as president, W. Worth as vice-president, and W. F. Collings as secretary-treasurer. Within weeks the Association grew to over a hundred members, adopted white and blue as the Club's official colours, and appointed Charles McQuillan as captain of football (rugby), and Harry Ritchie as manager of the track and field team. The formation of the Victoria Amateur Athletic Association was a milestone event in the development of sport in Charlottetown. While the Association lacked the experienced leadership and athletic prowess of the Abegweit AAA, the Club, nevertheless, provided strong competition for rival teams and experienced notable success in hockey, track and field, cycling, rugby, and baseball. Before the First World War, the Club won six provincial and three Maritime hockey championships, and numerous individual awards in track and field and cycling.

Why Summerside did not organize an athlete-centred multi-sport association at the turn of the century, similar to the Abegweits and Victorias, is a matter for conjecture. Certainly there was a need for a coordinated approach within the community, as there was a growing interest in hockey, cycling, baseball, and track and field. The Summerside Amateur Athletic Association, at the time the most active sport organization in the town, possessed the leadership resources necessary to form such an athlete-centred group; however, it opted to function as an administrative organization, e.g., acquiring outdoor sport facilities at the Summerside Raceway and sponsoring athletic events. The departure of its president, Alfred Lefurgey, to enter provincial/federal politics in 1897 left a critical leadership void within the SAAA, which eventually contributed to an inactive period for the Association. The Crystals hockey team, riding a wave of public support in the early 1900s, had an even more timely opportunity to form such an association; but it did not follow the lead of the Victorias Hockey Club, who were instrumental in the organization of the VAAA.

The Abegweits, of course, were anxious to play the Victorias in rugby, and informed *The Guardian* of their willingness. The Vics, however, shied away from such a match, opting to wait for their initial game with the vaunted Abegweits. Interest in rugby was at a high pitch when the Victorias finally decided to enter league play. The previous fall, 1902, the Abegweits and St. Dunstan's had battled to three successive scoreless games in their effort to decide the provincial senior championship. The third game, played in several inches of snow, drew upwards of four hundred die-hard fans to the CAAA grounds. With the score tied 0–0, the Abegweits wanted to continue play until a score was made, but St. Dunstan's declined, in order to preserve a streak of seven games over two years in which the team had not been scored on.

When the Vics gained entry to the PEI Football League in the fall of 1903, the much-anticipated game against the Abegweits became a reality. The Abegweits, well-prepared by playing coach Walter Jones, defeated the Vics 18–0. The superior tactical play of the Abegweits was evident as Jones utilized his experience gained the previous fall as a member of an All-Canadian rugby team that toured Great Britain. While the Vics were experiencing their baptism of fire, the serious competition for league honours was between SDU and the Abegweits. The game(s) drew the largest crowds "ever to watch a football game" in the province. St. Dunstan's prevailed, winning 3–0 and 5–3 to retain the league championship. The following season St. Dunstan's made its mark at the intercollegiate level claiming the eastern intercollegiate championship with a 3–0 win over St. Francis Xavier University, which in turn had won its way to the finals by defeating Dalhousie. With three highly competitive teams playing in Charlottetown, St. Dunstan's, Abegweits, and Victorias, the sport of rugby provided topnotch competition for its host of loyal fans.

The proliferation of new games and sport organizations continued into the first decade of the new century, with basketball and boxing finding a niche in the sport swirl, each with different contributions to make to the sport community. The first official game of basketball[28] played on Prince Edward Island was on December 12, 1903, at the YMCA, when the Abegweits defeated the Victorias 10–4. Bill Halpenny scored all the points for the Abegweits, as did Ernest Rice for the Vics. The low score undoubtedly reflected the players' lack of experience, but can also be attributed to restrictive rules which, for instance, prevented scoring after dribbling the ball. By 1906, a well-organized City League had formed at the Y, with teams representing the store clerks, businessmen, teachers, Prince of Wales, and the Charlottetown Business College (CBC). The membership reflected the sport's appeal to young businessmen/students in the community. The first league championship was declared on April 20, 1906, with the CBC team defeating the store clerks 16–9 for the Prowse Trophy. The victorious team consisted of

On April 3, 1911, the Prince of Wales College Basketball Team beat the Abbies 20–7 in the Senior YMCA Basketball League championship game. The victory evoked great enthusiasm amongst PWC students, who paraded through the streets of Charlottetown following the game. Top, l-r: Wendell McKenzie (Captain), V. Saunders; Middle: R. Fitzgerald, A. Seaman; Bottom: E. E. Jordan (Honorary President of the League), C. Balderstone, E. Warburton, C. J. Reily (Secretary, YMCA).
(AUTHOR COLLECTION)

Ernest Rice (captain), Hammond Steele, Fred Howatt, Art Gaudet, Louis Lafferty, and Fred Rice.

The popularity of basketball in the city was demonstrated by the infusion of new teams in city league play, intercollegiate competitions between SDU and PWC, interscholastic play for both boys and girls, the formation of the Church Athletic League (in April 1913), and the initiative of inter-provincial play against Pictou and New Glasgow. While it would be several decades before basketball would become a highly competitive, province-wide game, the sport was firmly entrenched as a major recreational activity in the capital city.

Boxing made its debut in Island sport circles prior to the First World War and during the early years of the 1920s. While the first boxing match in the province was staged in July 1888 at the Lyceum building on Prince Street, between Islander Joe Lannon and Dick Crowin of the United States Navy, it was two decades before boxing became a prominent sport on the Island. The main reason for the interlude was that many young Island men were displaying their fistic talents across the

United States. Lured by the prospect of employment, they travelled to Boston, worked at various trades, and learned the fight game, most likely at the Boxing School run by George Godfrey, and later by George "Budge" Byers.

George Godfrey, who grew up in the Bog Community of Charlottetown, was one of many Islanders who made the journey to Boston during the latter years of the 19th century, and the first to establish himself as a world-class fighter. While others would follow Godfrey in his quest for a world championship, including George "Budge" Byers and Tom "One Man" McCluskey of Charlottetown, William "Bill" McKinnon of Mt. Stewart and Eddie Tremblay of St. Louis, few, if any, possessed the fighting skills of Godfrey, the man they called "Old Chocolate." "Old" because he was an old-timer when he entered the fight game, and "Chocolate" because he was, as the *Police Gazette* in 1964 observed, as "black as a lump of charcoal." Wilf McCluskey, foremost authority on Island boxing, ranks Godfrey as the best "pound-for-pound" fighter to ever come out of the province.

Although comparatively small of stature at 5 feet, 10 ½ inches and 175 pounds, Godfrey possessed incredible stamina and skill. In his first ring appearance in Boston in 1879, he knocked out three heavyweights, all in the same evening, to win the New England amateur heavyweight title. After his impressive debut Godfrey turned professional and embarked on a sixteen-year pro career, 1879 to 1895, in the square circle. It was the era when boxing was poorly regulated in regard to the number of rounds, size of gloves, frequency of fights, and other aspects of the fight game. In some jurisdictions, bouts were held in secluded areas to avoid intervention by the police. In 1888, Godfrey fought a forty-four-round battle with McHenry Johnson, losing the "brutal battle" by a slight margin, and later the same year went nineteen rounds in losing to the coloured heavyweight champion of America, the great Australian fighter, Peter Jackson. But the fight he coveted most, a winner-take-all fight with the undefeated heavyweight champion John L. Sullivan, eluded him. Twice Godfrey issued formal challenges to Sullivan; on both occasions Sullivan evaded the challenge, using the colour line as his excuse. Those close to the situation maintained that Sullivan was afraid to place his title on the line. Deprived of his most sought-after opponent, "Old Chocolate" continued his illustrious career, winning his last professional fight at Baltimore in 1895.

Several years later, Godfrey returned to Prince Edward Island with his sparring partner, "Big" Danny O'Keefe of Campbellton, and staged

George "Old Chocolate" Godfrey grew up in the Bog community of Charlottetown and was one of many Islanders who travelled to Boston in search of employment during the latter years of the 19th century. He soon became involved in the fight game and was the first Islander to establish himself as a world-class fighter. (PARO 4349.1)

a series of promotional bouts across the province. Twenty years had passed since Godfrey had left his native home; they were twenty good years, and established him as a champion boxer and a worthy role model for Island fighters who would travel the same road.

The first big boxing match in the province was staged in Charlottetown on May 3, 1912, when "One Man" McCluskey fought Bob Stanley for the vacant Eastern Canadian heavyweight title. The fight attracted a large crowd to the Arena Rink, but the fight was of short duration. When the heavy-hitting McCluskey scored a knockout over Stanley in the first round, spectators were still lining up outside the rink, waiting to witness the much-anticipated fight.

When "Bill" McKinnon, formerly of Mt. Stewart, returned to the Maritimes from Roxbury, Massachusetts, to fight Roddie MacDonald of Glace Bay in two highly publicized bouts, one in Halifax, September 2, 1916, and one in Charlottetown, September 19, 1921, it helped to popularize the fight game in the province. McKinnon was a stylish boxer, who enjoyed the scientific aspect of the sport. During his career he fought nine world champions at the middleweight and light heavyweight levels, but was unable to claim a world title.

The bout in Halifax against MacDonald was a classic confrontation between MacDonald the slugger and McKinnon the boxer, and was declared a draw after fifteen rounds. The second fight between the two combatants, a ten-round main event at the Arena Rink in Charlottetown, was witnessed by over 3,000 spectators who cheered the fighters at every blow. When the smoke cleared, this bout was also declared a

William "Bill" McKinnon, formerly of Mt. Stewart, PEI, was a stylish boxer who understood the scientific aspect of the sport. His reputation was such that he was considered to be one of the most popular middleweights the ring has ever known. His two highly publicized bouts against Roddie MacDonald of Glace Bay, one in Halifax in 1916, and one at the Arena in Charlottetown, September 19, 1921, before more than 3,000 fans, helped popularize the sport of boxing across the province. He was inducted into the Prince Edward Island Sports Hall of Fame in 1973.
(PARO 2320/91-1)

draw, although the referee, Jack Ahern of Tignish, thought McKinnon had won the fight. Wilf McCluskey ranked McKinnon as "one of the most popular middleweight pugilists the ring has ever known." Commenting on the fight, *The Guardian* stated:

> The bout between MacDonald and McKinnon was something that Charlottetown sport enthusiasts really appreciated, and clearly demonstrated that boxing in the true sense should be given every support, especially from a physical culture point of view.

William "Wild Bert" Kenny of St. Teresa, was yet another Islander who travelled to the USA (New York) in search of employment, and ended up achieving world fame as a heavyweight boxer. Kenny was noted for his fight against the great Jack Dempsey on July 8, 1916, when he battled the future world heavyweight champion to a ten-round draw.[29] In his autobiography, Dempsey stated that his fight against Kenny was one of the most brutal of his life. Kenny tried desperately to get a return fight with Dempsey, but with Dempsey's reputation on the rise, fate and circumstance deprived him of the much-deserved encounter. Kenny's outstanding boxing career was duly acknowledged in his native province in 1992 when he was inducted into the province's Sport Hall of Fame.

The legend of "Big Jim" Pendergast grows with each passing year. Tales from Boston, New York, and the Klondike tell of his athletic exploits, notably in track and field, boxing, rugby, and a world record in throwing the 56-pound weight for height at the old Madison Square Gardens in New York in 1904. On his return to Prince Edward Island he successfully staged the New Annan races, promoted boxing, gymnastics, and fiddle music, which annually attracted crowds of over 5,000 spectators. (PEI SPORTS HALL OF FAME)

Big Jim Pendergast did much to promote boxing on his return to the province in 1910. Pendergast, a boxer of note and a world-class athlete in track and field, helped establish the New Annan horse races in 1912. His flare as a promoter of special events was evident in the New Annan initiative. Pendergast established a carnival-type atmosphere with vaudeville entertainment, gymnastics, and, later, boxing. The program format proved immensely popular as a major summer attraction for residents and visitors alike.

The races and special events of August 17, 1921, gave boxing wide public exposure, capitalizing as it did on the popularity of horse racing to attract a ready-made crowd of sport enthusiasts. Pendergast had enticed Eddie Tremblay, a native of St. Louis, PEI, to fight an exhibition bout with one of his husky sparring partners. Tremblay, a main event fighter and holder of the middleweight and light heavyweight titles of the US Navy, was an instant hit with the overflow crowd of over 5,000 spectators. It is generally accepted that the two fights between Bill McKinnon and Roddie MacDonald, the popularity of Wild Bert Kenny, and the appearance of Tremblay at the New Annan races were the key events in establishing the sport of boxing on Prince Edward Island.

Against a backdrop of heroes and world class boxers that was created by George "Old Chocolate" Godfrey, Bill McKinnon, Eddy Tremblay, and Bill "Wild Bert" Kenny, boxing emerged as a viable sport across the Island during the early years of the new century. While local boxers contributed to the public interest, notably Tom "One Man" McCluskey, Bob Stanley, and Barney "Kid" McCluskey, the promotion/develop-

Eddie Tremblay, a native of St. Louis, PEI, began his remarkable boxing career in 1916, while a member of the US Navy. While he only fought once on PEI, a 1921 exhibition bout where he demonstrated the art of boxing at the New Annan races was a big hit with the overflow crowd of 5,000 spectators. It elevated the popularity of the sport in the province. Tremblay was inducted into the Prince Edward Island Sports Hall of Fame in April 2000. (WILF MCCLUSKEY COLLECTION)

ment of the sport remained sporadic until the late 1920s and into the 1930s. On Prince Edward Island the 1930s and 1940s were boxing's "Golden era," and featured the fistic talent of Danny McCormack, George Leslie, the fighting McCluskey brothers, Tom, Ace, and Cobey, Irish Leo Kelly, and PEI's most outstanding boxer of the era, Harry "Kid" Poulton.

A distance-running craze swept across Canada during the pre-Great War period. Interest in marathons and long-distance running had been generated by the first Games of the modern Olympics in 1896 and the first Boston Marathon in 1897. Baron Pierre de Coubertin of France conceived the idea of a modern Olympic Games, and, with interest highest in Greece, the first Games of the modern Olympics were awarded to Athens in 1896.[30] Although the level of competition was not high, the Games were considered to be a huge success with enthusiasm and good sportsmanship demonstrated by both athletes and spectators. Appropriately, the highlight event, the marathon race, was won by a Greek peasant, Spiridon Louis, in a time of 2:58.50. The idea of a marathon race, 26 miles 385 yards, was inspired by the legend of Pheidippides, a runner who allegedly carried the news of the Athenian

The officials and participants in the Patriot *six-mile road race June 6, 1907. The race was the first organized road race to be held in the province, and it attracted widespread public and political interest. Colin McNevin was the winner of the inaugural event. Officials, back, l-r: L. B. McMillan, W. Matheson, L. B. Miller, Mayor Paton, J. Coyle, Fred K. Nash, Cyrus McMillan, G. F. Hutcheson, H. MacLean, P. Barlow, J. W. Jones; Contestants: P. Duffy, Ivan Reddin, H. Harley, C. McNevin, P. Macdougall, F. Jenkins, F. MacDonald, and (cross-legged) E. Arsenault, J. Macdougall, J. Ferguson.* (AUTHOR COLLECTION)

victory over the Persians at the Battle of Marathon in 490 BC. Upon his arrival in Athens he called out, "Rejoice, we conquer," and then dropped dead of exhaustion. While the Olympics provided a stimulus, the real frenzy for the sport stemmed from the societal conditions of the era. An intense interest in competition, ease of training for the sport, and a society not yet obsessed with the automobile, were all contributing factors. The legendary feats of Tom Longboat of the Six Nations Reserve near Hamilton, Ontario, added to the enthusiasm. Longboat was Canada's first great distance runner. A charismatic and sometimes controversial athlete, he won the Boston Marathon in record time in 1907 (2:24.24), and represented Canada in the London Olympics in 1908. Later, Longboat turned professional and raced primarily in the United States, but not before giving Canada one of its most charismatic athletic personalities.

The widespread public interest in distance running attracted major support and sponsorship to the sport, usually by local newspapers, which

Participants in the YMCA-sponsored 40-mile road race from Summerside to Charlottetown on September 22, 1908; time 4 hours,18 minutes. The era, which preceded the automobile, was one of great interest in distance running. The team included the top road racers in the province. Clockwise from 12 o'clock: A. Henry, F. Stewart, H. Pruner, I. Reddin, C. McNevin, L. W. Archibald (YMCA), H. Harley, J. McKay, A. White, H. J. McLeod, J. Ferguson. (PARO 4507/4)

gave prominent headlines to the distance races and track and field events. The first publicized road race to be held on Prince Edward Island was the *Patriot* six-mile race on June 6, 1907. While the race was plagued by heavy rain that deterred spectators, those who witnessed the event saw Colin McNevin run to victory. A month later on July 6, 1907, a seven-mile race was sponsored by prominent citizens, Dr. R. J. Ledwell, R. H. Sterns, and W. F. Boggis. Ivan Reddin of the Victoria Club won the race in a time of 42:29 1/5, followed closely by Peter MacDonald

IF ITS NEW AND TRUE THE PATRIOT HAS IT

THE DAILY PATRIOT

THE WEATHER

XXVIII, NO. 143 — CHARLOTTETOWN, PRINCE EDWARD ISLAND, CANADA, TUESDAY JUNE 22, 1909. — PRICE TWO C

The Patriot's Marathon Race Won By The Island's "Longboat

Dawson a Plucky Runner from Westville, was a Good Second, and Harley of the Victoria Athl Club of This City Was Third

Eleven Runners Waited for the Starter's Pistol and Nine of These Crossed the Finish Line—It was a Great Race on a Rare June Evening and Thousands of People Were at Every Vantage Point—One Most Exciting Finishes Ever Witnessed in This Province—The Fourth Regiment Band Rendered Choice Selections at the Finish Line Which Were Much Enjoyed by the Vast Throng

Michael Thomas made a sensational debut as a distance runner in winning the Patriot *Ten-Mile road race in Charlottetown, June 21, 1909. His victory created great excitement amongst the thousands of spectators who lined the race course.* (AUTHOR COLLECTION)

and Thomas McCluskey of the Abegweits. The excitement generated by the close finish evoked headlines in *The Guardian*, "Such a crowd and so much enthusiasm has not been seen in Charlottetown since the Boer War. A splendid race."

After these early forays, participation in road races escalated in the province and across the Maritimes from 1907 until the outbreak of the First World War. On July 6,1908, the second *Patriot* race, now ten miles, was held. It was won by a well-conditioned Colin McNevin. "There Was None So Fleet As Could Wrest The Trophy From Colin McNevin," claimed *The Daily Patriot* headline. McNevin covered the ten-mile route in 1:07.7 2/5, followed by Ivan Reddin and Harry Harley. "Practically all of Charlottetown was present at the finish line."

When Michael Thomas, a Mi'kmaq from Lennox Island, made his spectacular debut as a distance runner in the Island premiere road race in 1909, he gained headlines in *The Daily Patriot*: "The Patriot's Marathon Race Won by the Island's 'Longboat'." Under the guidance of Father John A. MacDonald, the parish priest of the Grand River area, Thomas trained for his first racing event on a crude quarter-mile track near his home and on long jaunts over dusty Island roads. He was a virtual unknown entering the ten-mile race, as Harry Harley of the Victoria Club and George Dawson of Westville were the race favourites. But it was Thomas who thrilled the thousands of fans lining the course with his stirring stretch run. "And the Indian won the race," was

Lennox Island Rugby Team, 1909. Interest in rugby on Lennox Island in 1909 was undoubtedly due to the influence of John J. Sark, Urban Gillis, and Fr. John A. MacDonald, who were introduced to the game while students at St. Dunstan's College. The rugby activity on Lennox Island coincided with Michael Thomas's victory in the Patriot Road Race, June 22, 1909. Back, l-r: Jacob Labobe, Dan Bernard*, — Toney*, Wilfred Copage*, — Toney*, Denny Lewis, Jim Sark*, John Francis; Middle: John J. Sark, Urban Gillis, Fr. John A. MacDonald, Teddy Knock-wood/Michael Francis*, John Paul*; Front: Michael Thomas, Jacob Sark, unidentified, Pat Bernard*.* (FRAN SARK COLLECTION)

**names unconfirmed*

The Daily Patriot's lead in describing Thomas' victory, seizing inevitably on Thomas' ethnic identity. Following his victory in the race, Thomas and his co-patriot, Michael Paul, joined the Abegweit track and field team, an arrangement that would prove mutually beneficial.

The distance running craze and the success of the Abegweit track and field program had created immense interest across the province. The sport was gaining a provincial flavour, with Thomas from Lennox Island, Paul from Rocky Point, and, later, John MacPherson and the talented Fulton Campbell, both from Montague. Over 3,000 spectators, one of the largest crowds ever to watch a track and field meet in the province, thronged the Abegweit Grounds in 1910 to watch the Maritime Track and Field Championships. Led by Thomas, Parker Hooper, Harold Stanley, and W. J. Donovan, the Abegweits dominated the meet, and received high praise from the Charlottetown press for staging "an outstanding event." Hooper, in particular, was superb in establishing a

The Abegweit Track and Field team of 1909 created a second wave of outstanding athletes that included Parker Hooper, Michael Thomas, and Harold Stanley. The team started a string of thirteen consecutive Maritime championships that, with the exception of the war years, extended to 1927. Front, l-r: Executive members G. Hughes, L. B. McMillan, S. F. Doyle, E. Rice, J. H. Lewis; Back: J. Parker Hooper, M. Paul, J. Gaudet, M. Robertson, Michael Thomas, Harold Stanley, W. J. Donovan (AUTHOR COLLECTION)

new provincial record in the quarter-mile. Two weeks later, at the Labour Day meet in Charlottetown, he established a new Maritime record of 50 4/5, a mark that would stand for twenty-four years.

It is noteworthy that on several occasions the strongest opposition faced by the Abegweits in their quest for a Maritime Championship came from the Victoria Club. Patrick Duffy, Harry Harley, George Prowse, and Percy Reardon in cycling carried the Vics' blue and white colours into Maritime competition. As was the case with the Abegweits, the Vics team was primarily a product of a vigorous junior development program at the Abegweits Grounds and a highly competitive interschool rivalry between West Kent and Queen Square Schools. Duffy, Stanley, and Hooper were each winners of the all-round athlete award during their interscholastic careers. Yet the story of track and field and its ally, distance running, on Prince Edward Island, remains a story of the Abegweits and its program of excellence.

J. Parker Hooper emerged from the Abegweit AAA junior development program to become the top middle-distance runner in Eastern Canada. His Maritime record of 50 4/5 seconds in the 440 yard race, which he established in 1910, stood for twenty-four years.
(AUTHOR COLLECTION)

Perhaps the biggest sporting event in the Maritimes of that era was the *Halifax Herald and Mail Star* ten-mile modified marathon. Inaugurated in 1907, the race consistently attracted upwards of 30,000 spectators, who lined the streets of Halifax for the Thanksgiving Day event. While Prince Edward Island was highly regarded as a power in track and field, it was not noted for its long-distance running prowess. Michael Thomas changed that perception.

On Thanksgiving Day, 1910, the Abegweit Club had Michael Thomas in Halifax for the now prestigious *Herald-Mail* half-marathon. Fifty-five runners lined up at the start, with an estimated 25,000 spectators lining the course that wove its way through the historic city of Halifax. As was the case in the *Patriot* race a year earlier, Thomas was not considered a race favourite. Thomas' tactics were basic — and successful: he took the lead and resisted every challenge in racing to victory. The *Halifax Herald* acclaimed it as a tremendous race:

> A successful race in 1907, a successful race in 1908, a successful race in 1909, but the success of all three of these was entirely eclipsed by yesterday's great race, which was won by Michael Thomas, the fleet Indian representative of the Abegweits.

When Thomas returned to Charlottetown, he was accorded a welcome like no other. After "vociferous cheering and fireworks at the wharf," he

Halifax Herald & Mail 10-Mile Modified Marathon

1907	Hans Holmer – 59:25 2/5
1908	Hans Holmer – 57:57
1909	Fred Cameron – 56:16
1910	Michael Thomas – 58:52
1911	Michael Thomas – 58:41
1912	Michael Thomas – 58:30¼
1913	Vic MacAulay – 55:43 4/5
1914	Competition suspended during Great War

was conveyed in a barouche to the Charlottetown Arena, where 2,500 people had assembled. The dignitaries included his former coach, Father John MacDonald, Premier F. L. Haszard, Mayor Benjamin Rogers, and his parents, Mr. and Mrs. Frank Thomas. An outpouring of "Island" pride followed, as prominent political and community leaders praised the accomplishments of Michael "Mick" Thomas, and the contribution of the Abegweit AAA to community life.

Following his impressive victory in the *Herald* race, the Abegweits entered Thomas in the 1911 Boston Marathon, the first Island athlete to run in the prestigious race. Characteristic of the Abegweits' concern for their athletes, the Directors sent Thomas to Boston a full month before the marathon, and provided the best training facilities available. While in Boston, Thomas gained valuable experience, placing seventeenth in the Boston YMCA run and a respectable twenty-sixth among eighty-five finishers in the Marathon. Considering that he ran most of the race without refreshments, Thomas's performance was remarkable. It was expected that each runner would provide his own supply of water and other fluids along the course. When his bicycle rider had an accident at the six-mile mark, Thomas ran on, alone and unrefreshed. His finish, in a time of 2:50:01 2/5, was actually faster than the winning time two years earlier. A gritty performance!

Taking into account the degree of difficulty of different marathon routes, a comparison of the times achieved by Island runners from a bygone era with those of our present-day runners reveals a remarkable consistency. One can rationalize the results for long distance events where performance is linked primarily to endurance training; other track and field events, however, would undoubtedly reflect a significant difference as technique, equipment, and facilities would each contribute to improved performance.

Comparison of Top Island Marathon Runners

1911 TO PRESENT
Standard Distance – 26 miles 385 yards

ATHLETE	LOCATION/ DATE	TIME	COMMENT
Michael Thomas	Boston, 1911	2:50.01 2/5	First Island athlete to compete in BostonMarathon. Finished 26th
John Paul	Boston, 1936	2:45.30	Finished 13th, ran a second time in 1946
Ewen Stewart	Island, 1979 (Cavendish to Charlottetown) Masters category 40 years and over.	2:47.00	48 years of age when he won the first of six straight Master races in Island Marathon. Awarded Honorary Roadrunner title in 1998
Paul Wright	Island, 1990 (Cavendish to Charlottetown)	2:43.15	Won Island marathon, six times
Pam Power McKenna	Island, 2000	3:15.16	Won Island Marathon four times
Marlene Costain	Island, 1983	3:29.08	Won Island Marathon twice, 1983 and 1984

- *PEI Roadrunners Club, the main promoter of distance running in the province, was formed in October 1978.*
- *Contributors, Don Harley and Parker Lund, PEI Roadrunners Club*

Over the long history of road races and marathons on Prince Edward Island, dating back to the first Patriot road race in 1907, few runners have demonstrated the determination and tenacity necessary to excel in the sport as has Ewen Stewart. He was the first recipient of the PEI Roadrunners Club (1971) Honorary Roadrunner Award for his dedication to the sport of distance running. (DON HARLEY COLLECTION)

The dominance of Island athletes in track and field, distance running, and road races was firmly established during the years prior to the First World War. When the Victoria AAA abdicated its direct involvement with rugby, track and field, and baseball at its Annual General Meeting in December 1911, to concentrate solely on hockey, it, in effect, relinquished its voice in the overall governance of amateur sport in the province. Consequently, with the Summerside Amateur Athletic Association inactive, the guardianship for Island sport at the regional level fell to the Abegweit AAA. The Club responded in a demonstrative way at the 1911 MPAAA Championships at New Glasgow, winning twenty-two medals, and scoring more points than their opposition combined. The New Glasgow press acclaimed it "An Abbie Day." It was a similar story in 1912, capped off by Michael Thomas's third victory in the *Herald and Mail* Marathon Championship race. There was much speculation in the Halifax press that Thomas might not run and that young Nova Scotian runner James MacKay would be the victor.

THE HALIFAX HERALD

VOL. XXXVII 12 PAGES HALIFAX, CANADA, TUESDAY, OCTOBER 29, 1912

GREAT MICHAEL THOMAS WINS HIS THIRD HERALD AND MAIL MARATHON CHAMPIONSHIP RACE

LARGER SHARE IN EXECUTION AND DIRECTION OF MATTERS OF IMPERIAL DEFENSE

Rt. Hon. L. V. Harcourt, Secretary of State for the Colonies, Addressing a Conference of Liberals, says he Would Welcome More Continuous Representations of Dominion Ministers, if They Wished it, in Matters of Defense.

But it Remained With James McKay, a Halifax Boy, to Push Him to the Hardest Contest of His Brilliant Career—Cameron's Record Holds—Enormous Crowds Cheer the Contestants as They Run and Finish the Banner Event of This Mammoth Series.

HON. FRANK COCHRANE IN HALIFAX TO INSPECT RAILWAY AND OCEAN TERMINALS

THOMAS McKAY ROGERS

Following his third successive victory in The Halifax Herald and Mail *(modified) Marathon Championship race in October 1912, Michael Thomas was the most dominant and highly publicized distance runner in Eastern Canada.* (AUTHOR COLLECTION)

Thomas left his entry until the last minute, almost as if to psyche out the Halifax establishment about his intentions. Thomas did run and won in his best time for the event, 58:30¼. The *Halifax Herald*'s front-page headlines read, "Great Michael Thomas Wins His Third Herald and Mail Marathon."

At the Annual General Meeting of the Abegweit Amateur Athletic Association on November 30, 1911, retiring president Dr. Ira Yeo stated that he did not think "there was an athletic organization east of Montreal as strong as the Abegweits. Some might be wealthier, but none is more active in athletics." One may wonder how an athletic organization based in Charlottetown could become so influential and successful in the development, promotion, and governance of amateur sport in the region. To place this in context, two main forms of sport governance were prominent in Canada during the era: the multi-sport clubs, and the autonomous sport governing bodies. The Halifax Wanderers, Saint John Trojans, and the Abegweits and Victorias of Charlottetown were prominent multi-sport clubs that promoted competition in most mass participation sports, i.e., track and field, hockey, rugby, and baseball. Lawn tennis, cycling, golf, horse racing, and rifle shooting were notable sports that affiliated directly with autonomous regional and national sport governing bodies.

In addition to their contribution to the Island sport scene, several Abegweits assumed leadership roles at both the regional and national levels. At the 1909 Annual General Meeting of the MPAAA in Halifax, Dr. H. D. Harry Johnson was elected president, and L. B. McMillan was elected secretary. Johnson and McMillan replaced two Halifax men, James C. Lithgow and Frederick Meyers, shifting the centre of power in the regional body away from the Nova Scotia capital for the first time. Lithgow and Meyers had served the MPAAA in a distinguished manner, but the election of the Abegweits representatives by the Maritimes' twenty-four registered amateur sport clubs was recognition of the Abegweit Association's emergence as a major administrative power in Maritime sport. At the end of their respective terms of office in 1913, Johnson and McMillan were duly honoured for their dedicated and competent leadership. The *Halifax Herald*, acknowledging Dr. Johnson's influence, described him as "the Tsar of athletics in Canada."

Later in the fall of 1913, Dr. Johnson was elected President of the Amateur Athletic Union of Canada during the Union's annual meeting in Montreal. His election to the top administrative position in amateur sport in Canada was a tribute to both his personal leadership ability and the national recognition accorded the Abegweit AAA. The Association's leadership role at the regional and national levels was complemented by the social activity it generated in Charlottetown. During its early years, the Abegweit Club routinely hosted visiting teams at social gatherings, and staged lavish banquets for its own teams at the end of their respective seasons. By 1910, the Club had expanded its social activities. Elaborate reunions brought former athletes, executive members, and friends of the Association together in an atmosphere reminiscent of past glories. Such formal dinners attracted many prominent political and business leaders of the province and became the formal social event of the year for many citizens.

Prior to 1912, the Abegweit AAA was a self-sustaining organization. From its own resources, it financed and directed all its activities, notably the maintenance of the Abegweit Grounds, the sponsorship and promotion of numerous athletic teams and events, and the cost of travel for regional, national, and international competition. The substantial budget for such programs was raised through membership fees, gate receipts, donations, and fundraising events.

The situation was dramatically altered in the fall of 1912. A spectacular fire at the Abegweit Grounds destroyed the grandstand and club house, plunging the Association into a financial crisis. Arson was suspected, and there were angry cries from citizens to bring the culprits to task. The anger was followed by an outpouring of community support for the Abegweit AAA, as the Charlottetown press lauded the Association for its contribution to the sporting and social life of the province.

Riding the crest of community support and prestige, the Abegweit Executive decided, for the first time in its history, to appeal directly to the public for financial assistance. Within one week of the fire the Abegweit Club ran a series of "Publicity Letters" in the Charlottetown press outlining the Club's achievements since its inception, and solicited financial support from the public. The response was most gratifying. President Gordon Hughes informed the 1913 annual meeting that all current expenses had been paid, including the new grandstand and club house; however, a mortgage of $1,400 was obtained to complete arrangement for purchase of the land. The financial burden incurred in gaining ownership of the Grounds would seriously encumber the operations of the Association during the late 1920s and into the 1930s.

The community involvement generated during the fire-induced financial crisis appears to have contributed not only to renewed support for the Abegweits, but also to increased sport activity throughout the province. While the hub of activity was centred in Charlottetown, where three multi-sport clubs existed,[31] complemented by athletic associations at Prince of Wales, St. Dunstan's, and increased interscholastic competition, there were reasons for optimism that a province-wide sport delivery system was now defined, a system that facilitated mass participation, membership in sport clubs, and the development of highly competitive athletes for regional and national competition. One of the main objectives of amateur sport — the sheer enjoyment of play and exhilaration of competition — had been achieved to a remarkable degree.

The leadership influence of the Abegweit AAA at both the regional and national levels was duly acknowledged on March 9, 1914, when the AAU of C awarded the Abegweit Club the Canadian Track and Field Championship, to be staged at the Abegweit Grounds in late August. The Abegweit Association made elaborate plans to stage the national Championship in connection with activities commemorating the fiftieth anniversary of the Charlottetown Conference on Confederation. By mid-June, entries had been received from all provinces and the United States.

However, by early August the Great War erupted in Europe, drawing Canada into the fray in support of the Motherland. Newspaper headlines conveyed the news, "The Die is Cast." On August 6, the AAU of C postponed the Canadian Championship indefinitely. In his outgoing address, Dr. Johnson advised "all the athletic forces to link up with the militia in defense of the Empire." The cancellation of what would have been a climactic achievement for the Abegweit Association did not diminish the magnitude of the Club's achievements over the previous two decades. While rugby, cycling, and hockey had achieved outstanding success at the regional level, it was track and field and distance running that had propelled Island athletes to national and international prominence prior to the First World War.

The legacy of sport excellence on Prince Edward Island was clearly scripted at the turn of the century and into the pre-Great War era. While the achievements of Island athletes received most of the accolades, other components of Island society were also involved in the rapid development of organized sport across the province. This involvement included the emergence of community leadership, the contribution of educational institutions at the college and public school level, intercommunity rivalry and competition, and commercial sponsorship and support that contributed to a sport/tourist industry. And then there was the ever-growing fan support that fueled feelings of community pride and identity. Taken in the context of a fledging social/cultural activity during the latter part of the 19th century, sport emerged as a dynamic component of Island society in the First World War era.

Government Pond provided, over many years, a natural ice surface for the citizens of Charlottetown to engage in sport and recreational activities. The activities included skating, shinny hockey, and winter carnivals. The site was filled-in during the early 1960s to provide parking space for the new provincial government offices on Rochford Street. (AUTHOR COLLECTION)

Part Two

The Morell Dreadnaughts, 1918, led by the outstanding play of Ish Murphy, who was considered to be an excellent hockey prospect, were an exciting attraction throughout King's County and Charlottetown during the early 1920s. Back, l-r: Claude MacEwen, Bill Ryan, Eddie Anderson, Ish Murphy; Front: Frank Jay, Ralph Dingwell, Birt McGraw (Coach), Layton Coffin. (SANDY CLARK COLLECTION)

7 War and Rejuvenation

When the Great War erupted in Europe on August 14, 1914, many of the Island's premier athletics and sport leaders enlisted for service in support of the Mother Country. Left behind were vivid reminders of a peaceful life on Prince Edward Island as young recruits eagerly responded to the wave of patriotism that gripped the province. Organized sport, heretofore the focus of mass participation and community emotions, was suddenly confronted with the reality that the athletic talent and administrative leadership that was so eminently successful during the preceding decades was now engaged in the escalation of hostilities in Europe. James Coyle in his book, *Prince Edward Island Athletes in the Great War,*[32] identified more than two hundred athletes who left the sport venues of the Island to display their courage and leadership on the battlefields of war. Men who excelled in sport, now as soldiers, included Lieut. Colonel Waldron B. Prowse, DSO; Lieut. Colonel A. E. Ings, Commander of the 105th (PEI) Battalion; Major D. A. MacKinnon, DSO; Captain J. P. Hooper, MC; Lieut. Alfred Murphy (Tignish), MC; Pte. Spurgeon Jenkins (Mt. Albion), an unofficial correspondent and Gunner Francis McCarey, star player with the Connaughts AAA; who was killed in action.

In spite of the exodus of Island athletes to the war effort, sport as a recreational pursuit remained an important activity for citizens at home as a diversion from the anxieties of the war. It has been postulated that sport and recreation are significant reducers of stress, and are viewed as important activities for individuals and communities in times of hardship and anxiety. Rifle shooting assumed greater importance, and hockey, bowling, curling, lawn tennis, golf, boxing, speed skating, and horse racing all succeeded in maintaining a public profile for their respective sports. Surprisingly, track and field, rugby, baseball, and road racing suffered the most significant decline likely due to the fact that the young men who participated most extensively in these sports were also of age for war service. Major sport events and competitions, such as the Canadian Track and Field Championships scheduled for Charlottetown during the summer of 1914 and subsequently cancelled, and the suspension of play by the Island Senior Hockey League in 1915, characterized the difficulty for maintaining an organized sport program across the province. What was apparently the last special train for hockey fans and players of the war years between Summerside and Charlottetown departed Charlottetown on February 12, 1915. The newspaper ad was terse: "Abegweit Hockey Special leaves at 4:00 p.m. today for Summerside, return fare $1.00." While the Crystals won the game, 7–6, the will was not there to continue league play. After several claims and counterclaims over possession of the Championship trophy, the League held the trophy and suspended play for the remainder of the war.

In the absence of senior players of military age, junior and interschool hockey between West Kent and Queen Square increased during the period, but not without controversy of its own. When Queen Square defeated West Kent 4–1 for the 1915 City Championship, West Kent protested on the grounds that "some players on the Queen Square team were not attending school." Periodically, controversies at all levels of sport in the province arose during the era. Since sport leaders were involved in the war, these stemmed more from a lack of governance than from any inherent problems with the sport.

While the standard of play in most sports declined during the war years, there was an earnest attempt by community leaders to organize competition at the recreational level that involved citizens and military personnel stationed in the province. The 105th Canadian Infantry Battalion (Prince Edward Island Highlanders) engaged both the Crystals and Abegweits in exhibition hockey games, and a Khaki league was formed in Summerside. Participation in sport was duly acknowledged as a diversion from stress and as a boost to the morale of the troops.

In the war's aftermath, as life regained a measure of normalcy— albeit in many ways changed— a new mood swept Canada. Sport was a prime beneficiary of the people's rejuvenation and escapism after the horrors of war, and, in Canada and the United States, the decade of the 1920s would be remembered as sport's "golden age." On Prince Edward Island, war veterans participated with the enthusiasm of their youth, and spectators crowded the sports fields and arenas to demonstrate their support of local athletes and teams. In this period of resurgence there was a need for strong leadership to reassemble the Island's fragmented sport scene, and rebuild facilities, team loyalties, and fragile motivation. In Charlottetown, the Abegweit Club took the initiative. At a special meeting of the Association on March 17, 1919, the first meeting of the Club since 1916, Dr. Ira Yeo emphasized the need for the reorganization of the Abegweit Club, and the revival of athletics in general. Major Dan MacKinnon, DSO, was appointed chairman of a publicity committee and S. A. McLeod, chairman of finance. A "Revive Good Old Sports Campaign" was launched and enthusiastically supported by war veterans and community leaders. A similar approach was taken in Summerside with baseball and hockey teams organizing under the Great War Veterans (GWV) identity.

During the spring of 1919, as more Islanders returned from the war zone, there were expectations for a summer of sport and relaxation. The Lawn Tennis Club convened its first meeting in several years, and there was a renewed spirit at the Charlottetown Golf Club. The Golf Club began to think seriously about major improvements to the Club House, and voted to abolish the use of cattle and sheep to keep the grass down on the fairways. One abiding issue faced the Club: ownership of the land on which the course lay. The Charlottetown Golf Club utilized the course, but the Belvedere Golf Club owned the land.[33] While both groups shared a mutual interest in developing the game of golf, the situation called for a resolution before major investments in facilities and changes in course design could be made. Ron Atkinson, in his book, *A Treasure Called Belvedere*, describes the chain of events when the Charlottetown Golf Club was incorporated in 1923 and immediately purchased all of the land in the Belvidere Woods owned by the Belvedere Golf Club, for the sum of $3,150. The historic event was concluded with several important notations: that the property was sold "in the interest of the game of golf, and secure that it always be maintained solely as a golf links," and that "from this time forward the club shall be known as the Charlottetown Golf Club Inc., but be called the Belvedere Links."

Horse racing, as always, seemed to be in the forefront of sport interests across the province, drawing huge crowds wherever races were held during the post-war era. On July 10, 1919, *The Guardian* commented, "The races at Kensington yesterday proved a big drawing card and a huge success. The attendance numbered close upon five thousand." A feature of the race card was the performance of Our Colonel, owned and driven by Major D. A. MacKinnon, in breaking the Kensington track record in 2:16. Horse racing was "big all over the Province" with race cards staged at Montague, New Annan, Summerside, the CDP, and at a host of rural tracks across the Island. The crowd of 5,000 that gathered at Kensington on that July day set the standard for the post-First World War popularity of harness racing in the province.

Baseball, inactive during the war years, expanded across the Island in 1919. Teams reorganized in Alberton, O'Leary, Souris, Georgetown, Mt. Stewart, Kensington, Summerside, and Charlottetown. The first game of the "new" season between Summerside and Charlottetown was played on July 9, 1919, at the now restored CAAA Grounds. Mayor Wright "cut one across the center of the pan" in delivering the ceremonial opening pitch. The inevitable analogy to "battlefields" was made by *The Guardian* in its account of the game:

> Prince Edward Island, in the past, has been famous for its athletes who won fame for the province in all parts of the world. The boys of today, many of whom have proved their courage and resourcefulness in the distant battlefields of Europe, will prove themselves — no less able — when it comes to contests in fields of friendly rivalry. Let the name of P.E.I. again shine forth as a symbol of all that is best in sport.

Perhaps no sport of the era evoked more nostalgia than rugby. It was a game for the purist, for players and spectators alike seemed to relish in the game, often played under the most adverse weather conditions of rain, mud, and snow in the late fall. For the pigskin brought young men to the gridiron to play during the season of The Hunter's Moon, the harvest, and Thanksgiving. Perhaps it was the aggressive nature of the game that was so appealing. It was played by "gentlemen" home from the battlefields of Europe, now transposed to the sport fields of the province.

St. Dunstan's was especially strong during the first season back (1919), bolstered by returning veterans and a record enrollment at the

The Summerside Great War Veterans (GWV) baseball team were Prince County Champions in 1920. In the years following the Great War, sport proved to be a strong antidote for the tribulations of the conflict. Clockwise: W. J. Whitney, F. Graves, F. McLeod, E. McQuarrie, H. Gillis, H. Whitney (Mascot), W. Daley, B. Waugh, L. McLellan, F. Daley, Don Stewart

(BILL STEWART COLLECTION)

Malpeque Road campus. The Saints won victories over Mt. Allison, Prince of Wales, and the Abbies, the latter game played appropriately on Thanksgiving Day. However, one gets the feeling that the score of the game was not so important; it was just good to be playing rugby once again.

In its millennium-ending story, "History Through the Headlines" feature, *The Guardian* would describe sport during the 1920s as active and province-wide:

> In the 1920s sports leagues started up again all over the province — everything from hockey, football [rugby] and golf to curling, swimming and harness racing. There were also numerous track and field meets, including the Maritime division of the Canadian track and field trials held here in 1920.—Other major events included the Maritime Golf Championship in 1922.—There were also plenty of local contests like ice sports, basketball, and gymnastics.

While the description is not intended to be all-inclusive, it does portray a grassroots participation in sport, combined with an emphasis on high performance. These constitute the essential elements of a sport delivery system, a system that became full-blown across the province during the "sport revival" of the 1920s.

The Charlottetown YMCA, which played an important role in the maintenance of sport and recreation during the war, increased its involvement during the decade of the 1920s. The local "Y" organized and promoted baseball, basketball, hockey, and bowling leagues, and stressed gymnastics and physical fitness as part of its three-fold philosophy of "Spirit, Mind and Body." The Association introduced the game of volleyball to the sport fraternity of Charlottetown on March 10, 1921, and formed leagues for businessmen of the city. Volleyball was a comparatively new game, invented at the YMCA in Holyoke, Massachusetts, in 1895. It first became popular in YMCAs and on military bases across Canada and the United States, and eventually became a highly competitive game the world over.

Both the League of the Cross, a Roman Catholic society, and the Church Athletic League contributed complementary programs to the extensive sport activity at the YMCA. The League of the Cross organized recreational basketball, volleyball, hockey, and bowling, but, with the exception of bowling, it was hampered by a lack of adequate gymnasium facilities. Later the League of the Cross would establish a high-profile athletic program in track and field, baseball, and basketball under the direction of ex-Olympian Bill Halpenny.

The role of sport as a character-builder was emphasized by the Church Athletic League, first organized in April 1913, and reactivated in the fall of 1921. The League, composed of representatives from four Protestant denominations (Presbyterians, Methodists, Anglicans, and Baptists), combined their resources and organized league play in basketball, baseball, hockey, and bowling. The leagues were well-organized and usually concluded their activities with banquets and the presentation of individual and team awards.

While the emphasis by the YMCA, churches, and related social organizations was primarily recreational, improvement in skill level and game strategies was not neglected. Bowling and basketball are games in point. New bowling lanes at the Market Building and YMCA led to the formation of a City league, and raised the level of competition significantly. At the time, there were four bowling facilities in Charlottetown and one in Summerside. Basketball showed a marked increase in scores, due to some modifications of the rules and increased competition in league play. When the YMCA team claimed the PEI Basketball Championship over the Abegweits in 1920, the score of the final game was 18–12. In subsequent years, scores in the thirties were the norm, with game totals occasionally over fifty points.

Functioning without the benefit of a multi-sport association, a YMCA (inactive), or post-secondary educational institutions in which to co-ordinate a sport system, Summerside introduced rugby, basketball, and volleyball to the community during the 1920s and maintained town leagues in both baseball and hockey. Until then, the staples of sport activities in the town had been harness racing, track and field, cycling, bowling, and hockey. This activity represented the most sustained effort to establish organized sport in the community since the formation of the Crystals hockey team in 1899, and the establishment of the Summerside Amateur Athletic Association in the mid-1890s.

Interschool sport, participation by women, and increased sport activity in rural communities were all products of the renewed sport activity that was gripping the Island. Previously, school sport was basically confined to West Kent and Queen Square Schools in Charlottetown, and their annual track and field competition, which began in 1900. The 1920s wave of activity included Summerside Academy, Kensington, Montague, and Prince of Wales Grades XI and XII. The prominence of school sport was highlighted in April 1923, when the Abegweit Club staged a Big Benefit Concert to raise money to send school athletes to an Interscholastic Track and Field Meet in Montreal. The team, composed of Lorne Wedlock, Fred McCarey, and Gordon White, made a commendable showing against the top interscholastic athletes in eastern Canada, with all three reaching the finals in their respective events.

Women's hockey, which had remained dormant since 1905 when several exhibition games were played, was also part of the sport revival. Teams were organized in Montague, Summerside, and Charlottetown, with the Abegweit Sisters the most active. The team played exhibition games against New Glasgow, Sackville, and Moncton, and were duly honoured by the Abegweit AAA at season's end, having gone undefeated during the 1922–1923 seasons. During the 1925–1926 season, the Abbies Sisters, Red Macs, Crystal Sisters, and Montague Imperials formed a provincial league that marked the beginning of a highly competitive era for women's hockey in the province.

Women also made their debut in basketball in the fall of 1922, when a Ladies' League was formed at the YMCA. Previously, several schools, Prince Street, and Prince of Wales, played exhibition games, but 1922 saw the first opportunity for play at the senior level. A problem that existed for women during the era was the absence of administrative leadership to promote and co-ordinate their involvement in organized sport. Hockey, as noted, had organized a provincial league, and, while both the Charlottetown Lawn Tennis Club and the Belvedere Golf Links included women as playing members, only the Tennis Club allowed women to serve at the executive level. Otherwise, the opportunities to participate in the core sports of track and field, curling, baseball, horse racing, rifle shooting, and rugby afforded only minimal opportunity for women to participate. It would be the mid-1930s and the post-First World War period before women would gain access to most organized sport activities across the province.

Alberton was the hub of organized sport in western Prince County during the mid-1920s, having established the first hockey and baseball teams in the area during the pre-war years. Baseball tended to be more localized than hockey during the era, with games played among Tignish, O'Leary, and Alberton. In one of the first games between Tignish and O'Leary, played on August 22, 1922, Tignish won 7–6. They immediately challenged the Summerside Pioneers for the Prince County baseball championship. It is doubtful that the game was played, but the victory over O'Leary marked the first sortie of a Tignish team into organized sport in the province. In later years, the Tignish Aces would become a strong athletic aggregation, contending for provincial honours in baseball and hockey.

By the mid-1920s, the Alberton Regals and O'Leary Maroons were part of a network of intermediate hockey leagues that had formed across the province. The first such league in the western part of the province consisted of the Regals, Maroons, Kensington Granites, Borden Nationals, and Victoria Unions, all playing for the MacLean Cup.[34] The League developed several outstanding players. The most notable was Everett "Moose" MacDonald, who played for the Regals during the first half of the decade. The exploits of MacDonald are legendary throughout Prince County. On a notable trip by the Regals to Kensington for a league game, MacDonald was unable to play, as his equipment was not available. However, in his determination to contribute to the team, he appeared on the ice at the start of the third period wearing only his skates and long johns. He boastfully proclaimed to the amused spectators that "The Moose is loose" in Kensington. Equally plausible is the story of his goal-scoring feat on his wedding night, when he registered fourteen goals for the O'Leary Maroons against Borden. While MacDonald had a flare for the dramatic, his vast hockey talent did not go unnoticed. He played for the Summerside Crystals, Saint John Beavers, and Boston Olympics. In Boston he had a try-out with the National Hockey League Bruins. According to sport columnist John McNeill, MacDonald was a "stick-handling wizard" and one of the finest hockey players of his era.

While there was a major focus on senior hockey during the first half of the decade, during the late 1920s intermediate level hockey gripped the populace, spreading to every corner of the province. There were new teams, new leagues, new trophies, open air rinks, and, where the train could not go, travel by horse and sleigh.

Perhaps the most noteworthy aspect of the resurgence of sport during the early 1920s was its expansive nature as it reached villages and towns across the province. Horse racing and hockey achieved the objective of province-wide participation during the early years of the new century, and of course certain physical recreation activities, such as skating, cycling, swimming, and fishing, had no geographic or social barriers. Organized sport, however, was still evolving, gradually engaging even the most rural communities of the province. Borden, Tignish, O'Leary, Murray Harbour, Beach Point, Hunter River, Winsloe, Cape Traverse, and others previously missing from the sport page of the Island's newspapers were now drawn into an energized sport environment.

Hockey fever swept across Prince Edward Island in March 1923, when the Abegweits defeated Windsor, NS, for their second Maritime Senior Hockey Championship. (AUTHOR COLLECTION)

8 Only Gold

Maritime Championships in Hockey/Track and Field

When the Abegweit AAA convened a meeting on October 30, 1919, to organize for the winter season, it was a "splendid meeting" with over one hundred members present. While there was optimism and enthusiasm, the news that neither of their arch rivals, the Vics nor the Connaughts, planned to reorganize, cast a shadow over the senior level of amateur sport in the province. The loss of the Connaught Club was not surprising. Its formation in 1913 was untimely as it occurred just prior to the outbreak of the First World War, and the fledgling club then faced a different sport dynamic in the postwar world. The withdrawal of the Vics was a particular blow, however, as the Victoria Amateur Athletic Association had contributed significantly to the development of amateur sport.

The absence of the two clubs in the Island Senior Hockey League caused a dilemma for League officials. The Crystals and the Abbies tried to keep the League intact, but, after several games, both teams looked for more competition. With a new ferry service operating between Port Borden and Cape Tormentine, New Brunswick, competition against mainland teams was an appealing alternative to an Island League.

When the Abegweit hockey team reorganized for the 1920 season, it brought to the fold a nucleus of star players from the pre-war years, and several key players from the Millionaires Club, a renegade team that formed in Charlottetown in January 1918, but which had disbanded when the Abegweits reorganized. John "Wacky" MacEachern, Lou Campbell, Fred Moore, Jack "Sugar" Gordon, Fred Kelly, and Ches Campbell comprised the nucleus of the squad. Such was the reputation of the Abegweit Club in track and field and rugby that there was an immediate clamour from Maritime centres for the appearance of the hockey team. After a series of convincing victories against Amherst and Stellarton, the Abbies were touted as the best amateur team in the East. The appeal of competition with mainland teams was so strong after the 1920 season that the Abegweit Association approved the team's entry into the New Brunswick Eastern Hockey League, comprised of Sussex, Sackville, Moncton, and Charlottetown. The decision was popular with Island hockey fans and propelled the Abegweits into the forefront of Maritime hockey.

In the final game of the 1920–21 League Championship series against Sussex, the team lost 7–4; however, impartial observers felt they deserved a better fate. Reminiscent of the Pictou Island adventure in 1907, the team experienced a hazardous crossing of the Northumberland Strait and arrived in Moncton travel-weary. *The Guardian* of February 24, 1921, provided a vivid description of their ordeal:

> If ever a hockey team deserved to win a Championship, the Abegweit team which left here yesterday morning to decide the winner of the eastern Hockey League certainly deserved victory. . .The car-ferry steamer yesterday had the toughest battle of the season with the ice of the real Arctic style. . .
>
> The Abbies pluckily determined not to let the elements hold them back and jumped overboard on to the ice and started to hike it on foot over the icy hummocks, the mate of the ship leading with a pole and the Abbies following the zigzag course holding on to ropes...The train started to pull out before they reached the landing, but a few lusty calls on the steamer's whistle brought the train to a standstill and the Abbies were soon on their way. . .
>
> In the second period they [Abbies] lead [*sic*] 3-2 but in the last period their opponent got a lead on them. . . It was hard luck but a good clean, swift game.

The following season, 1921–22, the Abbies played in the newly formed NB–PEI Hockey Association league along with Moncton, Dorchester,

Windsor Hockey Club, Nova Scotia Senior Champions, 1922, lost their bid for the Maritime Senior Championship to the Abegweits in 1922 and 1923. L-r: Frank Poole, Sam MacDonald, Vic McCann, W. A Ryan (Manager), George Smith, Doggie Kuhn, John Hughes, Ross Cochrance, Frank Clark, John "Chook" MacDonald, Ernie Mosher. (GARTH VAUGHAN COLLECTION)

and Sackville. The team went undefeated in league play and advanced to the playoffs against Sussex and Chatham. After defeating Sussex 2–1 in double overtime, in a game considered a classic in the annals of Maritime hockey, the Abbies travelled to Chatham for the first game of the NB–PEI Championship series. When the team defeated Chatham 3–1 in the first game of the series, there was great jubilation in Charlottetown, heralded by the ringing of the fire bell in the middle of the night. On return to Charlottetown following their impressive win, the Abbies were greeted with open arms. *The Guardian* reported the memorable occasion:

> The reception to the victorious Abegweit Hockey team on Saturday night was one which will long be remembered.—When the Borden train pulled in about five thousand citizens had assembled at the station and the members of the team, as they stepped from the cars, were received by the Abegweit officials and greeted with roars of applause which almost drowned the efforts of the

HE CHARLOTTETOWN GUARDIAN

The People's Paper Read by Everybody

CHARLOTTETOWN, CANADA MONDAY, FEBRUARY 27, 1922

CHARLOTTETOWN'S ROYAL WELCOME TO THE VICTORIOUS ABEGWEITS

he Boys Arrived Home Saturday Night and Were Received With Open Arms. Enthusiastic Reception at the Market Building, Speeches by the Lieut. Governor, Premier Bell, Mayor Jenkins, U. S. Consul Crosby and Others. President Sam Doyle Replies.

Headlines tell the story: Maritime Champions, 1921–1922.

> two brass bands which were playing for all they were worth "Hail the Conquering Heroes."

When Chatham arrived in Charlottetown for the final game of the championship series, they were given a warm reception by members of the Abegweit Club and civic leaders. The team were guests at a civic reception, and the Charlottetown press extended a cordial welcome to the hockey team and officials from Chatham. The goodwill carried over to the hockey game as the "home team" fans packed the Arena and cheered the Abbies on to a 7–3 victory. The win marked the seventeenth successive win for the team, climaxed an undefeated season, and with it the NB–PEI senior hockey championship.

With the NB–PEI championship secure, the Abbies waited a full month for the Nova Scotia winner to be declared. Finally, on March 24, 1922, the Abbies met Windsor in a sudden-death final at the Arena in Charlottetown. Amid wild cheering the Abbies prevailed, defeating the N.S. champs 5–3 for the Morton & Thompson trophy, and the Abegweits' first ever Maritime senior hockey championship.

The excitement of the 1922 championship play carried over to the 1923 season, which included several significant developments. The Summerside Crystals gained entry into the eastern section of the NB–PEI League, which included the Abegweits, Dorchester, and Sackville. The entry of the Crystals proved beneficial for Island hockey as it renewed the rivalry between the Crystals and Abegweits that had existed in the old Island League. Not willing to stand still in their position as Maritime senior hockey champions, the Abegweit Association engaged Mr. Frank Brown of Moncton as coach of the team. Brown, in effect, became the Director of Hockey for the city, as his duties extended beyond the senior Abbies to include all facets of hockey in Charlottetown: city league, women's, and school hockey. Not included in his job description was any control over the unpredictable weather that was typical of Island winters. A mild December in 1922 meant no natural ice on Government Pond, which forced the team to do dry-land training at the YMCA gymnasium. In contrast, several weeks later on January 13, 1923, a severe winter blizzard stranded the "hockey special" for six days at Emerald on its return trip from Summerside. *The Guardian* carried regular updates and headlines, e.g., "Besieged hockeyists return all the way from Emerald":

> Yesterday, the sixth day after the snow blockade, the railway line between Summerside and Charlottetown was cleared and the marooned hockeyists and hockey fans were released from snowbound Emerald and returned jubilant to Charlottetown yesterday afternoon . . . They report that the people of Emerald were very good to them and did what they could to fulfill the sudden demand for accommodation. There were 91 altogether placed upon their hands, including a number of ladies. . . . Luckily for everyone, there was no grouch in the party.

Oh, the perils of an Island winter!

The Abegweits extended their unbeaten streak to twenty-eight games during the 1923 season, becoming, in the process, the biggest hockey attraction in Eastern Canada. Sellout crowds watched the team play in Chatham, Moncton, Sussex, and Summerside. In the playoff game against Sussex, won by the Abbies 4–3 in overtime on a goal by Percy Rodd, scalpers were hawking tickets outside the Charlottetown Arena hours before the game. In the championship game against Windsor, for the Maritime title, the Abbies fought back from a 3–0 deficit to win 4–3. As it had done in the mid-1890s, hockey fever swept across Prince Edward Island. The Abegweits were true champions.

The excitement generated by the Abegweits attracted national attention. Art Ross, Manager of the National Hockey League's Boston Bruins, called the Abbies a "miracle team." When Fred Moore, a stalwart on the Abbies team, was injured in an exhibition game against Boston College as part of a tour of the Boston area, he received a telegram from Prime Minister MacKenzie King, wishing him a speedy recovery.

Prince Edward Island, too, was proud of the Abbies. Following the season, the Charlottetown Rotary Club launched a campaign to honour the team. At a gala musical revue at the Strand Theatre, the players were presented with gold medals. The Abegweit Sisters were also honoured for their unblemished record over the 1922 and 1923 seasons. In the inevitable speeches, Mayors Winsloe Lidstone of Summerside and R. H. Jenkins of Charlottetown each attested to the great honour the team brought to the cities and province.

The hockey team's momentum carried over into the fall of 1923, when the Abbies were selected to play an exhibition game against the Toronto Granites, Canada's representatives for the 1924 Winter Olympic Games in Chamonix, France. To the casual observer, the game was a natural: the National Champions and Allan Cup holders, the Granites, against the Maritime Champions, the Abegweits. To the astute hockey observer, the game represented an important contrast in hockey traditions. The "big city" Granites represented hockey sophistication; the Abegweits symbolized the free-spirited style learned on the natural ice surfaces of places like Government Pond, the Summerside Harbour, and the Ellis River. Few of the capacity crowd that jammed the Saint John rink to watch the game sensed the contrast, but it was there.

The game was a classic, with excellent individual and team play. Both teams emerged with their reputation intact. The Granites won the game 4–1 before 3,500 and were toasted on their departure for the Olympic Games. The Abbies, likewise, received glowing tributes, and were conceded to be the second-best amateur hockey team in Canada, worthy representatives of the country had it been their lot to play in the Olympic Winter Games. At Chamonix, the Granites won gold for Canada, defeating Sweden 22–0, Czechoslovakia 30–0, and Switzerland 33–0. It is no exaggeration to think that the Abbies would have carried home the gold had they been Canada's representative.

During the 1923–1924 season, jurisdiction of hockey in the Maritime Provinces was taken over by the Maritime Amateur Hockey Association (MAHA). The MAHA realigned existing leagues and placed the Abbies and Crystals in an Island league. While there was a long-standing rivalry between the two communities, the frequency of games and short schedule had an adverse effect on fan support. By ear-

The Summerside Crystals assembled a strong hockey team for the 1924–1925 season that included future NHL star Charlie Cahill and veteran Ernie MacQuarrie. The team broke the domination of the Abegweits in Island senior hockey on January 31, 1925, with a decisive 7–2 playoff victory. Back, l-r: Joe Wood (Coach), Llewellyn Rogers, Art Morris, Ernie MacQuarrie, Jack Wright, Art Johnston, Leo Wood; Front: Leo Gauthier, Charlie Cahill, Earl Corney, Carl Crockett, Ralph Silliphant, D. E. Cahill. (PARO CAMERA CLUB COLLECTION, 2320/93-8)

ly February, the Abbies had sewn up the Island Championship, and, still buoyant from their highly publicized game against the Olympic-bound Granites, the team departed for Boston for a series of exhibition games. The games against Boston College, US National Collegiate Champions, and the venerable Boston Athletic Association attracted more than 13,000 fans and were described as "sensational." While the Abbies lost both games, 2–1 to the college champs, and 3–1 to the Boston Athletic Association, the Boston Bruins were clearly impressed by what they saw, and placed John "Wacky" MacEachern and Roy Prowse on their negotiating list.[35]

While it was a credible overture by the Bruins, it did not bode well for the future of the Abbies. On return to the Maritimes, the Abbies were dethroned as Maritime Champions by their arch rivals Sussex. In the fall of 1924, MacEachern and Prowse departed for Boston. At the same time, several players decided to retire from hockey, and several

The product of the Summerside Crystals hockey program, Charlie Cahill became the first Islander to play in the National Hockey League. He was recruited by the Boston Bruins in 1925 and played for the team during the 1925–1926 season. Mid-way through the 1926–1927 season he was assigned to the Bruins farm club, the Springfield Indians, where he became one of the team's top scorers. (CIVIC STADIUM COLLECTION)

others defected to regional teams. The ingredients that had created one of the most spirited and successful hockey teams in the Maritime Provinces were now dispersed. Grantland Rice in his poem, "The Final Chapter," recommended caution in such circumstances: "Look out against the skyline, where training for the day, A better man than you are is always on the way." The Summerside Crystals were "on the way."

For the 1924–1925 season, the Crystals presented a strong aggregation that included Ernie MacQuarrie and Charlie Cahill. After dominating league play, the Crystals dethroned the Abegweits as Island Cham-pions, taking the deciding game of the playoffs 7–2 on January 31, 1925. With the Island championship secure, the Crystals advanced to the NB–PEI playdowns, winning against Amherst 5–1 and 4–2. The next series against Sussex, the defending Maritime Champions, produced excellent hockey, with Sussex prevailing 4–4 and 3–2 in a two-game total goal series. The competitiveness of the Crystals was aptly demonstrated by their close series against Sussex, combined with the slim margin in the ensuing Maritime finals between Sussex and Truro, with Truro winning the total goal series 3–2 and 3–3.

The calibre of Island hockey players during the era was outstanding. Charlie Cahill went on to play for the Boston Bruins in 1925–1926, becoming the first Island player to play in the NHL; Percy "Chick" Williams and Roy Prowse both played for Waterville, Maine, of the New England professional league; and John "Wacky" MacEachern and Everett "Moose" MacDonald were given tryouts with other professional teams. Collectively, they were the vanguard for the many Island hockey players who would etch their names on professional team rosters in Canada and the United States.

What the Abbies and Crystals senior hockey teams accomplished in winter across the Maritimes during the first half of the 1920s, the Abegweit track and field teams did in summer. When track and field did not rebound immediately to its pre-war status following the war, there was concern among the Abegweit executive. While the team, led by Fulton Campbell of Montague, successfully defended its Maritime Championship at Moncton in 1920 and Saint John in 1921, there was strong competition from the Saint John Trojans. The situation raised anxious moments for the Abegweits and prompted a pivotal decision by the Club; in the spring of 1921 they enticed Bill Halpenny to return to Charlottetown from Montreal to coach the track and field team. The decision reflected a philosophical shift for the Abegweit Association: the employment of coaches (and later players) to maintain the reputation and level of excellence that was expected from its extensive athletic program.

Halpenny approached coaching with the same flamboyance he displayed as an athlete twenty years earlier as the "Boy Wonder" of the Abegweit track and field team. During the first year of Halpenny's tenure, there was renewed optimism for track and field, led by a young and talented group of athletes. At a Dominion Day meet in Summerside, Phil MacDonald eclipsed the Maritime record in the long jump with a new mark of 22' 1". Days later, Barney Francis established a new provincial record in the half-mile with a time of 2:04 ¾, breaking a mark that had stood since 1900.

On September 10, 1922, in an atmosphere charged with excitement, over 3,000 spectators thronged the Wanderers Grounds in Halifax to watch the highly publicized Abegweits from Prince Edward Island defend their Maritime title. The Abegweits were up to the task. The excitement generated by the meet inspired *The Halifax Herald* to print the following headline: "Thrilling Scenes at Maritime Championship. . . Greatest Meet [in Halifax] since Canadian Championships in [1908]."

During the competition Barney Francis was deprived of a Maritime record in the mile event when "a zealous Charlottetown fan" (the *Her-*

Alf Groom clears the crossbar in establishing a new Canadian record of 14' 3" in the pole vault event at the British Empire and Commonwealth Games Trials in Toronto in 1962. Groom joined fellow Islander Bill Halpenny, of an earlier era, as a holder of the Canadian record in the pole vault. The event has changed dramatically over time, with new technology, new techniques, and high-level competition. (PARO 2320-99-3)

ald's description) embraced him as he raced for the finish. Phil MacDonald also lost a record-breaking jump when a well-meaning official raked the long jump pit before his jump could be measured. While Francis, MacDonald, and jumper Lorne Wedlock led the team to victory, it was Halpenny himself who drew the greatest ovation. Now forty years of age, he reclaimed his Maritime record in the pole vault, "making the most spectacular vault ever seen in Halifax," according to the *Herald*: "And the reception he was accorded when announcer J. D. Vair shouted, 'Halpenny clears at 11 feet, 4 ½ inches,' was fit for a King." As was the custom on Prince Edward Island, when the team returned to Charlottetown, "Our Boys" were given a rousing welcome, which included speeches from Lieutenant-Governor Murdock MacKinnon, Mayor R. H. Jenkins, and Abegweit Club president Sammy Doyle.

Comparison of Top Island Pole Vaulters

1880s TO 1960s			
ATHLETE	LOCATION/DATE	HEIGHT	COMMENT
James MacEachern	Caledonia Games/1888	10' 4"	Won Maritime Championship in 1888. First gold medal for Island athletes in Maritime track and field competition.
Marcus Henderson	Charlottetown 1888	10' 4"	Great rivalry with MacEachern. Lived in Clyde River, moved to Moncton early in his career.
Harry Harley	Halifax 1908	10' 11"	Was Maritime champion at MPAAA meet in Halifax. Consistently vaulted over 10'.
Wallie Scantlebury	Saint John 1921*	10' 7"	During the early 1920s Scantlebury was one of the most consistent vaulters in the Maritimes.
Bill Halpenny	Charlottetown 1903	10' 9½"	Canadian indoor record.
	Summerside 1904	11' 5½"	Canadian outdoor record.
	Stockholm Olympics/1912	12' 5½"	Injured after clearing the bar at 12' 5½".
Alf Groom	Toronto/1962 (BECG Trials)	14' 3"	Canadian outdoor record.
	Charlottetown 1964	14'	Provincial open record.

* *In preparation for the MPAAA track and field competition in Saint John, 1921, Scantlebury cut a small tree from the woods near his home and crafted it to his liking. He used the pole (tree) in winning the pole vault event at the Maritime Championships. Modern technology, such as the flexible vaulting pole and a better landing pit, has dramatically changed this event over the years, more than any other single event in track and field.*

Displaying a classic running style, Barney Francis of the Abegweit Team hangs on the shoulder of Roger Antliff from the Montreal AAA during the final lap of the one-mile race at the 1923 Canadian Track-and-Field Championships in Halifax. Over 5,000 partisan fans cheered Francis to a stunning victory. "The final sprint by the young Indian fairly ran Antliff off his feet..." (Halifax Herald). (AUTHOR COLLECTION)

The Abegweit track and field team, comprising athletes from various parts of the province, reached its zenith during the 1923–1924 seasons. When the 35th Canadian Track and Field Championships were staged in Halifax in September of 1923, the Abegweits made their most impressive showing ever in national competition. While Ontario won the meet with 55 team points, Phil MacDonald and Barney Francis scored impressive wins, each claiming a gold medal in individual events. MacDonald, "Charlottetown's Boy Athlete" (as he was dubbed by the *Halifax Herald*), won the hop, step and jump, and placed second or third in five other events. His aggregate 16 points in six field events was the second-highest individual total for the meet, trailing only Leigh Miller of Sussex with 19 points. Francis stirred the crowd of over 5,000 with an upset victory in the mile over Roger Antliff from the Montreal AAA. *The Herald* captured the drama of his triumph:

> Barney Francis, Charlottetown Indian, had too much speed and stamina for Ontario and Montreal runners in the mile. . . . Francis was a favorite with the crowd. . . . He allowed Antliff, a previous Canadian champion, to set the pace for practically the entire distance and waited for the final drive. . . . The final sprint by

Abegweit and League of the Cross athletes returning from the Maritime Track and Field Championships in Halifax, September 1924; one of the strongest teams to ever represent the province. Back, l-r: Bill Halpenny (Coach), Barney Francis, Gordon White, George Francis, unidentified; Middle: D. Cox, Phil MacDonald, Sammy Doyle, Dr. McGuigan, Elliot McGuigan, Fred McCarey; Front: Wallie Scantlebury, Alex Stewart. (AUTHOR COLLECTION)

> the young Indian fairly ran Antliff off his feet . . . . and the Islander won by two yards amid the wildest enthusiasm from the stands.

Francis set a Maritime record of 4:32 1/5 in the race, eclipsing a mark of 4:33 set in 1908 by Hans Holmer at the Maritime Championships in Halifax.

At the conclusion of the 1923 track and field season, which included the highly successful Canadian Championships, there were high expectations within the Abegweit Club for even greater achievements. There was the potential for three of the team's athletes, MacDonald, Francis, and newcomer Elliot McGuigan, to be selected to the Canadian Olympic team scheduled for Paris the following summer. However, administrative changes during the winter of 1923–1924 had an adverse effect on the track and field program. Seeking full-time employment, Bill Halpenny accepted a position with the League of the Cross as the Association's Physical Director. Within several months, he formed the

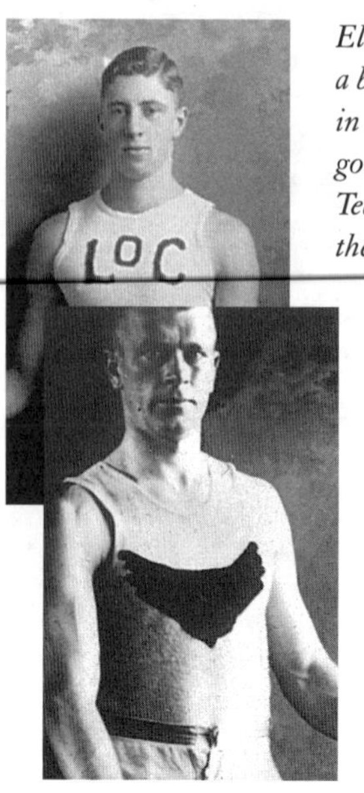

Elliot McGuigan of the League of the Cross AAA put on a brilliant display of talent at the MPAAA Championship in Halifax, September 1924. The young speeder won four gold medals in tying Phil MacDonald of the Abegweit Team for the individual aggregate points total during the meet. (AUTHOR COLLECTION)

During the early 1920s, George Walker was one of the top distance bicycle racers in Eastern Canada. He narrowly missed selection to the 1924 Summer Olympic Games in Paris. Walker overcame severe war wounds to pursue the challenging sport of long-distance racing where single events often extended over 100 miles. (AUTHOR COLLECTION)

League of the Cross AAA and affiliated with the Maritime Branch of the AAU of C. Phil MacDonald left the province to train with the Olympic team in Toronto, while Barney Francis sought employment in New Brunswick.

The dispersal of the previous summer's team was detrimental. Neither Francis nor McGuigan were at their best for the Olympic trials, and failed to qualify. George Walker of Brackley, considered the Maritimes' top long-distance cyclist, and a likely choice for the Olympic team, was not selected in spite of his valiant performance at the cycling trials at Montreal in July 1924. Walker finished third in the 105-mile road race, 14 minutes behind the winner, A. Laporte of Montreal. Many Maritime officials felt that both Walker and Francis were treated unfairly in the selection process. In the end, only Phil MacDonald was selected to the Canadian Olympic team, becoming the Island's second Olympian.

MacDonald proved to be a worthy representative of the province and Canada. Although his specialty was the long jump, he was entered in the 400-metre hurdles, an event in which he had little experience. His performance evoked praise from the Canadian head coach, Captain J. R. Cornelius, who lauded MacDonald's congeniality and natural ability. In his report to the Canadian Olympic Committee, Cornelius stated:

The Queen Square School track team of 1924, coached by Bill Halpenny, featured several future stars in track and field, cycling, and rifle shooting. L-r: E. Hornby, F. Lappin, H. Hennessey, R. Hogan, A. Gormley (captain), J. Ledwell, J. Trainor. W. Power, C. Arsenault; Front: Bill Halpenny (Coach). (PARO 2320-98-8)

> One of the most remarkable pieces of work was that of P. MacDonald in the 400-metre hurdle. Two months previously he had never run a race, let alone hurdles, and yet in his heat, two yards covered 1st and 3rd man, our man being nosed out by inches. The world's record at the time was 54 secs. The time for his heat was 54 4/5.

Reunited for the 1924 Maritime Championships in Halifax, Phil MacDonald and Elliott McGuigan put on an awesome display of talent. McGuigan, competing for the League of the Cross, won an unpreceddented four gold medals, and MacDonald, competing for the Abegweits, matched his former teammate with 20 individual points. MacDonald had strong support from Barney Francis, Wallie Scantlebury, Gordon White, and Fred McCarey, as the Abegweits won yet another Maritime title.

The League of the Cross team's rise to prominence can be attributed to the individual performance of McGuigan and the coaching of Bill Halpenny. When McGuigan finished his studies at St. Dunstan's University and entered the priesthood, the high-profile track and field

Phil MacDonald (left), one of the "great" Abegweit athletes, poses with Don Cable of Montreal at the Canadian Track and Field Championships in Halifax, September 1925. MacDonald was impressive in winning the Canadian championship in the long jump, and hop, step and jump, scoring 18 individual points at the meet. Teammate Wallie Scantlebury also performed well at the national meet, winning a bronze medal in the pole vault. (AUTHOR COLLECTION)

program at the League of the Cross diminished. The Association did remain active, however, with cyclist Ed Hornby, the province's premiere distance racer, representing the League during the latter part of the decade. When Hornby was transferred by his employer to Shelburne, NS, in the winter of 1929, the emphasis of the League of the Cross AAA reverted to a community sport program, notably baseball and basketball.

Following the 1924 season, with its memorable performances by Island athletes, there were signs of a general malaise affecting track and field across the Maritimes. While the Abegweits retained a strong nucleus of athletes, the continuance of the club's supremacy in Maritime track and field relied primarily on the individual performance of Phil MacDonald. In one of his last competitions, in 1927, he led the Abegweits to their thirteenth consecutive Maritime Track and Field Championship (1909–1913 and 1920–1927). In the meet, he accumulated 25 of his team's 47 points. Years later when Phil MacDonald returned to Prince Edward Island to be inducted into the province's Sports Hall of Fame, he spoke passionately about sport and its impact on his life: the competition, the friends, the Olympics. In his concluding comments characteristic of the champion he was, he modestly stated, "my cup runneth over."

It was inevitable that the Abegweit string of Maritime Championships would be broken. The first indication came in 1928 when the Maritime Provinces branch of the AAU of C failed to select a site for the annual competition, resulting in the cancellation of the champion-

A. Fulton Campbell of Montague joined the Abegweit track and field team in 1913, leading it to Maritime Championships in 1913 and 1920. The disruptions of the First World War prevented many of his outstanding performances from reaching the record books. (AUTHOR'S COLLECTION)

ships for the first time, war years excepted, since 1888. While the Abegweits technically retained the Maritime title for one more year (1928), the end of the Club's remarkable dominance of the sport came in 1929 when the Club did not send a team to the Championship meet in Saint John. Relinquishing its position as the most dominant track and field club in the history of the sport in Eastern Canada came with great anguish on the Island as diehard Abegweit officials and fans called for a return to the glory days of the early 1920s.

During the summer of 1929, in a series of public meetings, S. F. "Sammy" Doyle, president of the Abegweit Club, spoke passionately about the need for community support of athletes, and blamed "parents and cars" for the decline in public participation. While Doyle spoke with conviction, he seemed reluctant to acknowledge the decline of the Abegweit AAA as the most prominent organization in the governance of amateur sport in the province. Individual sport governing bodies were gradually eroding the influence and jurisdiction of the multi-sport club system at both the regional and national levels, a trend that Doyle would find difficult to accept in view of his personal/professional loyalty over the years to the Abegweit Amateur Athletic Association.

Notwithstanding the evidence of decline of the Abegweit AAA during the late 1920s, it did not diminish the significance of the achievements by Island athletes during the early years of the decade. The outstanding performances of Abegweit athletes in Maritime senior hockey and track and field came at a critical time in the rejuvenation of organized sport across the province following the Great War. Not only were the Abbies successful, they were hometown boys, the products of school and junior development programs, who represented the best of the Island's athletic talent. Phil MacDonald, Elliot McGuigan, Roy Prowse, Fred Kelly, and others were worthy role models, who contributed to the prominence of sport as an essential part of community life. Few, if any, cultural or social events evoked the level of emotion as did games at the Abegweit Grounds, races at the CDP, or a Sunday afternoon baseball game in rural PEI. Taken in the context of amateur sport during the early 1920s, the achievement of Island athletes represented a glamorous chapter in the history of sport in Prince Edward Island.

9 The Resilience of Sport

The mid-years of the 1920s were good years for sport on Prince Edward Island as the province continued to bask in the post-war revival of amateur sport. While track and field and senior hockey claimed the sport headlines throughout Eastern Canada, there was a corresponding ground swell of participation in community- and provincial-based sport across the province. While one might expect that the high-profile exploits of Island athletes in track and field and hockey would overshadow community/provincial participation, such was not the case during the postwar era, as all levels of the sport delivery system (i.e., recreation, community, provincial, and regional competition) functioned with momentum and optimism.

Baseball in particular was a beneficiary of the energized sport atmosphere. The 1920s saw the organization of local leagues, the declaration of provincial champions, and inter-provincial play. A controversy that threatened to disrupt the game, at least temporarily, confronted league officials in Charlottetown in 1923, when the Madison baseball team organized and entered city and provincial league play. The team, sponsored by city businessmen Joseph and Fred Lambros,[36] recruited the best baseball talent in Charlottetown, thereby depleting the other league entrants, the Abbies and League of the Cross, of their top players. The concern was for the competitive balance of the league,

Pioneer Baseball Club, 1938, Champions, Summerside Town League. Top: J. Millman (Captain), J. Schurman, J. Clow, D. Lidstone, D. Larkin, Rev. J. B. Wilson; Centre: Wilf Kelly, Manager, J. Hunter, H. Crossman, J. Dodds, D. Steele, Bruce Johnston; Bottom: Dr. H. Clarke (President), A. Gay, E. Arsenault, Jackie Kelly (Mascot). (CIVIC STADIUM COLLECTION)

as the uncertainty of outcome of a sport competition is an important factor in retaining player/spectator interest. While the Madisons swept through the regular season undefeated, the Summerside All-Stars provided, unexpectedly, strong opposition in the provincial playoffs, winning two games in the best of five series. The Championship game went down to the last out with the Madisons eking out a 10–9 victory.

When the Madisons convened a meeting at the end of the baseball season to discuss the organization of a hockey team and an athletic association, several respected citizens, including Fred Kelly of the Abegweits, were opposed. Kelly suggested that "Charlottetown could only support one athletic association for hockey." With the sentiment of the meeting running in support of the Abegweit AAA, the Madisons modified their hockey aspirations and entered a team in the City League. Meanwhile, the Madison baseball team became a one-season sensation.

By the 1925 season, baseball had regrouped, with strong local leagues in both Summerside and Charlottetown. The Prince County

The Souris Baseball Team, 1927–1928, competed successfully against teams from the Charlottetown City League and King's County teams, notably Murray River, Montague, and Georgetown. It was boastfully stated that Isaac Cheverie was so quick at shortshop that the opposition couldn't get a .22 bullet past him. In fact, the team was noted for its tight infield. Back, l-r: Michael Cheverie, Frank Cheverie, Arthur McCallum, James Brennan, Ivan Cheverie, Marcus Mooney; Front: Isaac Cheverie, Edmund Lavie, Warren Cheverie, Gordon MacLean, Harold Lavie. (PARO HERITAGE FOUNDATION COLLECTION, 3466 HF74.285.3.8)

League was revived with the Red Sox, Cardinals, Pioneers, and Torontos. In Charlottetown, the Anchors, Stars, and Rovers comprised a well-balanced City League. There was also renewed activity by rural teams, with Souris well-organized and playing exhibition games against teams from the Charlottetown City Baseball League. By 1929, the King's County League was in its formative years, with teams from Souris, Murray River, Montague, and Georgetown exhibiting strong interest in the game.

Under the patronage of Lieutenant-Governor Frank R. Heartz, an avid fan of the game of baseball, and President Dr. Charles Dougan, the City League proved to be immensely popular. The opening game of the 1926 season, between the Rovers and Stars, attracted more than 1,500 fans, and, by season's end, as many as 2,000 attended league games. When the Stars defeated the Rovers for the League Championship in September before a huge gathering, the consensus was that the game was "a (fitting) climax to a great City League season."

Rovers Baseball Team, Champions City League, 1928. The Charlottetown City Baseball League, comprised of the Rovers, Stars, and Anchors, was a popular sport activity during the late 1920s. Regular league and playoff games drew upwards of 2,000 spectators. Back, l-r: N. Whitlock (Manager), W. Murley, H. MacKenzie, D. MacLean, R. Doyle, P. MacInnis, L. Matheson (Coach); Front, l-r: G. Whitlock, J. Williams (Captain), F. Cronin, J. Whitlock (Mascot), P. Diamond, V. Blanchard, F. Connors. (PARO CAMERA CLUB COLLECTION)

Large crowds were the rule for baseball games during the period as the Prince County League and inter-provincial games attracted large numbers of spectators. On May 26, 1926 (Empire Day), two exhibition games between Moncton and the Abbies drew more than 2,000 fans to the Abegweit Grounds, with the Abbies winning both games, 5–4 and 5–3. During the 1929 season, the Abbies made their first sustained challenge for a Maritime Championship when they defeated the Moncton Catholic Club 2–0 and 4–0 to win the NB-PEI Championship. The series featured the outstanding pitching of "Putty" Connors and the stalwart play of battery mate George "Shonna" Francis. In the finals for the Maritime Championship the Abbies came up against a strong Yarmouth Gateways team, losing the best-of-five series three games to one. While the Abbies were outplayed by the Yarmouth Club in the battle for Maritime senior baseball supremacy, the presence of the Charlottetown team in the final series helped establish the competitiveness of Island baseball with mainland communities.

While the primary emphasis of baseball during the mid-1920s was on local leagues, a provincial league also functioned, with playoffs scheduled for late August to declare a provincial champion to advance to inter-provincial play. The 1925 playoff between the Crystals and Abbies was a classic series, with the Abbies winning the final game 2–0 behind the "no-hit" pitching of their young sensation, Vince "Lefty" McQuaid. Both the Abbies and Crystals developed outstanding pitchers during the era, including McQuaid, "Happy" Hobbs, Tom McFarlane, "Putty" Connors, Jim Wilson, and Lorne Monkley.

While baseball maintained its momentum into the early 1930s, the onset of the Great Depression and a lacklustre administration of the sport by the Maritime Amateur Baseball Association contributed to a decline of the sport throughout the Maritimes. The Depression, with its social and economic upheaval, seriously disrupted the vitality of the game on PEI, not only of baseball, but for sport in general. The financial and administrative resources that were readily available from the community during the 1920s were now diverted to the more pressing needs of the populace. High on the list of priorities for Island sport officials was to sustain the integrity of the sport structure at the provincial level, and to maintain inter-provincial play. This was difficult to achieve as sport traditionally received its financial support from membership fees, gate receipts, fundraising events, and contributions from private sources, of which volunteerism was a significant component. Now, with the Island's economy and social fabric in disarray, sport, at least temporarily, appeared to be a casualty of economic and social factors beyond its control. By 1933, Summerside reverted to an intermediate classification and won the New Brunswick/Prince Edward Island Championship over Newcastle, NB, in a best-of-three series. The team then waited six weeks, until October 31, before advancing to the Maritime final against the Springhill Iron Dukes. On that crisp October day the team lost to the Iron Dukes, 5–1. The Summerside AA squad had the chance to win the first Maritime baseball title for the Island, with a battery of Jim Wilson and Ben Schurman, and a group of talented players, had the MABA expedited the Maritime playdowns in a more efficient manner.

While the Abbies were successful in winning nine consecutive Island senior championships (1924–1933), and several inter-provincial series against Nova Scotia and New Brunswick teams, the Club was unable to annex a Maritime senior title to add to its long list of impressive victories in rugby, track and field, and hockey. In 1934 the Abbies also reverted to the intermediate classification, but they were unable to ful-

Key members of the Peakes Hawks baseball team celebrating the outstanding pitching performance of "Fiddler" MacDonald in shutting down the Charlottetown Dodgers with 26 strikeouts (24 via catcher) in 1936. L-r: George Smith (c), James "Fiddler" MacDonald (p), Earl MacDonald (ss).
(ANNE MORRISON COLLECTION)

fill playoff commitments due to a lack of funds. The junior Abbies faced a similar dilemma in their 1934 playoff series against Amherst. After defeating the St. Pats 5–2 in Charlottetown, behind the three-hit pitching of Bruce "Boo" McCallum, the team had to appeal for public financial support to continue the series. With funds forthcoming, the Junior Abbies were able to continue the series in Amherst, losing two games to one in their bid for a Maritime Junior Championship. While Island baseball teams were highly competitive during the era, the financial woes of a lingering depression kept them from competing more aggressively for Maritime honours.

It is unfortunate that the outstanding baseball talents of James "Fiddler" MacDonald developed during this downturn in Island baseball. His twenty-six strikeout performance for the Peakes Hawks in 1936 against the Charlottetown Dodgers was a superb athletic performance. The following year, MacDonald signed with the Amherst St. Pats of the NS Senior League, where he compiled a 29–4 win-loss record over the two years he toiled for the border team. Following the Second World War, "Fiddler" MacDonald returned to his native soil, where over a period of fifty years he continued his involvement with baseball, as a player and coach.

The organization of the Kings County Baseball League in 1935 had a stabilizing effect on baseball during a period of difficult transition. With its emphasis on local talent and knowledgeable fans, the League was somewhat immune from the problems besetting Summerside and Charlottetown, and prospered under the leadership of Father Michael

Teddies Hockey Team, Souris. Champions of Town League and Winners of Tip Top Tailors' Trophy 1934, 1935, 1936. During the 1930s, Souris operated a successful town hockey league with the Teddies, Beavers, and the Vics comprising the league. Back, l-r: Peter A. MacLellan (Coach), Bernie Dugas, John D. MacIntyre, Roddy MacIntyre, J. Wilfred Cheverie (Manager). Centre: Eugene Lewis, Frank "Darkie" Cheverie, Ambrose MacIntyre, Isaac Cheverie; Front: Leonard Condon, Bill Acorn, Jimmie MacIntyre (Captain), Maurice MacLellan (Mascot). (PARO MUSEUM AND FOUNDATION COLLECTION, 3466 HF74.285.3.3)

Rooney, parish priest of Cardigan, along with John A. Macdonald and Jab McConnell. The original teams were Peakes, Souris, Cardigan, Montague, Murray River, and Georgetown, communities where baseball was already ingrained in the sport psyche of the people.

During the decade of the 1930s, sport demonstrated a remarkable resilience to the oppressive atmosphere of the Depression by providing a range of social contacts and competitive experience to a broad sector of the Island's population. While baseball, track and field, and senior men's hockey[37] were the most adversely affected of the major sports, a cluster of other sports collectively maintained a public profile throughout the difficult years of the Depression. Most notably of this latter group was harness racing, intermediate, junior, and women's hockey, boxing, golf, curling, lawn tennis, yachting, rugby, softball, road racing, bowling, rifle shooting, and badminton. This variety of sport activities/opportunities had wide appeal to the people of the province, and provided a much-needed emotional and psychological outlet for a host of Island athletes and loyal fans.

Horse racing reached a new level of organization and popularity during the late 1920s and early 1930s. Local newspaper headlines conveyed the immensity of the sport on Prince Edward Island and throughout the Maritimes. During the month of August 1929, *The Guardian* carried the following feature stories: "Enormous Crowd Witness Races [at Montague], estimated at between 4500 and 5000 persons." "New Annan Races Splendid Success." "Over 12,000 Race Fans Witness Very Close and Exciting Finishes Yesterday" at CDP. The coverage was not confined to Island race tracks. On August 29, 1929, the *Canadian Press*, out of Halifax, stated: "Ch'town Horses Clean Up at Halifax Races," after Colonel Dan MacKinnon and Wellington MacNeil won all three events at the Nova Scotia provincial exhibition, driving Bingen Aubrey, Briar Mac, and Billy Cope to victories.

A contributing factor to the continued interest in harness racing was the leadership of the Provincial Exhibition Association and the Charlottetown Driving Park. In 1928, the Board of Directors of the Park moved the provincial exhibition and races from a late September date to mid-August to take advantage of the summer tourist season. The result was highly successful, attracting visitors and race fans from across the Maritimes and Eastern United States, to a much-enhanced exhibition, vaudeville acts, and race cards.

When Lieutenant-Colonel Dan MacKinnon assumed the presidency of the Driving Park in 1934 from Charlottetown businessman James Paton, it marked the continuation of competent leadership, with one additional attribute: MacKinnon was a horseman and he understood both the needs of the CDP and the expectations of horse owners and drivers. He started driving at the age of thirteen, and later owned and raced numerous horses that he kept at his private stable on Pownal Street.[38]

Coinciding with MacKinnon's election as president of the CDP in 1934, a group of prominent horsemen from across the Island met in Summerside to organize the PEI Harness Racing Club. The meeting elected George A. Calbeck of Summerside as president, and Willard Kelly of Southport as vice-president. The primary purpose of the meeting was to "encourage and promote the standardbred horse [breeding] and the racing of two and three year olds [colts]." The move was viewed as positive for harness racing in the province, as reflected by the inclusion of classes for the young horses on future race cards.

Joe O'Brien drove Scott Frost, considered to be his greatest horse, to victory in the 1955 Hambletonian. Five years later he again entered the Hambletonian winners' circle with a victory by Blaze Hanover. Scott Frost developed an unusual gait when trotting at high speed, drawing comments such as "Crazy Legs" and "spider-legged." Under O'Brien's care and training, the horse became "the greatest trotter of his decade." (JACK AND BEA O'BRIEN COLLECTION)

While the attempts to bring order to the harness-racing industry on Prince Edward Island were positive steps, the province could not function in isolation, as harness racing was a Maritime and Eastern United States activity that involved Island participation. What was accepted on a track in the state of Maine had an impact on what was acceptable on any race track on Prince Edward Island. It was this concern in 1938 that prompted the CDP to become a charter member of the United States Trotting Association,[39] a move that brought further stability and prestige to the horse-racing industry in the province.

While the CDP was conducting its affairs in a businesslike manner during the 1930s, one hundred miles or so to the west, in the rural community of Northam, dreams were coming true. For it was the personal ambition of Edgar Milligan to someday build a harness-racing complex on his farm in Northam. Milligan, along with his business partner George Morrison of Seattle, Washington, were highly successful entrepreneurs in the silver fox industry, where they accumulated substantial wealth and influence. The *Sackville Tribune* stated in an editorial that the partnership "had a line of silver fox ranches from the

Atlantic to the Pacific under their control. . ." The success of the business ventures of the Milligan/Morrison partnership greatly facilitated the realization of Edgar Milligan's personal dream on July 15, 1931. The *P.E.I. Agriculturist*, July 16, 1931, described the occasion:

> All roads yesterday afternoon led to Northam. It is estimated that over 7000 people were present at the big opening race meet of this magnificent race course – the largest it is said ever to have attended at a rural race track.

The race course was considered to be one of the finest in the province with a seating capacity for 2,500, an excellent view of all horses, a judges' stand, and a dance pavilion. In their effort to establish the race track as an entertainment centre, Milligan and Morrison added several attractions to the race program, notably boxing, step-dancing, and comedians, which had proven successful at the New Annan track and the CDP during the prewar years. An innovation that caught the fancy of horse owners and spectators alike was the staging of night races at the track. The event occurred on August 16, 1932, and is generally believed to be the first time in Canada that harness races were held under the lights. Night races became popular in this rural community, as the sport provided the opportunity for farmers and others who were committed to daytime responsibilities to enjoy evenings of leisure.

In the midst of progress tragedy struck. While en route to PEI on September 1, 1933, to attend a race event, Edgar Milligan and his partner George Morrison were killed in a car accident at Buffalo, New York. It was a grievous loss to the Milligan and Morrison families, to horse racing, and to the fox industry in the province. Eulogies portrayed Milligan as a man with great energy and vision. "His race track and buildings at Northam are evidence of the driving power and creativity that he possessed." In spite of the difficult situation, the track at Northam continued to operate, and made a valuable contribution to the racing circuit on the Island during the mid-years of the 1930s.

It is not surprising that the sport of harness racing maintained its popularity and overall level of success during the difficult years of the Depression, for the sport possessed significant resources: influential leadership, a network of race tracks across the province, and ownership of hundreds of thoroughbred horses trained and available for racing events. In its 1935 Sport Review, the *Charlottetown Guardian* conveyed the prominence of the sport across the Island: "Horse Racing Still Fa-

Homebred Steeds, the Harry O'Brien Stables of Alberton, typifies the grassroots nature of the horse-racing industry in the province during the 1930s. (PARO 2320-15-6)

vorite Island Sport. 'Kentucky of Canada' Stages Many Brilliant Meets in Season of 1935." And in 1936, a similar story: "Records Fell Before Flashing Hoofs On Island Racing Circuits." The claims can be justified by the number of regular purse races held at Alberton, Northam, New Annan, Charlottetown, Montague, Summerside, Georgetown, and St. Peter's, with matinee races also held at Kensington, Hamilton, and Northam. The 1936 season witnessed an assault on the record book with track records broken at Summerside, Montague, Alberton, and Charlottetown, with sub 2:10 miles commonplace. The Island tracks also produced the fastest trotter in the Maritime Provinces in 1936 with Heatherbell, owned and driven by Lieutenant-Colonel Dan MacKinnon, establishing a new track record of 2:08¼ over the Montague track. Taken in the context of the Depression years, harness racing provided a much-needed social/leisure experience, and in the process soothed the anxieties and worry of the populace. In the ensuing years, with the outbreak of the Second World War, a similar role would be expected of harness racing, and for sport in general: that of providing a diversion and solace from the horror of war in Europe.

What would the fall sport season be like in the City of Charlottetown without the annual fall ritual of a playoff for Island rugby supremacy between the St. Dunstan's Saints and the Abegweits? For decades the two combatants provided Island rugby fans with the utmost in competitive play and sportsmanship. Now, in the waning years of the 1920s, with competition keen and the impending Depression still in the offing, optimism abounded. For rugby was as much a part of autumn as burning leaves and the honking of Canada geese on their migratory flight southward.

While the St. Dunstan's senior teams accumulated a succession of five league championships from 1924 to 1928, the Abegweits experienced renewed vigour in 1929. A contributing factor was the leadership of W. J. "Billie Archie" MacDonald as playing coach of the Abegweits. MacDonald, a professor at Prince of Wales College, was noted for his aggressive style of play as a half-back, and for his exceptional kicking skills. His exemplary leadership as a player/coach led the Abbies to Island championships in 1929 and 1930. The 1930 Abegweit team was especially strong, led by the outstanding play of Ivan "Hickey" Nicholson and players developed through the interscholastic/intercollegiate programs. After defeating SDU for the Island senior championship in 1930, the team was touted as a legitimate contender for the McCurdy Cup, emblematic of the senior rugby championship of the Maritime provinces. However, with the playoffs between the Wanderers and the Caledonia Club still unsettled in late November, the Abegweits considered it impractical to continue play.

The 1932 season produced excellent rugby at all levels of competition: interschool, intermediate, and senior. West Kent defeated Queen Square 5–0 to win the Mcmillan Trophy; SDC won the intercollegiate title over PWC, and the senior Saints retained the senior league championship, defeating the Abbies 3–0. Typical of the closeness of the two teams, the winning try was scored in the final minute of play. With enthusiasm high amongst the players, the Abbies, now coached by Neil "Tiny" Matheson, considered an invitation from the highly regarded Caledonia Club of Glace Bay, holders of the McCurdy Cup, for a bid at the Maritime Championship. The game could have been a battle of the giants of Maritime rugby. But it was not to be. Although success was experienced on the gridiron, not so the financially troubled Abegweits Association. Seriously encumbered by the lack of financial support from the public, due in part to the continuation of the Depression, the Club was unable to support the team's participation in Maritime playdowns.

The decision apparently had ramifications for the following season, for in spite of several calls for practice, the Abegweits did not field a team in the Island Senior League in 1933. The withdrawal of the Abegweits from rugby marked the end of an era that dated back to 1885, when a group of young men formed the original Abegweit rugby team.[40] The significance of the event passed without fanfare; yet, undoubtedly, evoked nostalgia and memories in the minds of an older generation of the great gridiron struggles among the Abegweits, Pictou, New Glasgow, Wanderers, Dalhousie, the Saints, and Prince of Wales.

Yet, there were diehard rugby players, former Abbies, in Charlottetown. Calling themselves the Nomads, and coached by Lou Campbell, they formed a team and provided stiff competition for both SDU and PWC over several seasons. During the 1935 season they played St. Dunstan's to a 3–3 tie and lost 8–6 in a "bitter" game for the Island Championship. While the Nomads provided interesting competition for SDU and PWC, the long-standing spirited rivalry that had existed with the Abegweits was not evident. By 1938, the Nomads had suspended team play in the Island League, primarily for financial reasons.

Faced by a lack of competition on the Island, St. Dunstan's made their first serious sortie into intercollegiate play and entered the New Brunswick/Prince Edward Island league with the University of New Brunswick and Mt. Allison. The Saints made a credible showing in their first year in league play, losing to Mt. A. 3–0, winning over UNB 19–0, and then tying a must-win game 6–6 against the Mounties. Later Mt. A. went on to win the Maritime Intercollegiate Championship. The years following the Second World War would see a resurgence of rugby on the Island with the Saints, Abbies, and Nomads all vying for Maritime honours in the game.

Ironically, it was track and field and distance running that felt the brunt of the decline of the Abegweit AAA in the early 1930s. With only a remnant of the great track and field reputation of the Abegweits still evident, the officials turned to interscholastic athletes to rejuvenate the sport. At a well-publicized provincial school meet held at the CAAA Grounds on June 30, 1930, Island athletes broke two Maritime interscholastic records, with George Ayers of Prince of Wales college leaping 5' 4½" in the high jump, and Maurice "Sparky" Lodge covering the mile in 4:57 1/5.

Prominent among the other winners was Emmet Donahoe of Souris, son of the late Dr. Robert Donahoe, a star track athlete with the 1904 Abegweits and later at McGill University, where he won the top athlete award in track and field for four successive years. Competing for St. Dunstan's, the young Donahoe won both the 100- and 200-yard dashes. The following year, June 19, 1931, the performance of school athletes was even more impressive, with over 200 athletes competing and eleven new provincial records established. Reg Prichard of Summerside Academy won the all-round athlete award, placing first or second in five events.

PROVINCIAL MEET GREAT SUCCESS
West Kent Won Interscholastic School Title at Abegweit Grounds Yesterday – Reg Prichard, S'Side, New Alround [*sic*] Champion – 11 Records Go by the Board

In reporting the results of the meet, the *Charlottetown Guardian* commented:

> Depression may be the word of the hour in other parts of the world, but from an athletic point of view, the Island doesn't know such a word. Upwards of two hundred and twenty-five well conditioned young thoroughbreds, representing a big portion of the athletic citizenry —of the Garden Province toed the mark in the different events as worthy representatives of their respective schools and towns — To West Kent, the victors in the total aggregate of points congratulations — and to Reg Prichard, speedy Summerside individual, who won the all-round medal — hearty congratulations.

A nucleus of talented athletes emerged from the provincial school track and field program during the period 1930 to 1934, including Lodge, Ayers, Ken Beer, Lorne Calbeck, Stan Biggar, and a holdover from the Abegweit team, Gordon White. The group competed successfully under the Abegweit banner and consistently won individual events, but were undermanned when it came to team honours. Lodge, Beer, White, and the multi-talented Ayers maintained their interest in the sport over several years, competing in intercollegiate and Maritime competition. On May 16, 1934, Lodge established a new Maritime intercollegiate record in the mile run at 4:44 4/5, leading his University of New Brunswick team to the Maritime intercollegiate championship.

Even as track and field was kept alive by the exploits of Lodge, Ayers, Beer, and White, a group of distance runners were renewing interest in road racing. *The Patriot*-ten-mile event, dormant since the pre-war years, was revived in 1930, and a second ten-mile race, sponsored by Kelly and McInnis, a men's clothing store in Charlottetown, was added to the racing schedule in September 1932. Harry MacEwen, Wallie Rodd, Hugh Campbell, Russell Doyle, Edison Smith, and Kaney MacDonald were the premiere distance runners of the era, competing whenever they could afford to in Maritime races. Previously, it was the Abegweit Club that had provided the financial assistance needed, but, with the resources of the Club severely strained, it fell to other community groups, such as the YMCA, Charlottetown Fire Department, and *Patriot,* to assume the cost of inter-provincial competition. Following the 1930 race, which attracted a crowd of spectators numbered in the thousands, Arthur Gaudet of the *Patriot* and Ray Pendleton of the YMCA, in a joint statement, concluded that: "In all modesty *The Patriot* thinks that it has done much to revive marathon running on Prince Edward Island," and called for other community groups to contribute to the cause.

Patriot 10-Mile Road Race, re-established in 1930

1930	Harry MacEwen
1931	Wallie Rodd
1932	Harry MacEwen 59:22
1933	Wallie Rodd 58:03*
1934	Sr. Race cancelled
	Rodd finished 5th in Halifax race in 55:31 4/5

* *New Patriot race record*

The *Patriot* and Kelly and McInnis races attracted the top road runners in the Maritimes. Roy Oliver of New Glasgow and Noel Paul of Springhill were the most dominant, winning the *Halifax and Mail* Modified

Wallie Rodd of Highfield was one of the top long-distance runners in the province during a resurgence of the sport in the early 1930s. The Patriot ten-mile road race and other local races attracted thousands of fans to witness the popular events. Rodd's main rival in the province was Harry MacEwen of Bristol, while his Maritime opponents were world-class runners Roy Oliver of New Glasgow and Noel Paul of Springhill. (DAVID RODD COLLECTION)

Marathon on five occasions between 1931 and 1937. In the 1934 race, won by Oliver in 51:50, Wallie Rodd, now trained by Bill Massey, ran an outstanding race, finishing fifth in a career best time of 55:31 4/5. The exploits of Rodd, MacEwen, and other distance runners from across the province were a high point for sport during the otherwise difficult decade of the 1930s.

With the Abbies and Crystals senior men's hockey teams commanding the attention of Island hockey fans and sport administrators during the early 1920s, it was an uphill struggle to establish women's hockey across the province. Apart from a flurry of activity at the turn of the century, when the sport consisted of a series of exhibition games involving the Souris Ladies team, the Summerside Alphas, and two teams from Charlottetown, the Micmacs and Silver Foxes, the sport suffered from a lack of administrative support and a junior development program.

A turning point occurred for the sport on February 19, 1921 when the reigning Maritime Champions from New Glasgow, NS, came to Charlottetown for an exhibition game. The *Charlottetown Guardian* provided a colourful description of the contest and alluded to the close 3–1 victory by the Maritime champs, somewhat surprised by the strong showing of the local team:

> The followers of sport enjoyed a treat extraordinary last night when a ladies hockey team from New Glasgow — crossed sticks

> with the Charlottetown ladies in the first demonstration of hockey of the feminine persuasion played in this city for several yesterdays. — The local girls showed they had abundance of hockey talent — in the art of manipulating the "rubber".

Encouraged by their strong showing against the highly rated New Glasgow team, the Charlottetown players formed two teams, the Abegweit Sisters and the Red Macs, for the 1921–1922 season. The move proved beneficial for women's hockey, especially the Abbie Sisters, as the team went undefeated for several seasons and attracted the support of the Abegweit AAA. After several seasons of exhibition games, primarily against Sackville, Moncton, and Amherst, there was sufficient interest in the women's game on Prince Edward Island to form a provincial league. The League was duly set up for the 1925–1926 season, with the Red Macs, Abegweits, and the Summerside Crystal Sisters as members. The League expanded to four teams for the 1926–1927 season, when the Montague Imperial Sisters made their debut in Island hockey. After several seasons of play the provincial league was discontinued in favour of exhibition games and the lure of inter-provincial competition. The Abegweit Sisters were especially strong during the mid-1920s, featuring a group of talented players built around "Moo" Weeks, Lillian Duchemin, Kathleen "Tinker" Bourke, and Ruth Unsworth. The team won consistently against Moncton, Sackville, Amherst, Mt. Allison, and the Crystal Sisters. However, even as the Abegweit Sisters dominated women's hockey during the mid-1920s, the Summerside Crystal Sisters established a winning reputation of their own during the early 1930s.

Members of the 1934 Crystal Sisters

WHO PLAYED THE MONTREAL MAROON SISTERS TO A 2–2 TIE, MARCH 19, 1934.

Martha Nicholson – *goal*
Irene Linkletter – *captain*
Margaret Gallant – *centre*
Minnie Boswell – *defense*
Helen Montgomery – *defense*
Pat MacLellan – *winger*
Lillian Dickie – *forward*
Zilpha Linkletter – *forward*
Alice Noonan - *defense*
Irene Silliphant - *defense*
Anne Green – *winger*
Ralph Silliphant – *coach*
Clifford Montgomery - *referee*

The 1926 Abegweit Sisters Hockey team were Island champions. Back, l-r: Lillian Duchemin, Della Walsh, Inez Mutch, Muriel "Moo" Weeks, Norma Jamieson, Marie Mutch; Middle: Kathleen "Tinker" Bourke, Selma Owen, Ruth Unsworth, Marion Small, Eleanor Hall; Front: Helen Jamieson, Isabelle Bourke. (PARO CAMERA CLUB COLLECTION, 2320/93-4)

In 1932, when the team laid claim to the Maritime Championship by defending Kentville 2–0, the team set its collective sights on a national championship.

The opportunity presented itself in 1934 when the Crystal Sisters, as the reigning Maritime Champions, advanced to the Eastern Canadian Hockey playdowns. Skating onto the spacious ice surface of the Montreal Forum in March 1934, the Crystal Sisters engaged the Montreal Maroon Sisters for the right to advance to the Eastern Canadian Championship. Led by the hockey savvy of captain Irene Linkletter, the team made an impressive showing, battling the Maroons to a 2–2 tie in a game dominated by the Islanders. Unfortunately, after two periods of overtime failed to declare a winner, thus requiring another game, the Crystal Sisters were forced to forfeit the series due to a lack of funds.

The Souris Tigerettes, 1943–1945. The Tigerettes maintained the long tradition of women's hockey in Souris. Led by "Babs" MacDonald, the team competed against the Georgetown Eagles, the Montague Vikings, and the Abbie Sisters from Charlottetown. L-r: Rosie Paquet, Mary Paquet, Barb Cheverie, Joyce McLellan, Dot Mossey, Florence Arsenault, Gert McCormack (Coach), Kimball Jarvis, "Babs" MacDonald; missing from picture, Jennie Dugas.
(BARBARA "BABS" MACDONALD COLLECTION)

When financial help arrived from Summerside, the new playoff schedule was already in place, thereby depriving the Crystal Sisters a chance at the Canadian Championship. It was disheartening for the team to lose out on their bid for a national championship when the reason revolved around the lack of financial support. However, the reality was that women's hockey, as with other sports, was poorly financed during the period, a situation that was compounded by the lingering Depression.

The following season (1935), the team, now known as the Summerside Primroses, hosted the powerful Preston Rivulettes at the Crystal Rink in a two-game total-goal series. While the Primroses lost the opening game of the series 4–1 and tied the second game 1–1, a capacity crowd at the Crystal Rink accorded the home team lavish praise during their moment in the spotlight of women's hockey.

Women's hockey during the 1920s and 1930s on Prince Edward

The Primrose Sisters (formerly Crystal Sisters) of Summerside engaged the powerful Preston Rivulettes in a two-game goal series for the Eastern Canadian Championship, March 9–10, 1935, before capacity crowds at the Crystal Rink. While losing the first game of the series 4–0, the team played the Rivulettes to a 1–1 tie in the second game. Group picture: Patricia MacLellan, Alice Noonan, Helen Montgomery, Zilpha Linkletter, Irene (Linkletter) Silliphant, Anne Green, Martha Nicholson, Lillian Dickie, Minnie Boswell, Margaret Gallant, Ralph Silliphant (Coach), Clifford Montgomery. Played in games: D. Harris, Elia Gay, V. Jones. (*THE GUARDIAN*, MARCH 8, 1935)

Island was driven by a small group of talented athletes whose persistence established the sport at a highly competitive level. Stars of the era included Irene Linkletter, "Googs" McInnis, and others whose hockey skills extended the reputation of the Crystal Sisters and Abbie Sisters across the Maritimes and into the arena of national competition. The effect of their collective efforts would become more visible during the late 1940s when women's hockey would extend to all parts of the province.

In spite of the financial constraints that faced the province during the 1930s, sport remained a vital part of community life. Sport placed more emphasis on participation during the period as there were few occasions where large crowds would gather to watch a City League baseball game or attend a track and field meet at the CAAA Grounds. Softball was a game in point. The sport was introduced to the province in 1930 when the West End Ramblers played an exhibition game against an unidentified team. The following spring, members of the Abegweit senior hockey team became involved in the sport when

Tommy Oliver and Ray Stull organized a team and challenged any team on the Island to a game. The hockey residence rule in sport (Big Six and Big Four League) in Charlottetown meant that highly skilled athletes filtered into the sport system during the summer. Softball, baseball, and golf were the sports that benefitted most, as prominent athletes such as Stull, Oliver, Jack Kane, Johnny "Snag" Squarebriggs, and Pete Kelly became involved.

Softball became instantly popular with athletes across the province. Within two years, teams were organized in many Island communities, including Borden, Summerside, Georgetown, Lower Bedeque, Flat River, Cape Traverse, Uigg, and Eldon. A City League formed in Charlottetown with eight teams: CNR, Navy, Stewart's Bakery, Firemen, Hi-Y, Senior Y, 8th Battery, and Holy Name. On October 4, 1934, the 8th Battery defeated the Borden Nationals for the PEI Softball Championship, and, two years later, the PEI Softball Association was formed to cope with the rapid development of the sport.

The organization of a provincial governing body for the sport gave impetus to the formation of regional leagues, notably in the Borden/Summerside area, where four teams were competitive, and in King's County. The Kings League comprised teams from Cardigan, Georgetown, Montague, Souris, and the rural community of Newport. In a personal conversation with Michael MacDonald, a star outfielder with the Newport team, he related how the community's interest and support of the team elevated the players to the status of stars, and how the team often travelled to games in the back of the big truck owned by Leo Fay, the general store keeper, or by ferry from Newport to Georgetown. It was a rapid rise for the sport from an exhibition game four years earlier to a self-governing body under the presidency of prominent sport personality, Earl Goss. Softball was the prototype for sport development on Prince Edward Island during the recession period of the 1930s.

Soccer made its debut on Prince Edward Island during the summer of 1934, somewhat later than one would expect for a major international sport. Sport historians have postulated that the American and Canadian versions of football, combined with the popularity of rugby, cricket, and baseball during the summer, deterred the early development of soccer in Canada and the United States.

Actually, the international version of the game, as we know it today, with its millions of loyal fans and high-priced players, has a long and storied history going back in its origin to the Roman Empire. So remote and vague are the earliest forms of the game that historians consider it almost futile to try to identify the various influences that molded the most widely played game in the world.[41] What we do know is that soccer became immensely popular in Great Britain after the 14th century, from where the game spread throughout the world, most notably in Europe and South America.

The first organized soccer played in Canada was during the late 1880s when under the authority of the Dominion of Canada Football Association (DFA) an all-star Canadian team played a series of matches against a picked team from New Jersey. The results of the matches, played over two years, were deemed even, with each team recording two victories, two ties, and two defeats. Two years later the DFA sent a different team to England in an effort to stimulate the sport, but the public response back in Canada remained disinterested.

An attempt to organize soccer on Prince Edward Island occurred in 1934, during the height of the Depression, when the Eastern Prince County League, headed by Vaughan Groom, was organized. The League consisted of at least three teams, the Summerside Hawks, the Sea Gulls, and the New Annan Wanderers. There was also interest in the game in Charlottetown with the Abegweits maintaining a competitive edge by playing against navy ships visiting the capital city. During July of 1934, a team from HMS *Dragon* displayed superior skills by defeating the Abbies 4–0. Later in the season the Abegweits won what was undoubtedly the first Island soccer championship, by defeating the New Annan Wanderers, 2–0.

The attempt to organize soccer as a new sport on Prince Edward Island during the Depression met with only modest success. After several seasons of local league play, organized around the rural community of New Annan, the sport did not sustain a viable competitive presence.

Badminton was yet another game that attracted devotees during the stressful years of the Depression. While there is a reference to the game being played in Charlottetown as early as March of 1910, the sport did not become established as a recreation/competitive game until the mid-1930s. First played on the Island as a recreational activity in church halls and other community facilities, the game gained considerable status when Mr. L. G. Lewis, a young barrister from Summerside, donated a trophy for provincial competition. The first competition for the new trophy was played as a "home and home" tournament held in mid-May 1934. *The Guardian* gave prominent headlines to the tournament, won by Summerside: "Teams Display Brilliant Badminton in

Final Tournament for Lewis Trophy," and singled out several players for their outstanding play. The salutations went to Walter Goss and W. A. Smith of Charlottetown, and D. Harris, R. Pritchard, and Miss I. Linkletter of Summerside.

By 1938, local clubs were organized in Summerside, and at the Holy Redeemer, the Armories (Military), and the YMCA in Charlottetown. The network of clubs greatly facilitated the staging of inter-club competition and provincial level tournaments. It is significant to note that a nucleus of talented athletes who were members of lawn tennis clubs became influential in establishing the new game of badminton. The situation undoubtedly contributed to the fast rise of badminton as an organized sport in the province, and demonstrated the flexibility of sport participation during the 1930s.

While some of the mass participation sports struggled, the four most prominent private sport clubs, the Charlottetown Lawn Tennis Club, the Belvedere Links, the Charlottetown Curling Club, and the Charlottetown Yacht Club, each experienced increased membership and an expansion of facilities from the late 1920s to mid-1930s. The period was a banner era for lawn tennis in Charlottetown and Summerside. As early as 1902, the CLTC had established its membership at one hundred members and steadfastly held to that limit for twenty-five years. However, with a long waiting list seeking the opportunity to play, the Club cautiously increased the limit by twenty-five members in 1927. The *Char- lottetown Guardian*, noting the increased activity in the sport, made this comment following the CLTC 1928 Annual General Meeting:

> The great interest taken in Tennis during the past few years bids fair to continue without any signs of abatement judging from the tone of last night's meeting. The Club has now six first-class courts and the improvements contemplated will add greatly to the beauty and attractiveness of the historic club grounds at Victoria Park. The standard of the game is also rising year by year.

The observation on the improvement in play was well-justified. Elinor Bourke was the dominant women's player at the provincial level and was highly competitive in Maritime competition. The "invincible" G. F. Hutcheson of Charlottetown and Thane Campbell of the Summerside Club were ranked at the top for men's play.

When the PEI Tennis Association formed in 1930, the Association consisted of two clubs, Charlottetown and Summerside. By 1934, the Association had grown to five, including the Holy Redeemer Club, with three courts on Upper Queen Street, the Holy Name Club, and the Maple Leaf Club, both at Victoria Park. The combined membership of the five clubs exceeded 400 members. The infusion of new members and additional clubs into the heretofore staid sports of tennis energized the game, and greatly increased the level of participation and competition. Recreational clubs were formed in Souris and Georgetown, and a number of high-level tournaments were held at the Victoria Park complex. Thus, during the early years of the 1930s, tennis became a major contributor to the sport system across the Island.

The Charlottetown Golf Club also experienced sustained growth during the late 1920s and early 1930s. The layout at the Belvedere Links was increased to eighteen holes in 1929, when membership at the Club exceeded 300. Meanwhile, the opening of the Summerside Golf Club in 1927 marked a milestone in the development of golf in the province, adding, as it did, an inter-community rivalry to the sport.

When provincial championship play was inaugurated in 1932, Belvedere golfers, including Pete Kelly, dominated the tournament until 1938, when Harold Gaudet of the Summerside Club won provincial honours. Gaudet carded rounds of 83 and 78 in defeating Doug Saunders, and claimed the trophy donated by his father, the late J. J. Gaudet. In women's play, Elda MacKinnon of Belvedere defended her provincial title with rounds of 101 and 98, winning over Mrs. W. E. Cotton of Belvedere and Mrs. Alex Horne of Summerside.

The public impression of golf at the Belvedere Links, however, remained one of elitism, accessible only to those with social and professional status in the community. The membership approval system, and the personal financial resources necessary to participate as a full member, were the main factors contributing to the public's perception. Lawn tennis, to an extent, overcame the elitist connotation by forming new clubs and adding additional courts, an option not available to those involved in the organization and promotion of golf during the 1930s.

Both golf and lawn tennis hosted major competitions in their respective sports in 1937, golf the Maritime Championship, and tennis the Eastern Canadian Championships. The two events actually ran concurrently and dominated the Island press for a week-long period. The national media also provided coverage of the two events, alluding to the capability/hospitality of the Island to host major sport and tourist-related events.

Harold Gaudet of the Summerside Golf Club won the provincial golf championship in 1938 by defeating Doug Saunders of the Belvedere Golf Links with rounds of 83 and 78. The win interrupted the succession of Island champions by members of the Charlottetown Club that extended from 1932 to 1952. (*THE GUARDIAN*, AUGUST 25, 1938)

During the 1920s curling expanded when the Summerside Curling Club formally organized in 1923, and the Montague Club assembled three years later. The presence of three clubs in the province accelerated the development of the sport and enhanced inter-club bonspiels. Montague curlers, in particular, demonstrated a zest for the game and the social amenities the sport provided for its members and the community. One such occasion was described by the *Charlottetown Guardian* in its January 27, 1930, issue:

> A special train bearing 125 eastern metropolites left Montague Friday morning. Among the excursionists were the thirty-five curlers (to compete and win the McArthur trophy) in whose minds the excursion originated, and who financed the sporting crusade. The remainder of the concourse was made up of hockey fans eager to see the Abegweit Crystals hockey game, and music lovers to see the Burns concert.

It was noted that on the evening previous to the excursion, a banquet had been held at Mosher's Restaurant. The festivities adjourned in time for the members to witness a hockey game between the hometown Imperials and the Charlottetown Seagulls. The community support evident for organized sport in Montague during the era was certainly a factor in the development of strong teams in hockey, curling, and baseball.

Curling continued to prosper when the Provincial Curling Associa-

The Montague rink of "Big Jim" McIntyre was the first Island rink to represent the province in the national curling championships. The historic event took place at the Brier in Toronto in 1936. L-r: Art Younker (Lead), Robert Beck (Second), Cecil Wightman (Mate), Jim McIntyre (Skip). (PARO 2320-87-7)

tion was formed in 1935, and in 1936 the province was represented, for the first time, at the Macdonald Brier tankard, emblematic of the Canadian Curling Championship. The right to represent the province at the Brier in Toronto was won by the Montague team of "Big Jim" McIntyre, skip; K. C. Wightman, mate; R. W. Beck, second; and J. A. Younker, lead. While the rink was 0–9 in the national competition, they were philosophical about the experience gained, hoping that their participation in the National Championships would stimulate curling in Prince Edward Island.

Curling became a provincial sport, geographically speaking, when the Alberton Curling Club was organized in December of 1937, and immediately joined the Provincial Curling Association. W. P. Keenan, a businessman who had moved to Alberton from Fredericton, NB, is considered to be the "founder of curling" in the western town. Keenan, an enthusiastic curler, brought a set of stones with him and soon created interest in the game. While the first facilities were primitive, a lean-to attached to the skating rink with one sheet of ice, curling experienced an enthusiastic beginning in Alberton. James H. Myrick was the first president and J. Willard Waugh the vice-president. With curling facilities located in Montague, Charlottetown, Summerside, and Alberton, the status of the game rose to considerable prominence. During the early years of curling in the province, the sport was a male-oriented activity, but following the Second World War, curling would assume a more inclusive membership profile and gain prominence at the national level.

When the modern-day version of the Charlottetown Yacht Club was reorganized in 1937 and incorporated in 1938, it perpetuated the images of a sport that provided competitive racing for its members. Yet it retained the pleasurable experience inherent in the activity of sailing "and the delight of sailing along while the landscapes unfold with panoramic regularity," equally applicable to the members of the present era as it was during the era of George J. Rogers. The responsibility for the "tender" care of the club fell to Dr. J. E. Blanchard, who was re-elected as Commodore at the Club's AGM in 1928, while Malcolm "Mac" Irwin, a name long associated with the sport, was elected Vice-Commodore, and Fred Morris as Rear Commodore. Morris, in turn, became the Commodore of the Club in 1938 when the organization was apparently revamped and incorporated. In 1938, the Northumberland Yacht Racing Association was formed, bringing structure to a recreational/leisure pastime that for over half a century had resisted "organization." During the late 1930s, races were held at Summerside, Shediac, Pictou, Borden, Souris, and Charlottetown.

The late 1930s were particularly good years for members of the Provincial Rifle Association. Lieutenant A. F. "Brick" Gormley, who first took up rifle shooting at Queen Square School in 1927, was selected to the Canadian Bisley team in 1939. His selection placed him among an elite group of Islanders who had been members of previous Canadian Bisley teams. The members included Capt. J. M. Jones, 1905, Allan McCabe, 1920 and 1927, George MacLennan, 1928, and Percy Hooper, 1933. It is of interest to note that Mary MacLennan of Alexandra, sister of George MacLennan, created a considerable stir among the rifle shooting fraternity when she won the Lieutenant-Governor's Match in a shoot-off with Trooper Percy Landrigan in 1937. As the *Guardian* noted, she placed her last shot "fair in the center of the bull, winning the gold medal." MacLennan would later become the most accom-

PAGE SIX

BOWLING HOCKEY WRESTLING

NEWS OF THE SPORT WORLD

BOXING BASKETBALL OTHER SPORT

Mary McLennan Wins P. R. A. Gold Medal

Mary MacLennan achieved a career breakthrough in 1937 when she won the Lieutenant-Governor's Match during provincial rifle competition. In 1951 she became the first female shooter in Canada to be selected to the Canadian Bisley team. Bisley, located sixty miles southwest of London, is considered to be the Championship of the British Empire.
(PARO *THE GUARDIAN*, JULY 28, 1937)

plished female shooter in Canada after the Second World War, and would herself be selected to shoot at Bisley in 1951 as the first female member of a Canadian Bisley team.

Skeet shooting rose from the ashes of the Belvidere Gun Club of the 1880s and the Newstead Gun Club of the pre-Great War era. Following a period of inactivity, the sport reorganized as the Charlottetown Skeet Club in 1936, and became firmly established as a viable member of the sport commuity following the Second World War.[42]

Actually, private sport clubs appeared to be unaffected by the lingering Depression or by disruptions associated with governance of their sport. Lawn tennis, golf, curling, yachting, rifle shooting, clay-target shooting, and other private clubs possessed the necessary financial and leadership resources within their respective organizations to maintain business as usual.

Publicly supported sport— those sports that relied on a loyal fan base and the general public for financial and administrative assistance— were the most seriously affected during the era. Baseball, track and field, rugby, and senior men's hockey typified the dilemma, as each became a casualty of factors beyond their control. There were teams with the skills and aptitude to compete at the regional level, such as the Abegweit rugby team of 1932, the Summerside AA baseball squad of 1933, and the 1934 Crystal Sisters, in hockey; but the opportunity to compete in regional and national playdowns was usually confronted by

Earl Smith, one of the province's most versatile athletes, compiled a long list of sport achievements during his illustrious athletic career. His most notable success came in tennis, as provincial singles champion three times; in bowling, where he established a Maritime record for high triple (1042) in Maritime competition; in basketball, three times scoring champion (1945, 1946, and 1947); and in badminton, five times provincial champ. He also excelled in golf, softball, table tennis, and as a builder/promoter in the sport of boxing. (EARL SMITH COLLECTION)

a financial reality. The fact that there was grassroots activity in all four sports during the period, such as the Kings County Baseball League, intermediate and junior hockey, and interscholastic/intercollegiate competition in track and field and rugby, helped sustain the sports at a community/provincial level.

A distinguishable cluster of sports, not dependent on public financial support, nor directly associated with private sport clubs, became highly visible during the era. In many ways they became the foundation of the sport delivery system whose participants competed for the intrinsic pleasure gained, or as a diversion from the social and economic woes that persisted during the era. These participant sports sustained the base from which high performance and elite athletes emerged. The sports within this cluster gained their support from fraternal organizations, such as the YMCA and Holy Name Club; from employer-sponsored recreation; and through entrepreneurial initiatives, such as boxing and bowling. This group included softball, bowling, basketball, boxing, badminton, soccer, volleyball, speed skating, long-distance road racing, billiards, and gymnastics. Bowling, boxing, and softball represent a different approach to providing Islanders a leisure, sport experience. Bowling and boxing were both entrepreneurial initiatives; bowling emphasized participation, boxing entertainment. Three bowling alleys operated in Charlottetown during the 1930s: the Holy Name Lanes, the YMCA, and the Charlottetown Alleys, which were located

The mid-1930s were good years for boxing across the province, particularly for local pugilists. Among the top fighters of the decade were Benny Binns and Danny McCormack, who staged a "bloody fight" on December 24, 1937, at the LPU Hall. Binns won the hard-fought battle by a knock-out in the seventh round to claim the Island middleweight title.
(PARO *THE GUARDIAN*, DEC. 24, 1937)

in the basement of the Market Building. There were also alleys in Summerside and in several other communities across the province. Bowling remained one of the most popular winter games during the 1930s with competitive leagues at the Capitol Alleys in Summerside and the Holy Name, Charlottetown, and YMCA alleys in Charlottetown. The game, which had provided over half a century of competition and socializing for Islanders, attracted large numbers of bowlers during the period and experienced an unprecedented level of proficiency. During the 1937 season, the Five Aces team, bowling at the Holy Name alleys in regular league play, set a Maritime record in five-pins for a single game with a high total of 1497. The team members were G. McDonald, J. Callaghan, F. Tierney, R. McCabe, and E. Robin. The following season, in 1938, Miss Gertrude Doyle, considered to be the Island's outstanding woman bowler, "knocked the pins" for a high triple of 900, which, in turn, established another Maritime record. Meanwhile, in an informal match, Fred Gaudet exceeded the Maritime record in men's triple when he bowled an amazing score of 1112. Unfortunately, because it was a pick-up match, the record could not be claimed.

Boxing placed its emphasis on entertainment, a proven attraction ever since "Big Jim" Pendergast first staged boxing bouts at the New Annan races prior to the First World War. During the mid-1930s, Joey MacDonald regularly lined up cards at the Sporting Club and/or the Arena, where spectators could vent their aggressive feelings within a socially accepted venue. On July 17, 1936, for example, over 3,000 spectators watched George Leslie of Souris defend his Island heavyweight crown with a third round TKO over Stan Biggar. "It was the biggest crowd ever to watch a boxing match in this Island Province," stated the *Charlottetown Guardian*.

As the decade of the 1930s wound down, the impact of the Depression, combined with the change of governance of amateur sport in the region, had become clear. Not only had amateur sport survived, it had contributed to a social, cultural vitality in the province during a most difficult time. Sport was no longer a luxury or the hobby of a privileged few. It had become part of the fabric of Island life.

The Alberton Regals won their first major hockey championship in 1929 when they won the A. E. MacLean Trophy, emblematic of intermediate hockey supremacy in Prince County. The league consisted of the O'Leary Maroons, Kensington Granites, Borden Nationals, Victoria Unions, Cape Traverse Rovers, and the Regals. Back, l-r: W. R. Oulton, J. E. Millman, J. T. Larkin, G. K. Profit, Fred MacAlduff (Manager), C. E. O'Brien; Front: M. J. Albert, A. Jeffrey, J. C. Profit, Harvey Jeffrey. (ALBERTON MUSEUM, 986-12-243)

10 Turbulent Times for Senior Hockey

During the late 1920s and the decade of the 1930s, controversy swirled around senior men's hockey on Prince Edward Island. The sport dominated the Island's media and created a public fixation as two of the most eventful developments in its history unfolded: the clash of the Crystals and Abbies that caused the collapse of the Island Senior Hockey League, and the subsequent sojourn of the Abegweit Club into the Maritime Big Six/Big Four League. For thirty years, hockey had been played with the emphasis on skills and speed; rough play was decried, and fans flocked to the rink to witness the intricacies of the game. However, during the late 1920s and into the 30s, factors with long-term implications for the sport fuelled controversy and intense rivalries. The reinstatement of professional players to amateur status became a burning issue, as were player defections and a residence rule designed to control the movement of players. The issues were not confined to Prince Edward Island, as amateur hockey was in a state of turmoil throughout the Maritimes.

Over several seasons, rivalries had been escalating between the Crystals and the Abbies. The calibre of hockey was high, with outstanding talent on both teams. The Crystals featured the talents of George "Chick" Gallant, Jack Schurman, and Ralph Silliphant. The Abbies comprised a spirited group of young players, dubbed "Prowse's Colts,"

The opening of the Charlottetown Forum on December 9, 1930, provided Charlottetown — and indeed the province — with a state-of-the-art artificial ice arena. The new "Ice Palace," one of only three such facilities in the Maritimes, attracted the interest of hockey officials across the Maritime provinces, and launched the Abegweit Hockey Club into major senior hockey. The initial beneficiaries were hockey and speed skating (ice sports), and, later, figure skating, boxing, curling, and wrestling utilized the spacious facility. (DON BURNS COLLECTION)

a reference to coach Roy Prowse. They included Johnny "Snag" Squarebriggs, Walter Lawlor, Frank "Duck" Acorn, and Ivan Nicholson. The league games attracted capacity crowds, with over 2,000 fans witnessing the final game of the 1930 season in Summerside. Six hundred of them travelled by double-header special train from Charlottetown. But their loyalty paled beside that of Lowell Hancock. Hancock, an ardent Crystal supporter, had skied from Summerside to Charlottetown to attend a previous playoff game. The trek required twelve hours; leaving Summerside at 8:15 A.M., Hancock arrived at the Charlottetown Arena by 8:00 P.M., in time for the opening face-off. The sporting gesture by Hancock was applauded by both sides of the Arena Rink on that February night.

The opening of the Charlottetown Forum on December 9, 1930, had a profound effect on hockey throughout Prince Edward Island and, indeed, throughout the Maritimes. While the game had evolved from scrimmages and games on natural ice, usually formed as a result of a January thaw, the formalization of the game required more predictable circumstances. The Forum, with its artificial ice and spacious seating,

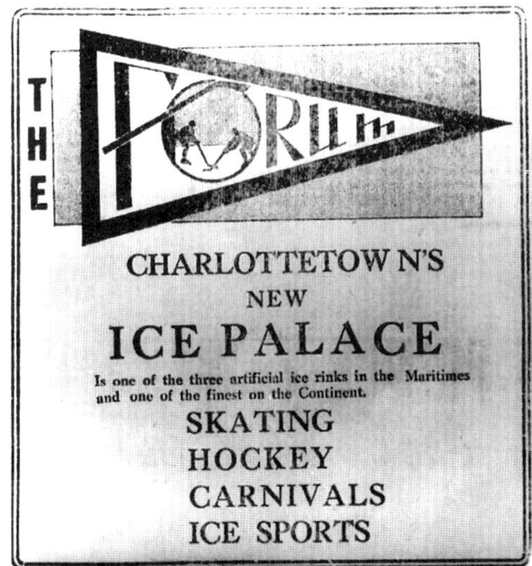

Sport officials in Charlottetown promoted the new Ice Palace with invitations and attractive ads that initially drew thousands of athletes and fans from across the Maritimes. The first hockey game to be played in the facility was on December 13, 1930, when the Moncton Victorias defeated the Abegweits 3–2 before a capacity crowd of more than 3,000 fans.

(*THE GUARDIAN*, DECEMBER 14, 1930)

added a new dimension to the sport of hockey, and in later years contributed to the popularity of speed skating, figure skating, curling, boxing, and even wrestling.

Ice sports (speed skating), in particular, was a beneficiary of the new facility as there was keen interest in ice sports in Island schools, both urban and rural. While a number of schools had previously held their own ice sports competition, the promotion of a provincial ice meet was new. Bill Gillespie, the manager of the new Forum, provided the venue, and invitations were sent to schools from Tignish to Souris. Arthur Gaudet, former Maritime Champion speed skater, offered his services as instructor during practice sessions, and winners of the events were recognized as provincial champions. The staging of Provincial Ice Sports became a huge event during the following decades, with special teams, buses, and other means of conveyance bringing students and parents by the thousands to the host community.

The first hockey game in the state-of-the-art facility was staged on December 13, 1930, when the Moncton Victorias defeated the Abegweits 3–2. There was a capacity crowd of 3,200 present in the Forum for the historic game, and the power of radio broadcasting extended the audience to those Island homes fortunate enough to have radio receivers. CFCY Charlottetown carried the game, with B. J. Murley providing the voice of Island hockey.

After a series of exhibition games with mainland teams to christen the Forum, the Island Senior Hockey League resumed play with only the Crystals and Abbies as entrants. Even the opening of the modern "Ice Palace," the Charlottetown Forum, did not subdue the hostility that developed between the two teams over several seasons. From 1927 to 1931, there was an increase in the incidence of rough play, altercations with the fans, disagreement with officials, and bitterness over player defections. In fact, it may have unwittingly contributed to it. A rough game to open the League was followed several games later by a "squabble" between Nicholson and Grady that resulted in a one-game suspension for each player. Summerside officials were incensed and threatened to withdraw from the League, and the matter was referred to the Maritime Amateur Hockey Association for resolution. Several games later, the Abbies were awarded a game when the Crystals left the ice to display their disagreement with the referee. Over 2,000 fans were in the rink to witness the fiasco. When Ralph Silliphant was suspended for the season by the MAHA, the Crystals protested vehemently. The gathering storm erupted on February 14, 1931, when a full-scale donneybrook broke out during a playoff game at the Crystal rink. With the score tied 4–4, fans swarmed onto the ice to take part in the ruckus, and it required strong intervention by the Summerside Police to restore order. While players from both teams received injuries, the most serious was a broken jaw sustained by the Abegweits' classy forward, Walter Lawlor. Even worse, in the aftermath of the game, Charlottetown's Ivan "Hickey" Nicholson was discovered beaten and unconscious in an alleyway near the Summerside Railway Station.

The MAHA intervened in the volatile situation and ordered that a sudden-death game be played in Moncton to determine an Island champion. The Abegweit Club protested the decision, claiming the removal of the game from Charlottetown would give a "black eye" to Island hockey. So intense were the emotions that, prior to the game, Johnny "Snag" Squarebriggs stated "a victory tonight would be as good as a Maritime title." Nevertheless, the ruling stood and the Abbies were ordered to play in Moncton or face suspension. While Abbies' coach Bill Gillespie praised the efforts of his injury-depleted team, the Crystals won 5–2, and laid claim to the coveted B. W. Robinson Trophy. While the deciding game was played with some civility, the season as a whole was a dark episode for senior hockey on the Island.

The disastrous 1930–31 season had major repercussions for senior hockey. The Island Senior League suspended play, and both the Crystals and Abegweits sought entry to mainland leagues. The Crystals

Ivan "Hickey" Nicholson made his hockey debut in the late 1920s, and became a star with the Abegweit senior team on the Island and in the Maritime Big Four leagues. In 1936–1937, Nicholson played hockey in England with the Harringay Racers, and the following season turned professional with the Kansas City Greyhounds of the American Hockey Association. During the season he was called up by the Chicago Black Hawks of the NHL, and scored a goal in his first game against the Boston Bruins, February 5, 1938. (PARO 2320-94-7)

elected to join the Central New Brunswick League, which included Amherst, Moncton, Sussex, and Charlottetown Millionaires. The Abegweits entered the high-profile Northern League against Fredericton, Moncton, Bathurst, Campbellton, and Dalhousie.

The decision by the Abegweits to enter the controversial atmosphere of Maritime Senior hockey had major implications for the Abegweit AAA, both philosophical and financial. To be competitive, the Abbies would have to import players and provide for their needs, including accommodation. The residency rule required players to live in the community for a period of six months in order to be eligible for league play. Therefore, jobs and accommodations needed to be found for each import player. That practice compromised the spirit, if not the letter, of amateurism. It also threatened the bond between the Abbies and its wholly Island roots. Great Abegweit teams of the past were made up of "Islanders," not players "from away." Nevertheless, the decision was made, and the Abegweit Club's Executive, with obvious reluctance, relinquished the administration of its senior hockey team to an influential hockey committee, consisting of Dr. Ira J. Yeo (who was also president of the Forum), Colonel Dan MacKinnon, and Dr. W. A. Smith. The time-honoured name of the "Abegweits," noted throughout Canada for its athletic excellence and support of amateurism, was suddenly a much sought-after commercial entity. In retrospect, the decision was ill-fated, and adversely affected the vitality of the Abegweit Amateur Athletic Association over the long term. In the short term, however, there would be moments of intense excitement and triumph.

Within weeks, the Hockey Committee commenced an aggressive

ABEGWEIT HOCKEY TEAM 1931-1932

JACK "HURRY" KANE was born in Montreal twenty-seven years ago, is five feet seven inches tall and weighs 155 pounds Hurry can play either right wing or centre. In the season 1930-1931 he was with the Hamilton Tigers, Allan Cup finalists, and led the O. H. A. in scoring. He is single.

DORAN "RED" DOUCET, born in Bathurst, N. B., August 11, 1910 which makes him twenty-one years old. His first senior hockey was with Bathurst Papermakers in 1926. He played with Shawinigan Falls Cataracts 1927-1928, Dalhousie 1929-30. Back with Bathurst 1930-31. Red's weight is 150 pounds and is five feet eight inches tall. He is a right winger and unmarried.

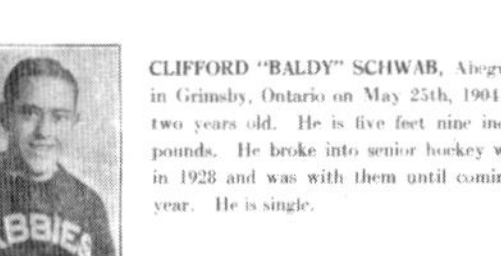

CLIFFORD "BALDY" SCHWAB, Abegweit left winger was born in Grimsby, Ontario on May 25th, 1904 and is therefore twenty-two years old. He is five feet nine inches tall and weighs 160 pounds. He broke into senior hockey with the Hamilton Tigers in 1928 and was with them until coming to the Maritimes this year. He is single.

WALTER BERNARD LAWLOR plays in centre ice for the Abegweits. He was born in Charlottetown, August 15, 1912 and is therefore not yet twenty years old. He played his first senior hockey with the Abegweits in 1929. He is five feet eight inches tall and weighs 160 pounds. Walter is the youngest member of the team and is single.

JOHNNY "SNAG" SQUAREBRIGGS, centre and left wing is twenty-one years old, having just seen the light of day November 6, 1910 in Charlottetown. Snag weighs 145 pounds and is five feet nine inches tall. He has been playing senior hockey with the Abegweits since 1929. He is single and one of the most popular boys on Charlottetown's line up.

IVAN "HICKEY" NICHOLSON, left wing was born in Charlottetown, September 9, 1911. Is five feet nine inches tall and weighs 165 pounds. Played senior hockey first with the Charlottetown [illegible] This is his fourth season with the Abegweits. Hickey is married.

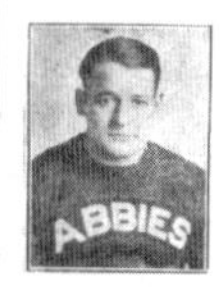

CHICK WILLIAMS, defence and right wing. Born in Charlottetown on October 25, 1899. Is five feet six inches tall and weighs 170 pounds. Started playing senior hockey with Abbies in 1915. Overseas from 1915-1919. Then was with the Maples of Boston 1921-1925, and has played Abegweit ever since. Chick is one of Charlottetown's favorites and very popular with players and fans alike.

HIBBERT SAUNDERS better known as "HIB" was born in Charlottetown, September 25, 1907. Is a right winger and got his first taste of senior company with the Abegweits in 1927. He is five feet ten inches tall and weighs 165 pounds and is single.

RAYMOND FRANCIS STULL, Goal was born in St. Catherine's, Ontario on 13th day of May, 1909. Ray is five feet six inches tall and weighs 165 pounds. Played with Jordan, Ontario Intermediates 1928-1929; with the Abbies 1929-30. Ray is married.

Abegweit Hockey Team, 1931–32. The Abbies, long sought-after as a commercial entity, entered the Maritime Big Six Hockey League in 1931–1932. In a major policy change, four of the nine members of the team were recruited from out-of-province. Left page: Jack "Hurry" Kane, Doran Doucet, Clifford Schwab, Walter Lawlor; Right page: Johnny Squarebriggs, Ivan Nicholson, Chick Williams, Hibbert Saunders, Ray Stull. (AUTHOR COLLECTION)

recruitment program, attracting Harold Gross from Kentville Wildcats, plus players from Campbellton, Sussex, and Moncton. Seeking players with speed and an adept scoring touch, the Abbies lured Jack "Hurry" Kane from the Hamilton Tigers. Notified that Kane was en route from Hamilton to Halifax to discuss playing for the Wolverines, the Charlottetown group intercepted the train as it passed through Amherst, Nova Scotia, and convinced Kane that he should play for the Abbies. The rest of the story is legend in Island sport history.

The first season of play for the "Big Six" League, 1931–1932, was immensely successful on Prince Edward Island. By January, special trains were running from Souris and other Island communities for home games, and fan excursions were offered for games in Moncton. While the team finished out of the playoffs, optimism remained high.

With the "Big Six" League enjoying success on the ice, a major jurisdictional battle loomed between the Canadian Amateur Hockey Association and the MAHA. Apart from the residency rule, the CAHA required that players not receive any financial remuneration for hockey

The 1934–1935 Abbies were leading the Maritime Big Four hockey league when the CAHA ruled a number of players in the league ineligible for amateur play. The Abegweits lost seven players. The decision led to the demise of the once powerful Big Four Hockey League. Front, l-r: Joffre Desilets, Des Smith, Jimmy Kelly, Frank Currie, Jack "Hurry" Kane; Back: Leo Sargent, "Nig" Brennaman, Ray Getliffe, Harold Gross, Pete Kelly, Ivan "Hickey" Nicholson, Jerry McCabe, Pat Adair. (AUTHOR COLLECTION)

services. The CAHA claimed there were eleven players in the Maritimes receiving at least $75.00 per week, and that $100,000 would not cover the operating expenses of Big Six teams. When the Moncton Hawks won the Allan Cup in 1933 (and 1934), defeating the Saskatoon Quakers with a team stacked with "tourist" hockey players, it caused embarrassment to the CAHA for its inability to take the Maritime Clubs to task. In January of 1935, the Abegweits were leading the new Big Four League with a team featuring future NHL stars Pete Kelly, Ray Getliffe, Joffre "Dizzy" Desilets, and "Nig" Brennaman, when the CAHA issued an edict declaring a host of players ineligible for Allan Cup play. The ruling caused an outcry from hockey officials in the Maritimes, as all four teams were adversely affected. The Abegweits alone lost seven players. The team's situation was compounded by the departure of their leading scorer, Pete Kelly, who in view of the uncertainty of the situation, signed with the NHL's St. Louis Eagles.

The protests were to no avail, and senior hockey in the Maritimes was thrown into disarray. Saint John withdrew from the League, and the Moncton Hawks, one of the great amateur hockey teams of the era, disbanded. Only Halifax Wolverines and Charlottetown persisted with

Pete Kelly was recruited by the Abegweit Hockey Club in May 1933, and became the leading scorer in the Maritime Big Four League during his tenure as a right-winger with the team. His stellar play caught the attention of the St. Louis Eagles of the NHL, and later he was signed by the Eagles in January 1935. After his hockey career, Kelly returned to live in Charlottetown and married Pearl Marguerite "Peg" Hobbs. As a member of the Charlottetown Golf Club he became one of the leading golfers in the Maritimes.
(AUTHOR COLLECTION)

league play, with the Abbies recruiting Johnny "Snag" Squarebriggs, Harry Currie, and Windy Steele to replenish their line-up. By season's end, Halifax had won the League Championship, and went on to win the Allan Cup, which carried with it the right to represent Canada at the 1936 Winter Olympic Games. By November of 1935, Halifax had withdrawn from the Big Four League to protect its Olympic eligibility. The decision by the Wolverines was for naught, as the CAHA replaced the Allan Cup holders with the Port Arthur Bearcats as Canada's hockey representatives at the Olympics. The ruling brought a torrent of protests from the Halifax press and Maritime hockey officials. Led by prominent Halifax sports columnist Alex Nickerson, they campaigned furiously against the disqualification of the Wolverines. The efforts proved fruitless, for as the committee debated the issue in a Halifax hotel room, the Port Arthur Bearcats sailed out of the Halifax harbour en route to the Winter Olympics at Garmisch-Partenkirchen, Germany.

The Bearcats, considerably weaker than the Wolverines, lost the gold medal to Great Britain, the first time Canada had suffered a defeat in Olympic hockey since the Winter Games were inaugurated in 1924. In an ironic twist, a major squabble developed over the eligibility of two players on the British team. Alex Archer and goalie James Foster were Canadians who had moved to England the previous year. The day before the Olympic tournament began, the International Ice Hockey Federation voted unanimously to ban the two players. However, two days later, Archer and Foster, along with several other Canadian-born players, appeared on the ice playing for Great Britain against Sweden. Although the USA and Canada raised protests, the controversy sudden-

Kensington Silver Wings, of the North Shore Hockey League, winner of the Baker Trophy in 1937, and the Lea and Wright Trophy in 1936 and 1937. The team was part of the widespread interest in rural hockey that swept across the province in the 1930s and late 1940s. Back, l-r: G. Simms, G. Webster, A. Taylor, A. Bernard, M. Waite, L. Howatt, B. Lawson; Front: R. Crozier, D. Whitlock, B. Champion, G. Cooke, H. MacFarlane.
(COMMUNITY GARDENS COLLECTION)

ly subsided and Canadian-born players played a pivotal role in Great Britain's gold medal victory at the 1936 Olympic Winter Games.

Back in the Maritimes, the Big Four Hockey League was essentially defunct, the Charlottetown Abegweits the only remnant of the once-proud league. With great anguish, on November 28, 1935, the Abbies disbanded, leaving no senior hockey for the first time since 1896. By early January, all of the team members had left Charlottetown to play for other clubs — several, including Johnny Squarebriggs, to the Baltimore Orioles, and others to the Denver Canadians.[43] With the players went the fan support, along with the enthusiasm and pride that had been manifested by the people of the province.

The disillusionment that remained had a negative impact on the Abegweit AAA, as the organization struggled with its identity. Quite apart from the issue of disillusionment, the resources of the Association, in terms of leadership, energy, and finances, were severely taxed. The problem was not wholly internal to the Abegweit Club, as the administration and governance of amateur sport in Canada was undergoing fundamental change. Commencing in the late 1920s and extending into the decade of the 1930s, the formation of separate governing bodies for the major sports reflected the trend toward autonomy in the

The 1940 Freetown Maple Leafs (later the Royals), North Shore Hockey League Champions, was one of the most successful rural hockey teams in the province during the 1940s and early 1950s. The team played in the South/North Shore Hockey Leagues against such well-known teams as the Albany St. Pats, Middleton Bombers, Bedeque Beavers, and Cape Traverse Rovers. Much of the credit for the success of the team has been accorded to the leadership of Robert Jardine, manager and coach over seventeen years. Back, l-r: Horace Paynter, Walter Campbell, Morris Deacon, Walter Hogg, Walter Stavert, Robert Jardine (Coach); Centre: Allan Clow, Walter Simmons, Walter Paynter (goal), Allison Deacon, Horace MacFarlane; Front: Wilfred Burns, Gerald Jardine, Wilbert Deacon, Reg Bradshaw. (ROBERT JARDINE COLLECTION)

governance of sport. The Amateur Athletic Union of Canada and its regional branches, until then the most influential sport governing organization in Canada, were experiencing an erosion of power in the governance of sport previously regarded as within their respective domain.

The evolving administrative framework had important implications for the Abegweit AAA. Both by tradition and reputation, the multi-sport Association had been the main governing authority for amateur sport within the province. As the number of autonomous sport governing bodies increased, the role of the Abegweit Association declined. During the 1930s, the club entered teams in provincial and Maritime competition, hockey, baseball, and rugby that were administered by

From 1929 to 1939, the Victoria Unions won five provincial intermediate hockey championships and three Maritime titles. At various times during their hockey dominance, the team was composed of five MacLeod brothers, Danny, Bill, Louis, George, and James, and two MacLeod cousins, Lester and Lou. Front, l-r: Bill MacLeod, Donald MacLeod (Captain), Stanley Stewart, Whitfield Howatt, Crilly Lea; Insert: Rev. Kaye (Coach); Rear: Danny MacLeod, Hedley Miller, Frank Pidgeon, Jim MacLeod, Charlie Hogan.
(PARO CAMERA CLUB COLLECTION, 2320/94-3)

regional and provincial sport governing bodies. It was a far cry from the authority and power that had resided in the organization for over thirty years.

While both the Abegweits and Crystals were experiencing turmoil in Island senior hockey, and while the Abbies' fortune rose and fell with their sortie into Maritime commercial hockey, a groundswell of interest in intermediate hockey was sweeping the Island. Commencing in 1927, there was, for over a decade, highly competitive hockey on Prince Edward Island that was based on local talent and community support. The accomplishments of hometown players generated immense excitement in their respective communities, and represent an illustrious period in the annals of hockey history on the Island.

While numerous communities were represented by their team, ranging from Alberton to Murray Harbour, in historical perspective the

Borden Nationals, Island Intermediate Hockey Champions, 1930–1931 season. The Nationals defeated the Victoria Unions 2–0 and 1–1 in claiming their first pro-vincial intermediate hockey championship. The team would repeat as provincial champions in 1936 and as Maritime champions in 1945. Back, l-r: Ray Smallwood (Coach), W. McWilliams, L. Inman, E. Campbell, D. MacPherson, E. McInnis, L. Bell, T. Paquet; Front: C. Howatt, O. Campbell, Mayor William Leard, R. MacKenzie, L. McAleer, L. Peters. (OSCAR CAMPBELL COLLECTION)

era belongs to the Victoria Unions and the "MacLeod Boys" of the picturesque seaside village. The MacLeods, numbering seven and representing two families, were talented hockey players who were led by the scoring wizardry of Dan MacLeod. Following their third Maritime Intermediate Championship in 1939, when they defeated the Glace Bay Consuls 6–5 at Glace Bay, and 10–3 at the Charlottetown Forum in front of 2,000 fans, the *Guardian*'s sport columnist paid tribute to the Unions: "Hats off to what is undoubtedly the finest squad of intermediate puck chasers ever developed in the Island and one that is composed of entirely home brews from one of the smallest centres on the Island."

In May 2001, Lester MacLeod, then in his 88th year, reminisced about the Unions' team. When asked which game evoked the most satisfying memories, he replied with a twinkle in his eye, "against the Truro Primroses in 1930." He continued, "The Primroses agreed to come to Victoria for $300, bolstering their team with three members of the senior Bearcats, just to insure victory. After arriving, the Primrose players visited the General Store and questioned how such a small place could have a hockey team, let alone a good one. The Unions skated to a 4–3 victory over the Truro Primroses that night in Victoria, claiming the NS-PEI intermediate hockey championship." Lester MacLeod leaned back in his chair, smiled, and for a moment savoured that moment of triumph, when he was just a boy, a MacLeod Boy.

MAHA Intermediate Hockey Provincial Champions, 1927-1939

YEAR	ISLAND CHAMPIONS	PROVINCIAL FINALISTS
1927	Charlottetown Vics**	
1928	Charlottetown Vics	Charlottetown Abbies
1929	Victoria Unions*	Charlottetown Abbies
1930	Victoria Unions	Charlottetown Abbies
1931	Borden Nationals	Victoria Unions
1932	Cape Traverse	Alberton Regals
1933	Charlottetown Abbies	Summerside Hockey Club
1934	Montague Primroses	Charlottetown Abbies
1935	Charlottetown Abbies	Montague Primroses
1936	Borden Nationals	Montague Primroses
1937	Victoria Unions*	LPU
1938	Victoria Unions	Montague Primroses
1939	Victoria Unions*	Montague Primroses

* *Denotes Maritime Champions*
** *Old Victorias Hockey Association revived*

While the achievements of the Victoria Unions and other Island intermediate hockey teams of the era marked a glorious decade for "rural" hockey on Prince Edward Island, junior hockey was emerging from the shadow of the senior Abbies. Coached by Lou Campbell and Harry Richardson, and led by team captain Gordon Stewart, the Junior Abbies made a valiant run in the 1934 season for the Memorial Cup, emblematic of junior hockey supremacy in Canada. After disposing of

The Montague Primroses, Island Intermediate Champions, 1934. Intermediate hockey was highly competitive during the 1930s, with the Primroses annual contenders. In 1934 they defeated the Abbies of Charlottetown to claim the coveted provincial championship. Front, l-r: Norbert Grant, Wilfred Waterworth, Ted McEwen, Pete McCarron, Ken Beer; Back: Bruce Currie, Stewart Vickers, B. MacDonald, Randolph Carruthers, Bill Garrick (Coach), Martin Currie, Lowell Poole, Calvin Hitchey. (DICK MACLEAN COLLECTION)

the Bathurst Papermakers and Halifax Canadians for the Maritime Championship, the Abbies defeated the highly favourite Quebec Champions, the Mount Royal Cranes, to advance to the eastern finals. The games against the Cranes were played in Charlottetown, with the first game ending in a 4–4 tie, and the Abbies winning the deciding game in a two-game total-goal series, 8–1. The *Charlottetown Guardian* declared the victory "a smashing triumph for the Maritime Champions and one that brought a glow of pride to the hearts of all Island hockey followers." In the eastern finals the Abbies encountered the St. Michaels Majors of Toronto, considered to be the strongest junior team assembled in Canada for twenty years. The local squad was outclassed in "everything but courage," losing 12–2 and 7–2 to the eventual Memorial Cup Champions.

The junior Abbies' stirring quest for the Memorial Cup in 1934 created considerable interest in both Charlottetown and Summerside. A new team, the Royals, was formed in Charlottetown, and Kensington

The Charlottetown Junior Royals, Maritime Junior Hockey Champions, 1939. After disposing of the Saint John Pontiacs and Dartmouth Rough Riders in Maritime playdowns, the Junior Royals advanced to the eastern Memorial Cup semi-finals against the Perth Blue Wings. The series played in Charlottetown displayed hockey at its best, with the Royals featuring such stars as Wes "Bucko" Trainor, Bert Steele, and Jack Coyle. The series proved to be a roller coaster, with the Blue Wings winning the deciding game 7–6 in double overtime. Front, l-r: N. Whitlock (Manager), A. Perry, W. MacDonald, J. Davis, L. Jay, E. Corbett, D. MacLeod (Treasurer); Back: G. MacLeod, A. Blacquiere, V. Peters, E. MacNeill (Secretary), J. Roach, A. Steele, W. Trainor, A. Rogers, J. Coyle, J. Whitlock, V. Roach; Insert: Walter Lawlor (Coach). (JOE COYLE COLLECTION)

and Summerside also organized teams. Within two years, the Summerside Soviets were contending for provincial junior honours against the Abbies and Royals, and, while they did not win any provincial titles, they did provide a competitive challenge for Island playdowns. It was the junior Royals who emerged in 1939 with a highly talented group of hockeyists that included Wes "Bucko" Trainor, John Coyle, Bert Steele, and John "Tarky" Whitlock, all ready for a run at the Memorial Cup. After annexing the Maritime Championship with victories over Saint John Pontiacs and Dartmouth Rough Riders, coach Walter Lawlor

Beach Point Stars, ca. 1939. Hockey across rural Prince Edward Island during the decade of the 1940s, and into the 1950s, reached every corner of the province. Pictured are three members of the Beach Point Stars, who played their home games on an open-air rink. An indoor rink was built in Murray Harbour in 1946. L-r: Gordon MacKay, Louis Harris, Willie Harris. (BARRY HARRIS COLLECTION)

prepped his team to meet the Perth Blue Wings, the Ontario District Champions.

A classic series ensued. Led by the adept scoring of "Tarky" Whitlock, the Royals forced the Blue Wings to double overtime in the deciding game. *The Charlottetown Guardian* captured the drama of the moment:

> In the first overtime session Royals held the lead twice on goals by sharp-shooting Tarky Whitlock, but with only forty-two seconds remaining and the 3,000 fans that packed the Forum to its capacity in a mad uproar, Blue Wings tied it up.

In the end, the Blue Wings prevailed, 7–6.

A fragile senior hockey league operated during the 1937 and 1938 seasons, but it was a brief stint for both the Crystals and Abbies, as the upstart Charlottetown Rangers claimed the 1939 Island Championship. Following their provincial victory, the Rangers barely managed to fulfill their playoff obligations to Fredericton and Saint John, due to a lack of funds. It was a far cry from the good old days of the early 1920s, when keen rivalries, loyal fan support, and solid club administration made senior hockey in the province a viable sport enterprise. It was intermediate, junior, school, and women's hockey that sustained the game across the province during this difficult period of transition.

Junior men's hockey, in particular, restored hockey to a level of public confidence and support, flashing as they did their youthful exuberance for the game. Unfortunately, it would be the same young men who would, in the ensuing years, fight another kind of battle, that of the Second World War in Europe.

Part Three

Prince of Wales College Intercollegiate Champions, 1941–1942. Intercollegiate hockey competition between St. Dunstan's and PWC filled a void during the early years of the Second World War. Standing, l-r: T. Hooper, F. MacTague, Professor G. Bennett (Coach), W. Simmons, Ivo Cudmore, Mac Beck; Sitting: E. Bagnall, I. MacArthur, B. Hodgson (Captain), B. Auld, R. Peppin; Missing: D. Bagnall. (DR. MAC BECK COLLECTION)

11 Sport Battles

When Great Britain declared war on Germany on September 3, 1939, it marked the beginning of the Second World War; tragically, the conflict would last from 1939 to 1945. Canada followed Britain into the fray with its own declaration of war one week later. The forthright decision demonstrated the degree of loyalty held by Canadians for the Mother Country, and the commitment Canada was prepared to make to the war effort. The decision prompted an overwhelming response at recruiting centres across the Island, and, indeed, across the country. Young men and women in the prime of their lives left family, friends, and jobs, when available, and declared their willingness to fight for freedom and country.

Many of the men and women who joined the service were the cream of Island athleticism, the rugby players, golfers, boxers, and members of baseball, basketball, and hockey teams, who laid aside their personal aspirations to serve their country. So compelling was the response that Island newspapers boasted that Canada's smallest province had the highest rate of enlistment in the country. Over the course of the War, 49.6 per cent of Island males between the ages of eighteen and forty-five would serve in the armed forces.[44] It seemed that a whole generation of Island men had gone off to war. Initially, the exodus of athletes to serve in the war effort was highly disruptive to sport leagues and club competition across the province. However, as the reality of the conflict impacted the lives of people at home, there was a return to sport and recreational activities. For sport provided a significant diversion, entertainment for people who were fraught with worry as they anxiously awaited news from the battlefields of Europe. An afternoon at the race track, rink, or other sport venue could provide a respite from the constant stress revolving around the daily lives of citizens.

The 1941 *Guardian* Sport Review underscored the fact that the ranks of Island athletes were depleted: "List of participants in various (sport) branches reduced through enlistments." Nevertheless the Review was optimistic, positive. While baseball, basketball, senior hockey, boxing, lawn tennis, golf, and badminton suffered an initial decline, other sports maintained a public profile. The Junior Royals won their third successive Maritime title, while the Victoria Driving club enjoyed its greatest season of winter racing over the speedway in front of Victoria Park. Other sports that regained their prewar vigour included curling, bowling, rugby, speed skating, rifle shooting, yachting, boxing, wrestling,[45] and a new sport attraction, figure skating. While "fancy" skating, later figure skating, was performed in Island rinks dating back to the turn of the century, it was due to the efforts of Wallie Scantlebury that the sport gained acceptance in Charlottetown. The first public presentation of the sport came in 1941, when skaters under the tutelage of Scantlebury performed in front of a large crowd of interested parents and spectators. Subsequently, figure skating became a bona fide member of the amateur sport system in the province.

The appearance of servicemen on the Island's sport scene was a welcome sight for Island sport officials, bringing, as it did, a high level of skill and experience to the senior level of competition. Commencing in 1941, an influx of military personnel was created by the construction of eight air bases spread across the Island. The bases with the most notable impact on sport were located at Summerside (St. Eleanor's), Mt. Pleasant, and Charlottetown. The General Reconnaissance School (RAF) in Charlottetown was of particular interest in that it contained personnel from the Royal Air Force whose members tended to seek out different kinds of sport and leisure activities, such as rugby, yachting, and boxing. The airmen who were stationed across the Island were highly competitive in local sport. P/O George Millard won the island's golf championship in 1942 and 1943; others stimulated interservice boxing; entered teams in rugby and city league hockey; and contributed to an increased activity at the Charlottetown Yacht Club.

Charlottetown Figure Skating Club, 1947. Under the creative talent of Wallie Scantlebury, figure skating blossomed as a full-fledged sport during the 1940s. Back, l-r: unidentified, Jane Giddings, Claudette MacMillan, Wallie Scantlebury, unidentified, Arlene Lavers, Elaine Murley, Sheila Praught; Front: unidentified, Jean MacDougall, Teresa Gallant; Missing: Velma Carmody, Adele Vickerson, Margery Gillespie, Pat Richard. (GEORGE SCANTLEBURY COLLECTION)

The contribution of servicemen, army, navy, and air force to the sport environment of the Island was highly significant in stabilizing the Island's fragile sport system and, in effect, replaced, at least temporarily, our Island athletes who were serving in other theatres of war.

While the overall sport system gained a measure of organization during the mid-years of the War, it was the sport of harness racing that attracted spectators by the thousands to racing ovals across the province. The 1942 Old Home Week races and Provincial Exhibition were a case in point. In its attempt to attract tourists and horse-racing fans, the CDP advertised the event as the "Maritimes' Greatest Holiday Week." Special trains ran from Tignish and Souris, and the president of the Provincial Exhibition Association called it "the largest attendance since the Exhibition opened in 1889." The off-track program was resplendent, with eight vaudeville acts and a nine-piece Royal Orchestra Band. Lieutenant-Colonel Dan MacKinnon, as president of the CDP, revived the concept of Old Home Week in 1940, and combined it with harness racing as the main component of a four-day program.

Joe O'Brien had a way with horses. Fellow drivers often commented that he could communicate with horses by the way he held the reins. Whatever the reason, Joe O'Brien from Alberton, Prince Edward Island, became one of the most successful trainers/drivers of standardbred horses in the world.
(PARO 2320/89-4)

The impact of the sport was equally impressive in 1943, as huge crowds, fast horses, and expert drivers highlighted the season. The 1943 Harness Racing Review, as compiled by "D. A. MacK.," and published in *The Charlottetown Guardian,* conveyed the state of the harness racing industry in the province,[46] noting the expertise of drivers Joe O'Brien and Johnny Conroy. O'Brien was the leading driver at the Old Home Week event, and Jollity, driven by Conroy, paced the "two fastest heats, in one race in Canada" during 1943. The sensational racing continued in 1945, with numerous trotting and pacing records set. The most notable trotting record was established by Island favourite Christie Budlong, 2:09, owned and driven by George Brookins of Kensington, and the top pacing record was set by O.U. Volo, 2:10½, owned by Harold Stead of Brackley.

Taken in the context of the war years, harness racing provided a meaningful social/leisure experience to many thousands of Islanders and tourists alike; and, in so doing, indulged the social and psychological needs of a populace weary of the stress and anxiety of the War.

The year 1944 marked a turning point in the revitalization of amateur sport in the province. Even as the battles on the war front in Europe continued, there were signs, locally, that the War was coming to an end. While the involvement of servicemen in the sport system of the Island was at its peak, with teams competing in numerous leagues and sport activities, the closure of military bases across the province was imminent. Four of the five installations were closed in 1945; only St.

Racing into the Paddock turn before an overflow crowd at the CDP. Picture taken before the grandstand fire of 1961. (PARO 2320-88-8)

Eleanor's — later CFB Summerside — survived the government cuts. CFB Summerside remained active in promoting/competing in sport by entering teams in provincial competitions, notably baseball, softball, and hockey, and by joining teams representing the Town of Summerside. The involvement of servicemen in Island sport competition during and after the War was of considerable importance, and helped sustain a fragile sport system during the most difficult of times.

There was a feeling of optimism throughout the sport community in 1944, as former athletes trickled back from the war front in Europe and citizens of the province sensed that the War was winding down. The appointment of S. F. "Sammy" Doyle as Sports Co-ordinator for the city was a positive sign as he and Professor Gordon Bennett worked tirelessly to re-energize basic sport leagues and competitions. While the response was more subdued than during peacetime, it nevertheless provided, as noted by *The Guardian*, "one of the best years of athletics since the outbreak of war in 1939." Features of the revamped program included a four-team city hockey league, and increased interest in rural hockey; an active program at the four curling clubs; a banner year of ice racing at the Victoria Driving Club and the Brackley Driving Club; increased activity at the lawn tennis clubs, with an emphasis on junior programs; softball regaining its popularity across the Island; bowling alleys "thronged from early fall"; and the sports of golf, rugby, yachting, and boxing maintaining basic programs.[47] Of the major sports, only baseball, track and field, and basketball were absent from the sport headlines of the Island's news media.

Following the end of the War, the demand for sport and recreation facilities across the province increased dramatically. As in the post-Great War period, citizens' exuberance for activity confronted community leaders and politicians with the deficiency in athletic programs and facilities. In Charlottetown, the City Council, previously reluctant to become directly involved in the provision of sport facilities, was faced with the reality that the Abegweit Grounds, long taken for granted, were no longer available. Not only were the Grounds gone — sold to a real estate speculator during the War — but the Abegweit Amateur Athletic Association, which, for nearly half a century had provided volunteer leadership for the city's and province's sport and recreation needs, was in a disorganized state, lacking leadership, finances, and an administrative mandate. A similar situation existed in Summerside and numerous rural communities, where prewar sport facilities were no longer adequate to the sport and recreational needs.

The first overt response came from the provincial government, the first time the elected officials of government had acknowledged any responsibility for the provision of sport and recreation as an essential service. In 1945, the Jones government appointed Lieutenant Colonel W. W. "Bill" Reid as Director of Physical Fitness for Prince Edward Island. Later, two regional representatives were appointed, James T. Hogan of Summerside for Prince County, and Arthur Perry of Charlottetown for King's County. The mandate of the new appointees was to promote and coordinate sport and recreation programs throughout the province.

Reid was ideally suited for the leadership role placed upon him by the provincial government. While his first athletic test came as a goalie for West Kent School in 1931, it was his leadership as a soldier where he made his greatest contribution to the Allied cause during the First World War. Reid possessed an extraordinary ability to lead and motivate his troops, and, during combat in Italy, he was duly honoured for his heroic actions against the Italian and German armies. Upon his return to Prince Edward Island in 1945, he became the first commander of the new Prince Edward Island Regiment, and in 1949 he was promoted to the rank of Brigadier General.[48]

Reid inherited an arduous task, essentially to reassemble a provincial sport delivery system that had been severely disrupted by the demise of the Abegweit AAA and the advent of war. That the premier of the province at the time was former Abegweit great J. Walter Jones was fortuitous, to say the least. Jones was a versatile athlete, a member of

In 1945, the provincial government of J. Walter Jones appointed Brigadier-General W. W. "Bill" Reid as Director of Physical Fitness for the province. It was a strategic appointment, as Reid was able to restructure the amateur sport system across the province during the mid-1940s and early 1950s. (AUTHOR COLLECTION)

the Abegweits' 1899 Maritime rugby champions, a member of the All-Canadians' rugby team that toured Great Britain in 1902, Maritime record holder in the hammer throw, an accomplished basketball and baseball player, and a former director of the Abegweit Association. His long involvement in sport as an athlete and an administrator provided him with a canny appreciation of the situation and undoubtedly influenced his and his government's decision to direct provincial funding and leadership resources to the development of sport and recreation services to all parts of the province.

A contributing factor to the government's action was that public opinion was strongly in favour of decisive action to address the situation. The most aggressive position was taken by Prince of Wales College, whose administrators and Student Athletic Association presented a formal petition to the provincial government in October of 1945. The petition decried the lack of sport facilities in the city, and outlined the need for a football (rugby) field, a 440-yard cinder track, and an outdoor rink. The College needed the facilities in an urgent way, as it was, like St. Dunstan's University, experiencing a dramatic increase in enrollment due primarily to the influx of veterans returning from the War. With the Abegweit Grounds only a memory, the attention of sport officials was directed towards picturesque Victoria Park as the site for the much-needed outdoor athletic complex. The only long-term sport tenant of the Park at the time was the Charlottetown Lawn Tennis Club; consequently, there was suitable property available for such a sport development. Reid quickly assembled the main user groups: PWC, the public schools, and representatives from baseball, track and field, and rugby, and proceeded with the design and construction of the much-anticipated outdoor sport complex. On September 20, 1947, the project was realized when Memorial Field was christened by hundreds of school track and field athletes, and dedicated by Lieutenant-Governor Joseph A. Bernard and Premier J. Walter Jones "to the memory of former athletes who had died in two World Wars."[49] While all fatalities were grievous, the deaths of three members of the Maritime Champions Junior Royals Hockey team, whose last athletic feats contributed to the success of the team in 1939, were especially poignant to the sport community. Killed in action were FO John Coyle, PO George MacLeod, and Gunner Jimmie Roach.

The opening of Memorial Field was the first in a series of major sport facilities constructed after the war. The Summerside Recreation Centre, a multi-sport complex located in the heart of Summerside at Queen Elizabeth Park, evolved over several years during the late 1940s and early 50s, and provided much-needed outdoor sport facilities for the town. Track and field, baseball, softball, lawn tennis, and rugby utilized the Park's expanded facilities for public school programs and community use. A new artificial ice plant, Civic Stadium, which opened in 1952, was also part of a long-term sport facilities development program in the western capital.

While the War seriously disrupted the sport system of the province during the early years of the conflict, sport as a component of community life demonstrated a remarkable resilience to the turmoil. By 1944, there was a noticeable increase in sport activities that ranged from the popularity of horse racing to the solace of yachting. With leadership demonstrated by both the civic and provincial levels of government, there was optimism that organized sport would once again contribute in a significant way to the normalization of community life during the postwar period. "Reclaiming Excellence" would demonstrate that such optimism was justified.

12

Reclaiming Excellence

While there was an enthusiasm for the reorganization of all sport and recreation activities across the Island following the War, the spotlight belonged to hockey and baseball. Other sports, notably harness racing, lawn tennis, curling, golf, boxing, track and field, and rugby would regain their previous vigour in the sport system, the reclaiming of excellence would first become evident in the hockey rinks and ball diamonds of the province. Both sports were in disarray at the senior level during the prewar years, so a return to excellence was a refreshing change from the difficult period of the late 1930s.

In Charlottetown, Sammy Doyle, one of the province's truly dedicated sport volunteers, headed up City leagues in both sports. In hockey, with a military presence still in evidence, the league comprised teams from the Navy, Legion, SDU, and PWC. The League was well-organized and attracted large crowds to the Charlottetown Forum. Abegweit greats of the prewar era returned to the game as coaches: Johnny Squarebriggs to PWC, Jack "Hurry" Kane to SDU, Roy Prowse to the Legion team, and Walter Lawlor as coach of the Navy squad. The Legion featured the "smooth" trio of Wallie Shepherd, Allie Carver, and Cecil Dowling. PWC had goalie Jack Proud, and the "dynamite kids," Willie Robertson, Clayton "Nick" Nicolle, and Elmer Blanchard. SDU responded with their own array of stars: Joe Mahar, A. J. MacAdam,

The Collegians Hockey Team, comprised of players from St. Dunstan's and Prince of Wales of the 1945–1946 City League, won the NB-PEI Junior Championship by defeating Moncton CYO Club 26–11 in a two-game total goal series. The team later lost 13–5 to the powerful St. Mary's Club of Halifax. Front, l-r: Gordon Bennett (Manager), Nick Nicolle, Willie Robertson, Elmer Blanchard, Jack Proud, unknown, Brighton MacDougall, Toey Richard, Father Fred Cass; Back: Tubby Quigley, Mike Hennessey, Wendell Murphy, George Smith (Equipment Manager), Knucker Irvine, Johnny Squarebriggs (Coach), Cecil Dowling, Stan Millar, A.J. MacAdam, Angie MacDonald.
(NICOLLE FAMILY COLLECTION)

Cart MacDonald, and Mike Hennessey. The Navy featured Roy "Buck" Whitlock, John "Tarky" Whitlock, and Cliff Jackson. The quality of play in the local league was exceptional. In that first season, 1945–1946, the combined PWC/SDU Collegians went on to win the NB–PEI junior championship by defeating Moncton 26–11 in a two-game total-goal series. "Nick" Nicolle, a highly talented product of the natural ice ponds around Murray River, scored seven goals in the series: the Collegians later lost 13–5 in a Maritime two-game total-goals final against the powerful St. Mary's team of Halifax. Meanwhile, teams at the intermediate level were attracting the attention of hockey buffs across the province. Picking up from where the Victoria Unions left off in 1939, the Borden Nationals capped a valiant effort by winning the 1945 Maritime Intermediate hockey championship. Led by Oscar "Big Hero" Campbell, Lester MacLeod (a former Victoria Union), and goaltender Ellsworth Noonan, the team skated to a suspense-filled 7–6 overtime victory over the defending champions, the Berwick Bruins of Nova

A. J. MacAdam, a native of Morell, was a "Four Letter Athlete" during his student years at St. Dunstan's University. He excelled in hockey, rugby, basketball, and track and field, and is the only SDU athlete to receive this athletic distinction. (MACADAM FAMILY COLLECTION)

Clayton "Nick" Nicolle learned his hockey fundamentals on the frozen ponds around Murray River. His first organized hockey was played at Prince of Wales College in 1941, where his exceptional skills were noted by officials of the Saint John Beavers and NHL hockey scouts. As a member of the Beavers, he became one of the best senior hockey talents in the Maritimes. In 1989 he was inducted into the Saint John Sports Hall of Fame. (NICK NICOLLE FAMILY COLLECTION)

Scotia. In 1946, the Charlottetown Legionnaires, coached by ex-NHL star Gordie Drillon, continued the dominance of Island teams in Maritime intermediate hockey when they also defeated Berwick 16–15 in a two-game total goal series, and then repeated as Maritime Champions in 1947 with a victory over the Antigonish CYO. In addition to Drillon, the Legionnaires included such stars as Cecil Dowling, Art Perry, and Ted Strain.

The postwar years were a period of exceptional achievement in sport for the two academic institutions in Charlottetown. Both SDU and PWC experienced an influx of war veterans, many of whom were talented athletes from the prewar era. There was also a younger group of student athletes eager to assume a role in the exciting swirl of sport activity across the province. Even as PWC was experiencing unparalleled success with its athletic program, having won the provincial intermediate rugby championship for six successive years and riding a wave of exciting competition in hockey, St. Dunstan's was on the verge of one of its most outstanding athletic accomplishments. In 1947, the Saints squared off against the highly touted St. Francis Xavier team from Antigonish for the Maritime Intercollegiate Hockey Championship. The teams met at the Charlottetown Forum on March 12, 1947, to play a sudden-death game to determine the winner. In a thrilling game, played in front of more than 2,000 boisterous fans, the Saints defeated the Xaverians 8–6. The SDU team, coached by Jack "Hurry" Kane,

Maritime Intercollegiate 1946-1947 Hockey Champions. On March 12, 1947, the St. Dunstan's Saints created one of the great moments in Island hockey history by defeating the St. F. X. Xaverians 8–6 at the Charlottetown Forum, to win the Maritime Intercollegiate Hockey Championship. The highly rated X-men were expected to win; not so, said the talented St. Dunstan's Saints. Top, l-r Joe Mahar, Allister MacIsaac; Second row: Bill Ledwell, Reg Rogers, Des Burge, Cart MacDonald, Bert Methot, Brighton MacDougall, Allison Farmer; Third row: Jacques Thibeault, Jack Kane (Coach), Francis MacKinnon, Rev. G. A. MacDonald, Francis Strain; Bottom: Claude D'Amours, Robert Carmichael (Manager), Francis MacIntyre (Trainer), Elmer Blanchard.

(COURTESY: U.P.E.I. ATHLETIC DEPARTMENT COLLECTION)

was led by the four-goal performance of smooth-skating Joe Mahar, two by Cart MacDonald, and key markers by Brighton MacDougall and Reg Rogers. When Rogers scored late in the third period, the Saints realized they had the championship in their grasp. When the final whistle blew, fans swarmed unto the ice to mob the victorious St. Dunstan's team. It was a tremendous upset, one that ranks amongst the greatest in the long history of the venerable educational/athletic institution on the Malpeque Road.

The resurgence of baseball following the war paralleled that of

Montague's Dick MacLean's involvement in hockey has spanned more than six decades, initially as a seven-year-old star at the minor, school, and juvenile levels, and later with Prince of Wales, Old Timers, and Senior competition. Dick is typical of the many players who made the game of hockey an important part of their youth and adult life.
(MARY MACLEAN COLLECTION)

hockey; there were well-organized local leagues at the intermediate level, a superior level of play, and a return of fans to the stands. The Summerside league comprised the RCAF Flyers, Red Sox, Legion, and Junior Kinsmen, while the Charlottetown league consisted of the Rovers, Anchors, and Legionnaires. The game was also on the rebound in both Prince and Queen's Counties, with Morell and Lennox Island fielding new teams in their respective leagues.

It is easy to understand why baseball and hockey were so popular with athletes and spectators during the post-war period. Social and sport historians tend to attribute the prosperity to the pent-up expectations for sport entertainment among returning veterans, and a whole society lifted from the shadow of war. Another likely influence was the prominence of both sports at the national level. Riding the crest of hockey popularity, the Toronto Maple Leafs were on a run of three successive Stanley Cup championships in 1947, 1948, and 1949, boasting such stars as Ted "Teeder" Kennedy, Syl Apps, and Turk Broda. The popularity of the Maple Leafs was fueled by the distinctive radio voice of Foster Hewitt, whose Saturday night salutation of "Hello Canada and hockey fans in the United States and Newfoundland" echoed across the winter countryside.

In baseball, it was the Jackie Robinson story. In 1945 Branch Rickey, the general manager of the Brooklyn Dodgers, assigned Robinson to the Dodgers' farm team, Montreal Royals, as part of a move to launch Robinson into the big leagues as the first black player in major league baseball. The highly publicized signing vaulted Montreal baseball to international prominence, and reflected the general surge in the popularity of professional baseball in the postwar years, with new attendance records set almost annually in the major leagues. Robinson, an ideal role model, played his first game as a Dodger on April 15, 1947,

The Charlottetown All-Stars, Maritime Intermediate Baseball Champions 1946. Front, l-r: Frank Strain, Cart MacDonald, Buck Whitlock, Jimmy MacQuarrie and John Ryan (Mascots), Jack "Hawk" Gallant, J. Higson, H. Hennessey, Had McInnis; Back: Elmer Rice, Irv MacKinnon, Charlie Ryan, Fred McCabe (Manager), Art Perry, Elmer Larter, Lefty McAleer–McKinnon.

(PARO *THE GUARDIAN*, OCTOBER 19, 1946)

and subsequently opened the door to a succession of highly talented black players in professional baseball.

In the Maritimes, there was a move towards semi-professional baseball leagues as talented players moved into the Maritimes from Maine and US colleges, hoping to catch on with one of the local teams. The most prominent league was the Halifax and District League, which began play in 1946 with a mixture of local and import players.[50] Saint John was also a hotbed for import baseball players during the period.

While Summerside and Charlottetown resisted the temptation to get caught up in the rapid expansion of the game with its semi-pro, import players, both centres experienced a surge of interest in the sport at the junior and intermediate levels. Charlottetown boasted such stellar players as Charlie Ryan, Art Perry, "Lefty" McAleer, and "Buck" Whitlock, and Summerside presented Gerard "Joe" Bernard, Bob Schurman, Gordie MacKay, and Henry "Hank" Landry as the core of its talented players.

In the first post-war Island playdowns (1946), the City League All-Stars defeated Summerside 3–0 in a best of five series that featured the pitching of Charlie Ryan, who struck out sixteen batters in the final

The Abbies junior baseball team was a product of a sport development program in Charlottetown. Back, l-r: Bobby Lund, Don LeClair, Randy Edwards (Coach), Lorne MacDougall, Willie Dunn; Middle: Forbie Kennedy, Kip Ready, Ron Stanley, Ken MacDonald, Richard St. John, Jack Kane; Front: Billy Purcell, Lorne MacGuigan, Archie MacFadyen (Bat boy), Malcolm MacFadyen, Don "Duck" MacLeod, John Squarebriggs, Jr. (DR. BOBBY LUND COLLECTION)

game. The All-Stars went on to claim the Maritime Intermediate baseball championship by defeating St. Joseph's of Moncton 10–1 and 2–0 for the NB–PEI title, and later split the first two games with a best-of-three series with the Sydney Mines Ramblers. When the Ramblers were unable to make the trip to Charlottetown to complete the series, the All-Stars were declared Maritime Champions. What Island baseball teams were unable to accomplish in the prewar era — win a Maritime baseball championship — the Charlottetown All-Stars had achieved in their first season back.

The intense rivalry that soon developed in baseball between the Abegweits (reorganized from the All-Stars), and the Summerside All-Stars (later Curran and Briggs), elevated baseball to its highest level of popularity in the history of the sport in the province. Both teams possessed senior-calibre players who undoubtedly would have contributed to teams in the Halifax and District League. It was to the advantage of Island baseball that Joe Bernard, Charlie Ryan, and others decided to cast their lot with their home team.

The Summerside Curran and Briggs Baseball Team, Maritime Intermediate Champions 1948, 1949, 1950. The Summerside team reigned supreme over Maritime intermediate baseball for three successive years (1948–1950), and for five successive seasons at the provincial level. Contests against the Charlottetown Abegweits were often the team's biggest challenge. Front, l-r: Bill Allen (Captain), Syl Bernard, Benny Grady, Hank Landry, Emmett Mulholland, Charlie Hogan (Coach), Russ Phaneuf, Gordie MacKay, Jim Grady, and Dee Lefurgey (Bat Boy); Back: Ron Campbell, Charlie Deighan, Alan Stewart, Roy "Pony" Daley, J. K. Curran (President), Bruce MacWilliams (Vice-President), Les Gaudet, Bob Schurman, Gerard "Joe" Bernard, Henry Gallant; Missing: Cecil Powell, Frank Oatway, Norman Macdonald (Secretary-Treasurer).

(PARO CAMERA CLUB COLLECTION, #2320/83-3)

The decision by J. K. Curran, president of Curran & Briggs,[51] to become involved personally in the sponsorship and promotion of baseball in Summerside in the spring of 1949, was a significant factor in increasing the popularity and success of baseball across the province. Curran took over what was already a winning team, the Summerside All-Stars, and added a flamboyance to the game not previously witnessed in Island baseball. During the period 1947 to 1952, the team won five successive provincial and three Maritime intermediate championships. Not surprisingly, the hardest-fought games were usually against the Abbies whose roster also included an array of stars. The game that perhaps best characterized the intense rivalry between the arch rivals was played at Memorial Field on July 17, 1949, during a regular Island league game. The teams battled to a 0–0 tie over twelve innings behind the superb pitching of Joe Bernard and "Lefty" McAleer. Hank Landry in centre field and Syl Bernard at second base starred for Curran and

Fire-balling Joe Bernard, shown here as a member of the Summerside Legion baseball team, 1946, became one of the best baseball pitchers in the history of the sport on Prince Edward Island. During his career he helped pitch the Summerside Curran and Briggs intermediate team to numerous victories, including three Maritime championships and five provincial titles. (PEI SPORTS HALL OF FAME)

Alan Stewart rose to stardom in baseball in 1950 when he pitched the Summerside Curran and Briggs Juniors to a Maritime Championship over the highly rated Saint John Kinsmen. Stewart also excelled in intercollegiate hockey, swimming and badminton. (ALAN STEWART COLLECTION)

Paul H. Schurman, a multi-talented athlete, was equally adept at playing different positions in baseball and hockey. His versatility made him a valued member of both the Curran and Briggs junior and senior baseball teams, which won the Maritime Championship for the town of Summerside in 1950. (AUTHOR COLLECTION)

Briggs, while Charlie Ryan at first base and "Buck" Whitlock at shortstop excelled for the Abbies. Die-hard baseball fans consider the game to be "a classic in the annals of baseball history in the province." The Summerside C & B squad went on to win the Maritime intermediate title, defeating Metaghan, NS, and Chatham, NB, for the Three Province Crown.

While intermediate baseball was experiencing a period of sustained popularity, junior ball was also benefiting from the public's interest in the sport. Coach Charlie Ryan took his 1946 junior team to the Maritime finals against Liverpool, losing 3–2 and 8–6 in a well-played series. The following year, Summerside ascended to the top of junior baseball in the province, winning the Provincial Championship over the Charlottetown Kinsmen. The Junior program produced several outstanding players who later contributed to the success of the intermediate league. Donnie "Funnel" MacLean, Jack "Spy" Ready, Don "Duck" MacLeod,[52] Harold "Red" Howatt, Alan "Stew" Stewart, Paul H. Schurman, and smooth-fielding Eddie Lund were among the brightest stars emerging from the junior level of play.

The team that elevated junior baseball to its highest level during the era, however, was the 1950 edition of the Curran and Briggs Juniors.

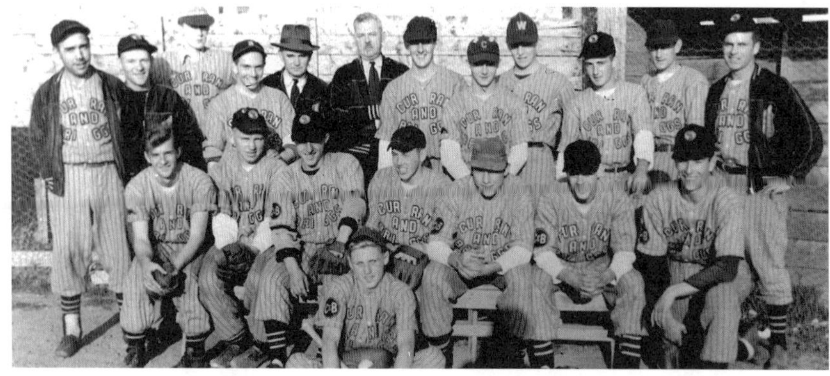

Curran and Briggs Juniors Win Maritime Title. The Summerside baseball team defeated the Saint John Kinsmen Juniors 5-2 in the deciding game of the Maritime finals played at Summerside, October 9, 1950. The series featured the stellar pitching of Alan Stewart, who out-pitched major league prospect Jackie Bowes over the final two games of the series. The victory marked the first junior baseball championship for Summerside. Back (l-r): Bill Allen, Henry Landry, Edward Dalton, "Chuck" Hulme, Norman Macdonald, J. K. Curran, Jack Murphy, Bob Timmins, Donald Simmons, Gordon MacKay, Stan Richards, Charlie Hogan (Coach); Front: Leigh Cooke, "Cokey" Grady, Paul H. Schurman, Gerard Dalton, Mark Delaney, Neil Walker, Alan Stewart, John Whalen (bat boy). (*SUMMERSIDE JOURNAL*, OCTOBER 11, 1950)

After winning the Island title over the Charlottetown Knights of Columbus, the team engaged the highly touted Saint John Kinsmen in a best-of-three series for the Maritime Championship. As was often the case with Island baseball teams, their Maritime counterparts took them for granted. In this case, Saint John agreed to play all of the games of the final series at Summerside over the Thanksgiving weekend. The confidence of the NB–NS Champions was bolstered by the presence of their ace pitcher, Jackie Bowes, who was on the negotiating list of the New York Giants and later attended the Giants' training camp. After losing the first game, 7–4, Summerside rallied with exciting wins in the next two games to claim its first Maritime Junior baseball championship. The series featured excellent baseball with Gordie MacKay, speedy right-fielder of the C and B squad, stealing home in the fifth inning to seal a victory in the second game, and batting over .600 for the series. While there was praise all-around for the supporting cast, including Gordie MacKay, Jack Murphy, Paul H. Schurman, Chuck Hulme and Neil Walker, the most outstanding performance of the series was the pitching of Alan Stewart. In sixteen innings of hurling,

Stewart gave up a meagre four hits and three runs, basically shutting down the Saint John offence. *Summerside Journal* sports columnist, John McNeill, in his own inimitable way, heaped praise on coach Charlie Hogan, Alan Stewart, and the team as a whole, for bringing the first Maritime Junior baseball championship to the town. It was a well-deserved tribute to a classy group of athletes. Two weeks later, the intermediate team annexed the Maritime Championship, making it a true "baseball double" for the western town in 1950.

While baseball and hockey were attracting headlines in the Island's news media for their success in Maritime competition during the post-war years, the sport of harness racing was experiencing unprecedented expansion and popularity across the Maritimes and into the eastern United States. The 1946 season witnessed "Sensational Racing over Maritime Tracks," with Island favourite Christie Budlong dropping her trotting record to 2:06 ¾ in a race at Rochester, New York, and Chuck Worthy, owned by Harry Hirsch of Sydney, recording a new record of 2:06 ½ at the Covehead oval. While the excitement generated by the speed and competition of Maritime horses was paramount to the ever-increasing attendance at the CDP and other Island tracks, three innovations were introduced at the track during the mid-1940s that would have a profound impact on the sport. The new technology included night racing, the photo finish, and the mobile starting gate. While night racing had been held at the Milligan and Morrison track at Northam as far back as 1932, it became established as a regular feature at the CDP only during the summer of 1946. Later, with encouragement from Lieutenant-Colonel Dan MacKinnon, Rupert Godfrey installed the first photo finish camera in the province at the Montague track in July 1947, and later at other rural tracks and the CDP. While there was skepticism initially, the new technology proved reliable and gradually gained acceptance from drivers and race-goers. Perhaps the most practical innovation was the introduction of the mobile starting gate. Considered standard equipment by the USTA for all its member tracks by 1946, the first time it was used in Canada was during Old Home Week of that year. The drivers would marshal their horses at the top of the stretch, follow the gate at an increasing speed under the direction of the starter, and, at the word "go" the race was on. While the starting gate eliminated the practice of "scoring" in order to gain a fair start to a race, it also deprived race fans of the commanding voice of starter Dr. Charles Dougan, whose instruction to drivers to "take a hold of that horse" was thought to be an essential part of horse-racing culture.

One of several innovations adopted by the sport of harness racing during the late 1940s was the installation of the photo finish. The technology was first used on Prince Edward Island at the Montague race track in July 1947. Other innovations adopted during the period were the mobile starting gate and night racing. (PARO 2320-89-10)

While the installation of new technology attracted fast horses and throngs of spectators to the sport (18,000 for an Old Home Week afternoon and evening race card), the impact on smaller, rural tracks was detrimental. Unable to install the technical equipment necessary for night and paramutual racing, the smaller tracks relinquished their provincial charters and racing dates to the CDP.[53] It was a difficult transition, for the horse race was, and remains, the focus of one of the Island's great sporting traditions.

Amid the enthusiasm and excitement of the postwar period, there was a sincere effort to rejuvenate the Abegweit AAA and to restore the venerable Association to its former position of prominence in Maritime sport. To that end, on November 12, 1947, a large gathering of former Abegweits and sport-minded citizens was held. The assembly elected Colonel L. T. Lowther as the new president, with a full slate of executive and committee members. What was lost in the enthusiasm of the meeting was the reality that a multi-sport organizational format was no longer a viable system for the administration of amateur sport in the Maritimes and/or Canada. As successful as the Abegweits, Victorias, Halifax Wanderers, Saint John Trojans, or Montreal AAA had been for

The 1948 Abegweit track and field team restored the brilliance of Abegweit teams of a by-gone era by winning the Maritime Championship at Fredericton, NB, the first since 1927. Led by George Walters, Windy LePage, Dave Boswell, and Bill Brawley, the team's victory evoked widespread enthusiasm on Prince Edward Island. Front, l-r: Bill Brawley, A. Coady, J. MacCormack, John Cash, Dave Boswell, H. Warren; Back: Bill Massey (Coach), J. Nicholson, F. Foy, George Walters, E. Matheson, B. Jay, Walter LePage, W. Scantlebury (Manager). (AUTHOR COLLECTION)

nigh on fifty years, they had, in essence, been replaced by autonomous sport governing bodies during the late 1920s and the decade of the 1930s as the organizational format for the administration of amateur sport in Canada. Nevertheless, the meeting persisted, the memory of Abegweit achievements remained strong, vivid, even embellished, and the venerable organization was revived to once again excel in Maritime sport.

Track and field was the immediate recipient of the revitalized Abegweit athletic program. Under the guise of the Abegweit banner, Lieutenant-Colonel Bill Reid assembled a group of athletes, none of whom had previously competed as "Abegweits," to compete in the 1947 Antigonish Highland Games. The team surprised even die-hard Abbies by finishing second to a new power in Maritime track and field, the Antigonish Highland Society. Founded in 1861, the Society had come to the forefront in athletics in the 1930s. When the Maritime Championships resumed in 1947, the Highlanders were poised to be a legitimate contender for the track and field dominance previously shared by the Abegweits and the Halifax Wanderers.

Walter "Windy" LePage of the Abegweit Team raises his arms in triumph after defeating highly touted Harold "Casey" Power of Halifax and Dave Stothard of UNB in the 100-yard dash at the 1947 Maritime Track and Field Championships in Halifax. Time: 10 seconds flat. In addition to his outstanding ability as a sprinter, LePage excelled in rugby and basketball. (WALTER LEPAGE COLLECTION)

The 1948 season marked the return of the Abegweits to Maritime track and field supremacy. The new athletic complex at Memorial Field created renewed interest in the sport, and the prevailing mood was one of optimism, to once again place the Abegweits' name at the highest level of the medals podium. Following a series of competitions during the summer in Halifax, Antigonish, and Amherst, the Abegweits swept to victory in the Maritime Championships in Fredericton. The team was led by the inspired performance of veteran George Walters, who amassed 16 individual points, and a talented group of new recruits, including Walter "Windy" LePage, Bill Brawley, and Dave Boswell. The victory evoked widespread enthusiasm on Prince Edward Island, as notions of re-establishing an Abegweit dynasty in track and field teased the imagination of sport followers in the province. While a new dynasty was not in the offing, the achievements of the 1948 track and field team brought respectability to a sport that had languished for two decades. One outcome of the renewed interest in track was the achievements of Dave Boswell. A native of Victoria, Boswell emerged as one of the Maritimes' top middle-distance runners and was selected to participate in the British Empire and Commonwealth Games Trials in Toronto in 1949. His time of 49.7 seconds established a new provincial

David Boswell was the premier middle-distance runner of the Abegweit Club during the resurgence of track and field in the late 1940s and early 1950s. Boswell established provincial records in both the 440- and 880-yard dashes, and was invited to the British Empire and Commonwealth Games trials in Toronto in 1949. (AUTHOR COLLECTION)

native record in the event. While he was not selected to the Canadian team, Boswell's performance at the trials reinstated an Island presence at the national level in track and field for the first time since Phil MacDonald's heyday in the mid-1920s.

The Abegweits' last serious bids for Maritime track and field honours occurred in 1950, and again in 1952, when the Abbies assembled strong teams to compete against the Highland Society, the Wanderers Club, and a Halifax Navy team. The games staged at elm-shrouded Columbus Field in Antigonish attracted over 5,000 spectators for the 1950 meet, the largest crowd in the history of the annual gathering. The Abbies team boasted their junior sensation, Wendall Barrett, John Cash, and the senior sportsman of Maritime track and field, George Walters. While the Abbies won individual events, the team's aggregate points placed the team a close third in both the junior and senior categories. The Abbies continued to sponsor teams in Maritime track and field competition until 1953, when a small group of athletes, Ron Atkinson, Nick Day-Lewis, Bill Deane, Ev Cutcliffe, George Walters, and Bill Wells carried the colours of the once most dominant team in Maritime track and field.

The outstanding achievements of Island athletes continued throughout the postwar period, 1945–1950, claiming thirteen Maritime team championships. The Borden Nationals (hockey), Charlottetown Legionnaires (hockey), Charlottetown All-Stars (baseball), Summerside Curran and Briggs, intermediate and junior (baseball), St. Dunstan's (hockey), Abegweits (track and field): all victors in Maritime competition. The temptation, on the basis of such success, is to state "excellence reclaimed." But there was still more to come, for other teams and individual sports were marshalling in their respective domains to demonstrate their own particular level of athletic excellence.

The 1952 Abbies shown at the Highland Games in Antigonish was one of the last Track and Field teams to be sponsored by the Abegweit Club. The presence of Bill Halpenny at the meet represented fifty years of his personal involvement in Track and Field as an athlete, coach, and administrator. Front, l-r: Bill Wells, Bob Mills, Earl Beaton, Barney McGuigan, Ron Atkinson; Back: Bill Acorn, unidentified, Ev Cutcliffe, Wendall Barrett, George Walters, and Bill Halpenny. (RON ATKINSON COLLECTION)

Lawn tennis, golf, curling, and yachting were quick to reorganize after the War, due in part to the leadership and financial resources residing within the respective clubs. Lawn tennis regained a presence that had sustained the sport for seventy-five years and in 1947 staged the Island Open Championships, the first time in six years that the event was held. A major factor in the resurgence of the game was the development of several outstanding players who would have an impact at the junior and senior levels across the Maritimes. Bill Moreside, who began playing tennis at the tender age of ten, developed into the top-ranked player in the province, and successfully competed against the top-ranked in the Maritimes. Later, while a student at Dalhousie University, Moreside became the top intercollegiate tennis player in the Maritimes, and, upon his graduation, was awarded the Dalhousie Gold "D" for his outstanding contribution to intercollegiate tennis, the Dal Glee Club, and university hockey. Other players who excelled in the

Bill Moreside Winner Of Intercollegiate Tennis Singles Crown

HALIFAX, Oct. 17 — (CP) For the second straight year, Dalhousie University swept the intercollegiate tennis tourney, winning the championship today without losing a set.

ever, in the finals 6-0, 6-0, and 6-2.

SUMMARY

Men's Singles:

Bill Moreside, Number One ranked tennis player in the province during the 1940s, was also the leading intercollegiate player in the Maritimes. Upon his graduation from Dalhousie University, he was awarded the "Gold D" for athletic excellence in tennis, hockey, and the Dal Glee Club. (*THE GUARDIAN*, OCTOBER 18, 1946)

sport during the late 1940s were Audrey DeBlois, Beryl DeBlois, Elinor Bourke, Ivan "Lefty" Reddin, Walter Cullen, Ivan Connors, and Earl Smith of Summerside.

With Moreside's departure from Island tennis, Earl Smith became the top-ranked player in the province, winning both singles and doubles titles in 1949 and 1950. Smith's partner in doubles was Walter Cullen, a talented player in his own right, who played out of the Holy Redeemer Club on Upper Queen Street. Later in his athletic career, Smith expressed the opinion that the singles game in tennis, especially those against Moreside, was one of the most physically demanding of the several high-level sports in which he excelled.

The postwar years were ones of rapid expansion for lawn tennis in Charlottetown, especially at the Charlottetown Lawn Tennis Club (CLTC) at Victoria Park. The expansion included the construction of a new club house in 1951, and the upgrade of the courts surfaces. The guest list for the official opening of the new faculty, rated as one of the finest in the Maritimes, included Lieutenant-Governor T. W. L. Prowse, Premier J. Walter Jones, and Brigadier General W. W. Bill Reid. Reid was singled out by Club President J. E. Wran "for his assistance which made the erection of the new club house possible." Lawn tennis, during the era, was at the forefront of sport development that included competitive and recreational play, first-class facilities, and a growing interest in the game province-wide.

Lawn tennis experienced a resurgence during the late 1940s and into the decade of the 1950s. Pictured above are the 1950 provincial winners, l-r: Walter Cullen (men's doubles), Wanda MacMillan (ladies' doubles), Helen Larter (ladies' singles and doubles), Audrey DeBlois (mixed doubles), Earl Smith (Summerside, singles and doubles); missing from picture: Jim Palmer (mixed doubles). (*THE GUARDIAN*, SEPTEMBER 1, 1950)

At the Belvedere Links, membership that had been depleted during the war was on the rebound, with an emphasis placed on provincial and regional competition. The opening of the Green Gables Golf Course on July 19, 1939, provided an attractive alternative to the golf facilities in the province as it broadened the impact of the game, both competitively and recreationally. Players who chose to play golf at a recreational level now had access to a well-designed and maintained golf course. Until then, the Belvedere Links and the Summerside Golf Club were semi-private clubs with restrictive membership policies. Green Gables was a public course designed to attract tourists and Islanders to the Island's National Park at Cavendish.

Competition took the spotlight at Belvedere during the late 1940s with the renewal of the NB/PEI Championship. The tournament in 1945 was held at the Charlottetown Club, where a Belvedere team of Doug Saunders, Bill Beer, Boyd Britton, and Tom Stewart won the coveted *Telegraph-Journal* Trophy as the best four-man team in the competition. The emphasis placed on competitive golf produced several outstanding golfers during the last half of the 1940s and into the 1950s, most notably Cecil "Bubby" Dowling, Maurice "Mousie" Dowling, Bill "Pud" Beer, and Art MacKenzie. In that time, Cecil Dowling, the Bel-

Later in their respective careers, the Dowling brothers, Maurice, Cecil, and Bob, pulled off a remarkable sport achievement when each won a major golf championship on the same day, l-r: Maurice, senior champion; Cecil, tournament; and Bob, amateur champion. The extraordinary feat occurred at the Maritime Professional Golf Association Tournament at the Belvedere Golf Club in 1978. (BOB DOWLING COLLECTION)

vedere pro, would go on to win every title available in the Maritimes. In the ensuing years golf would continue to expand, providing access to the game for recreational players and the most affluent echelon of Island society.[54]

The status of curling on Prince Edward Island was considerably elevated in 1945 when the Hon. Thane A. Campbell was appointed a trustee of the Macdonald's Brier Tankard. Campbell, a former premier of the province and Chief Justice of the Supreme Court of Prince Edward Island, had a long and abiding interest in the sport, having curled his first stone at the Summerside Curling Club in 1928.

The year 1948 was a banner year for competitive curling across the province. The Alberton Rink of Jack Profit, Edward Millman, Eric Corbet, and Fred Millman won the prestigious Regal Trophy; George Hawkins skipped his Charlottetown Rink of Rankine McLaine, J. Andrew Likely, and Wendall Worth to the Lieutenant-Governor's Prize at the Quebec International Bonspiel, and the Gerry Hayes Rink of Summerside won the Provincial Championship. The Hayes Rink included Fred MacRae, lead, "Curley" MacLellan, second, and T. D. Morrison, mate. The Rink was competitive throughout the Brier, which was held in Calgary, losing seven of its games by a single rock. During the period, curling in the four Island Rinks attained a high level of provincial and national parity. It was a long look back to 1887, when the first curling stones were thrown on the natural ice of the Excelsior Rink, with barely enough players and spectators to form two rinks.

The Gerry Hayes Rink from the Summerside Curling Club, the first team from Summerside to represent the province at the Brier, in Calgary in 1948. L-r: Fred MacRae (lead), Curley MacLellan (second), T. D. Morrison (mate), Gerry Hayes (skip). (DAVID MORRISON COLLECTION)

Charlottetown Curling Club "Big Four," Provincial Champions and Brier Representatives, 1938 and 1939. L-r: C. M. Williams, Dr. H. McIntyre, G. G. Hughes, and F. R. McLaine. (PARO 2320/87-12)

Boxing also claimed major headlines during the postwar period, featuring, as it did in the late 1930s, the talent of local fighters. Joey MacDonald and Ivan Doherty were the active promoters of the sport, staging fight cards at the old Sporting Club, the Forum, and Union Hall in Charlottetown. It was the era of George "Big Boy" Peterson, Irwin "Jinx" Jenkins, Don "Duck" Trainor, Walter "Peanuts" Arsenault of Summerside, "Bud" Ramsay of Alberton, Syd Murray of Bedeque, and the McCluskey brothers, Tom, Ace, Cobey, and Wilf. While Wilf was considered to be "too good-looking" for the sport, Tom, Ace, and Cobey had outstanding careers. Their combined total fights, amateur and professional, during their illustrious careers numbered close to four hundred.

Tom, the oldest of the three, was described as a "natural fighter," and had a brilliant but brief career before an injury while serving with the Royal Canadian Navy changed his involvement in the sport. No longer able to sustain a career that involved fighting, Tom became one of the best-known and capable trainers in the business. Among his many successes as a tutor/trainer were his two brothers, Ace and Cobey, Richard "Kid" Howard, Ralph Howlett of Dartmouth, and the stylish Harry "Kid" Poulton of Charlottetown.

"Ace" (Bernard) McCluskey ruled the Maritime middleweight class following the war, and established a reputation as a strong, gifted fighter throughout eastern Canada and the USA. He was a leading contender for the Canadian middleweight championship, losing only 5 of his 127 professional bouts. Cobey, not known for this knock-out punch, relied on his speed and adeptness as a boxer to outmanoeuvre his oppo-

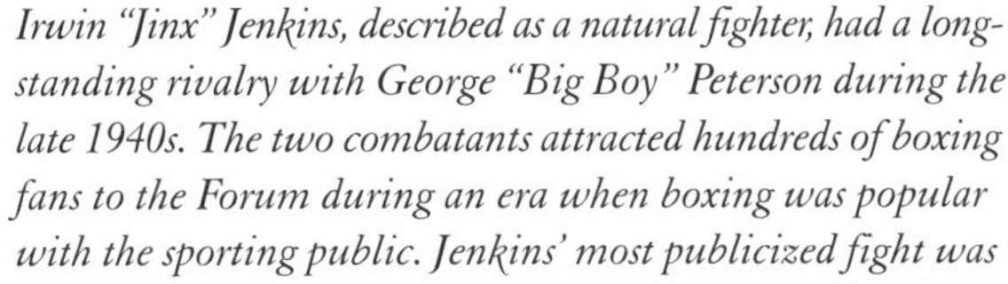

Irwin "Jinx" Jenkins, described as a natural fighter, had a long-standing rivalry with George "Big Boy" Peterson during the late 1940s. The two combatants attracted hundreds of boxing fans to the Forum during an era when boxing was popular with the sporting public. Jenkins' most publicized fight was against "Tiger" Warrington in 1949 in Kentville, NS. He fought the former Canadian heavyweight champion over ten rounds, losing the bout by a decision. Jinx Jenkins fought 50 bouts over his career compiling an impressive 32-8-10 record. (IRWIN JENKINS COLLECTION)

Tom McCluskey, a member of the fighting McCluskey family, had a brilliant career in boxing, cut short by an injury. He remained active in the fight game and experienced outstanding success as a trainer/manager of several of the top-ranked fighters of his era. (WILF MCCLUSKEY COLLECTION)

Harry "Kid" Poulton is considered to be one of the great fighters in Island boxing history. In 1976 he became the first professional boxer from the Island to be inducted into the Canadian Boxing Hall of Fame, the same year he was inducted into the Prince Edward Island Sports Hall of Fame. (PEI SPORTS HALL OF FAME)

nents. Amongst his many ring achievements was his high-profile victory on August 15, 1950, in Halifax, over Yvon Durelle of Baie Ste. Anne, NB, when he scored a unanimous decision over the then NB and Maritime Middleweight Champion. On the same card, "Ace" won a 10-round unanimous decision over former Canadian Middleweight Champion Roger Whynott. Such victories attest to the impact the McCluskey boys had on the sport of boxing during the period.

Harry "Kid" Poulton, whose boxing career spanned twelve years, March 1943 to June 1955, is considered to be one of the great fighters in Island boxing history. Dubbed the "Fighting Ghost" for his ability to feint opponents, Poulton relied on smart tactics, reminiscent of the style of Mt. Stewart's Bill McKinnon, a fighter from an earlier era, to accumulate an impressive string of victories. Trained by Tom McCluskey and Lem Moore of Boston, Poulton fought some of the top fighters in the business, including a controversial bout for the Canadian Middleweight Championship against Yvon Durelle. Poulton lost the fight in a hotly disputed split decision. While his career-long ambition to win the Canadian middleweight crown eluded him, he was duly recognized by his peers as one of Prince Edward Island's finest boxers. In 1976 he became the first professional boxer from the Island to be inducted into the

Wilf McCluskey has made a unique contribution to Island sport, notably the sport of boxing. His vast knowledge as a researcher/writer has earned him the reputation as Canada's foremost boxing authority.
(BARB MORGAN COLLECTION)

Canadian Boxing Hall of Fame, and that same year was inducted into the PEI Sports Hall of Fame. The selections were a fitting tribute to one of the province's elite athletes.

Outside the ring, Wilf McCluskey made his own unique contribution to Island sport, notably the sport of boxing.[55] He was often consulted by Nat Fleischer, then editor of *Ring Magazine*, boxing's bible, for evaluating Canadian fighters.

What Wilf McCluskey was unable to achieve as a fighter in the ring, he has achieved in what may well be an even more important dimension, the preservation, not only of boxing, but of great moments in Island sport in general. It is to the benefit of Island sport history that Wilf was "too good-looking" to pursue a career in boxing as did his celebrated brothers.

While the high profile sports of baseball, hockey, boxing, track and field, and harness racing were making sport headlines during the post-war era, it remained for rugby to make its sortie into the highly competitive environment of Maritime play. While the sport was active, during and after the War, with the senior "Saints" participating in the Maritime Intercollegiate league, and SDU and PWC intermediate teams

The Abegweit Rugby Team, 1952: an outstanding array of talent, played in the Maritime Senior League, and lost in playoff to Saint John Mariners. Front, l-r: Noel Wilson, Red Howatt, Ray Sark, Charlie Ready, Art Perry, Bill Ledwell, Ebbie Devine, Roy Campbell; Back: Clifford Gillis, George Scantlebury, Johnny Bradley, Howard Glover, Jim Coyle (Coach), Walter LePage (injured), Frank Strain (injured), Gordon Bennett (Coach), Jim Flanagan (injured), Elmer Blanchard, Reg Rodgers, Fred "Spic" Coyle. (AUTHOR COLLECTION)

playing their annual fall series, it was the absence of a senior team, the Abbies or the Nomads in Charlottetown, that presented the major deterrent to the revitalization of the sport. For the Abbies it was a seventeen-year hiatus, going back to 1933, that the Club was unable to field a team; for the Nomads it was 1938. While there were several attempts to assemble a team immediately following the War, it was the fall of 1949 when the Abbies made their return to the gridirons of the Maritimes. Two nemeses from the past stood ready to greet them: the senior "Saints," and the Caledonia Club of Glace Bay.

The 1950 season established the Abegweits as legitimate contenders for provincial and Maritime honours. While not subduing their arch rivals, losing the provincial championship to SDU 12–5 and dropping a 3–2 decision to Glace Bay, the team nevertheless created considerable excitement in Maritime rugby circles. On November 8, 1950, during the provincial championship game against SDU, Art Perry of the Abbies scored on a drop-kick from 55 yards out to send the pigskin on a "perfect spiral through the uprights." It was an outstanding athletic feat, one that placed Perry among the elite kickers in the sport. A week later the team travelled to Glace Bay for a showdown with the Caledonia Club in what was expected to be a classic game of rugby. The Abbies featured a talented group of players that included Perry, "Red" Howatt, "Spy" Ready, Noel Wilson, George Scantlebury, and Elmer Blanchard. The teams battled into the second half of the game when a controversy

The Charlottetown Nomads, winners of the McCurdy Cup, Maritime Senior Rugby, 1955. Gaining possession of the McCurdy Cup was, at times, as difficult as it was to win on the field. It was 29 years after the Nomads' victory over Acadia in Charlottetown that the team finally brought home the coveted trophy. Back: Dr. Frank Jelks (Coach), Dave Nicholson, George Kelly, Neils Hansen, Aquinas Ryan, Fred Driscoll, Hillson Carr, Dave MacLeod, Cliff Gillis, Dick Carroll, Gerard Burge; Front: Ron McIvor, Charlie Ready, Joe Coyle, Jack Ready, Claude Fields, Charlie Huestis. (DICK CARROLL COLLECTION)

erupted. With the Caledonia Club leading 3–2 and the Abbies carrying the play deep inside Caledonia territory, the timer declared the game over with twelve minutes remaining on the clock. The Abbies reacted in disbelief, but to no avail. Abegweit coaches Gordon Bennett and Lieutenant-Colonel W. J. MacDonald considered the tactic a travesty of sport. The immediate consequence of the infamous "short game" was that it deprived the Abegweit Club of a legitimate chance to win one of its most sought-after sport achievements, possession of the McCurdy Cup for the Maritime Senior rugby championship.

The next several years were exceptional years for Island rugby teams. In 1952 the SDU "Saints," coached by John Eldon Green and A. J. MacAdam, and employing an explosive offense, scored a Maritime double in the sport, becoming Maritime Intercollegiate Champions, and winners of the McCurdy Cup. While it was the first intercollegiate rugby title for the Saints, who defeated St. F.X. 16–2, and 4–0 over Mt. A., it was the second time that the Maritime Senior Championship had been won by an Island team. Back in 1899 the feat had been accomplished by the Abegweits when they defeated the Halifax Wanderers 6–5. In a personal conversation with Green, he attributed the team's success to a high-powered offence and the adept kicking skills of Jack Reardon as the main factors in the Saints' victory.

St. Dunstan's Saints win their second McCurdy Cup in three years (1952 and 1954) by defeating the rugged Saint John Mariners 10–0 in Charlottetown, November 20, 1954. The team, coached by A. J. MacAdam and John Eldon Green, and led by Aquinas Ryan, Gus Dorais, and Dick Wedge, displayed a versatile offense and a hard-tackling defense to win over the proven Mariners. L-r: A. J. MacAdam, Jerry Johnston, Rodney MacInnis, Robert Mooney, John Kelly, Aquinas Ryan, Gus Dorais, Paul Jay (Co-captain), Basil Campbell, Lloyd Gaudet (Co-captain), Jack Reardon, Thomas McGaugh, Lewis MacDonald, Kimball Jay, Arnold Mullins, Willard McCarron, Frank Slowey, Dick Wedge, Eugene Mooney (Manager). (PARO – *THE GUARDIAN*, NOVEMBER 20, 1954)

Two more McCurdy Cup Championships would follow. In 1954, the Saints, led by Lloyd Gaudet, picking quarter John Kelly, Aquinas Ryan, and Gus Dorais, defeated Saint John Mariners 10–0 to claim the Maritime Championship, and the following year (1955), the Charlottetown Nomads, led by Dick Carroll, Aquinas Ryan, Dave MacLeod, Joe Coyle, and coach Dr. Frank Jelks, would take the crown. The Nomads, revamped from the prewar years, won hard-fought victories over the Acadia Hatchetmen, 15–0, and Acadia University, 3–0, to win the championship. Clearly, it was a period of outstanding play and success for Island rugby teams.

Even with the outstanding success enjoyed by St. Dunstan's and the Nomads in winning successive Maritime rugby championships, the success could not be sustained. The reason wasn't from a lack of commitment to the game on the part of the two teams; rather, it was the popularity of Canadian football gaining momentum at other Maritime universities that was the determining factor. By the fall of 1956, St. Dunstan's was caught up in the shift and introduced Canadian football to the campus through an intramural touch football program. The following season the team engaged in a series of exhibition games against PWC, Moncton, St. Mary's, and St. F.X. junior varsity team, going undefeated in its initial season. The events marked the end of a great rugby tradition in Island sport, and expectantly the beginning of a new one in Canadian football.

A perusal of the sport section of Island newspapers of the late 1940s reveals a wide range of sport activities, including horse racing, hockey, baseball, rugby, badminton, boxing, golf, curling, lawn tennis, track and field, long-distance running, rifle shooting, clay-target shooting, figure skating, basketball, soccer, softball, speed skating, bowling, yachting, horseshoe pitching, billiards, road races, bicycle races, volleyball, swimming, and wrestling. From a single sport club, the Charlottetown Cricket Club, in 1850, to this impressive glossary of active sports one hundred years later, is a story with social, cultural, and community impact.[56]

By the late 1940s, the profile of sport activities across the province included participants and teams from even the most geographically remote communities, and reflected an awareness of the social, ethnic, and gender issues that resided within the sport delivery system. Critical to the successful evolution of the system was the provision that the individual had access to meaningful participation in organized sport and recreation within the confines of his or her own personal lifestyle. Athletes from the two minority races of the Island's population, Mi'kmaq and Afro-Canadians, had an increased opportunity to participate in organized sport, albeit with greater social and economic obstacles than for the Island's Anglo-European society. Even with the enlightenment of post-Second World War society, social, gender, and financial affluence remained as significant determinants to gaining access to various components of the sport delivery system.

Lennox Island, with a small population from which to draw athletes, was successful during the postwar period in both baseball and hockey. The "Micmacs" claimed their first Island baseball title in 1950, when they defeated the Peakes Bombers for the Provincial Intermediate "B" Championship. Peakes were the winners of the Kings County League, which included teams from Tracadie, Georgetown, St. Peters, Souris, Murray Harbour, and Morell, while the Micmacs were the Prince County champions. A contributing factor in the success of Micmac athletes in both baseball and hockey was the presence of Father Emmett McInnis, the parish priest of Lennox Island, as Father John A. MacDonald's leadership had been crucial to the development of runner Michael Thomas early in the century. Father McInnis, an accomplished hockey player in his own right, was keenly interested in sport and worked untiringly to develop athletes to represent the small Reservation in provincial sport competition.

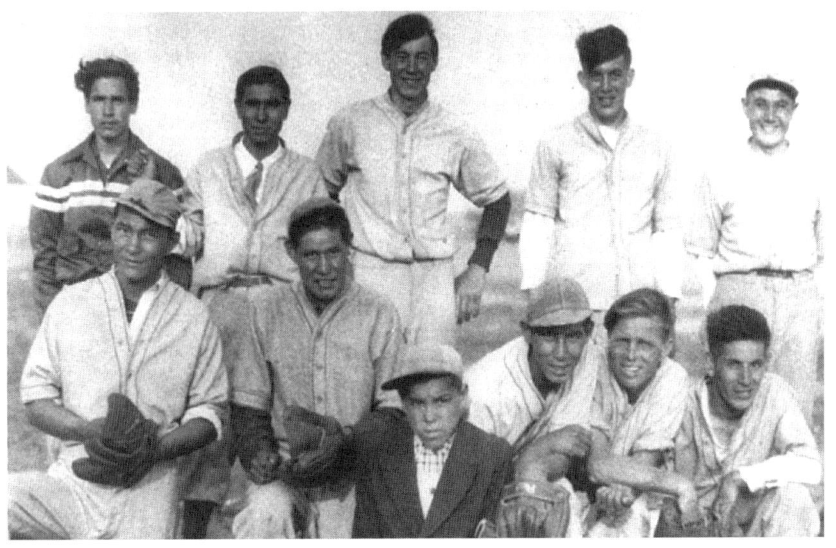

Lennox Island Micmacs, Intermediate B Baseball Champions, 1950. Front, l-r: Raymond Lewis, Leo Peters, Freddy Scully (bat boy), Albert Bernard, Lawrence Maloney, Mosey Bernard; Back: Alfred Callow, Joe Labobe, Charlie Tuplin, Rubin Tuplin, unidentified; Missing from picture: Louis Mitchell.
(CHARLIE SARK COLLECTION)

Lennox Island Micmacs, Provincial Intermediate C Hockey Champions, 1950–1951, defeated Nine Mile Creek Bulldogs. Front, l-r: Mosey Bernard, J. D. Scully, L. Mitchell (Captain), F. Knockwood, A. Bernard; Middle: P. Sark, M. Sark, J. Labobe, L. Maloney, Leo Peters, R. Lewis. Back: C. Tuplin, R. Sark, R. Tuplin, Alfred Callow, Rev. E. W. McInnis (Coach); Missing: Charlie Sark.
(CHARLIE SARK COLLECTION)

Tignish Aces, Island Intermediate B Baseball Champions, 1952. Back, l-r: Joe MacDonald (Manager and Coach), Melvin Gallant, Louis Doucette, Raymond Richard, Aneas Doucette, Rusty Callaghan, Ralph Gaudet (Assistant Manager); Front: Max Callaghan, Rodney McInnes, Henry Gaudet, Lloyd Gaudet, Melvin LeClair, Gerald Keough (bat boy). (GERALD KEOUGH COLLECTION)

The Peakes Bombers have a long and storied past in the annals of Island baseball. Teams bearing the name "Peakes" have consistently played with commitment and skill. The 1949 team carried on that tradition. Back, l-r: Joe Gillan, George Smith, Doug George, Earl MacDonald, Mike Handrahan; Front: Alf "Bingo" Handrahan, Merlin Devine, Peter Dunphy, Ebbie Devine; Missing: Fred Handrahan, Ernie Grant. (KAREN SMITH COLLECTION)

Charlie Ryan: PEI's "Mr. Baseball." During his illustrious career as an athlete, coach, and administrator, Charlie Ryan displayed exceptional talent and passion for the game he loved. Driven by a competitive spirit, he helped re-establish baseball on Prince Edward Island following the Second World War, and was a key player in bringing the first Maritime Championship to Charlottetown in 1946. In 1986 he was inducted into the Prince Edward Island Sports Hall of Fame. (WILF McCLUSKEY COLLECTION)

Black athletes, the remnant of the proud Black community that had existed in Charlottetown a half-century earlier, maintained a presence in boxing, baseball, softball, bowling, and horse racing. Going back to the turn of the century, black athletes achieved notable success in speed skating and hockey, albeit with overtones of racial discrimination. Over the years, Island society has become more racially tolerant, with black athletes now more fully integrated into the sport system. Benny Binns in boxing and Charlie Ryan in baseball represent a group of athletes who are recognized for their talents and contribution to organized sport in the pre- and postwar period. Ryan, highly respected for this athletic talent and administrative ability, was one of the Island's most prominent athletes during and after the war era and served as Director of Recreation for the City of Charlottetown from 1966 to 1989. His contribution to the development of sport for all members of the community was duly recognized in 1986 when he was inducted into the PEI Sports Hall of Fame, and a memorial was erected in his honour at Memorial Field.

There was greater opportunity for women to participate in organized sport during the postwar period with basketball and softball attracting players and spectators to the games. The PWC Co-Eds were perennial winners of the women's basketball league, with their strongest opposition coming from the nurses' team of the PEI Hospital. Regular league games were played in the spacious PWC auditorium and in a small gymnasium in the former carriage house at the nurses' residence at the Cundall Home. Spectators at the latter needed to stand single file around the court in order to watch the fast-paced game. In 1947, the Co-Eds advanced to the Maritime playdowns against the

The PWC Co-eds were perennial winners in provincial competition during the the mid 1940s. During the decade they also established a competitive presence in inter-provincial play. Top, l-r: Joan Sherren, Lyle Farquharson, George Young (coach), Eileen Landrigan, Geraldine Robertson; Centre: Stephanie MacDonald, Joan Miller, Barbara Quigley, Helen Behem; Bottom: Evelyn Henry, Florine Evans. (UPEI COLLECTION)

CYO Club of Moncton, and, while they lost the two-game total-point series, the inter-provincial competition served to confirm women's basketball as a viable sport in the province.

Women's softball also thrived during the period, with good rivalries among teams from Summerside, Georgetown, and Charlottetown. The Jack Hennessey-coached Knights of Columbus All Stars of Charlottetown won the Island Championship in 1946, with the team hitting five home runs in a 13–8 decision over Summerside. The consensus of the large crowd of spectators was that they had witnessed "good softball." The Knights of Columbus then advanced to the Maritime playdowns against Truro. While the Island champions displayed a lack of experience in losing the series, the exposure for the game clearly contributed to the development of women's softball on the Island.

Elmsdale Sisters, Island Champions, 1949–1950. The unheralded Elmsdale Sisters hockey team, coached by Perley Hardy, won the Provincial Women's Hockey Championship in March 1950, defeating the Charlottetown Abbies 3–2 in overtime at the North River rink. The victory evoked widespread excitement across western Prince County. The team was composed of four Adams sisters and their friends. Back, l-r: Heber Ramsay, Anna Ramsay, Janet Profit, Ruby Adams, Blanche Adams, Perley Hardy (coach); Front: June Fraser, Norma Matthews, Roberta Adams, Thelma Adams, Dorothy Adams, Evelyn Kinch; Missing: Betty Rennie, Olive Matthews, Tike McNeill. (RUBY ADAMS COLLECTION)

The venture of the PWC Co-Eds in basketball, and the Knights of Columbus All-Stars in softball, to engage in Maritime competition, established new opportunities for female athletes in the province. Previously, women gained most of their sport experiences within the sport club system, notably lawn tennis, golf, and badminton, or in hockey, bowling, and figure skating. Now, with leadership and administrative assistance from the Department of Physical Fitness, the opportunity to participate in community-based sport expanded significantly.

Women's hockey experienced a resurgence with teams organized in numerous communities across the Island, including Souris, Georgetown, Montague, O'Leary, Elmsdale, Borden, Summerside, and Charlottetown. There was a surprising level of parity within the sport, in view of the experience and reputation of the Summerside Crystal Sisters and the Abegweit Sisters that carried over from the mid-1930s. Nevertheless, with pride as the great equalizer, it seems that few events

Helen (Jelly) Kennedy starred for the O'Leary Maroon Sisters hockey team during the late 1940s and early 1950s. The Maroon Sisters, led by Kennedy, won the Physical Fitness Trophy for the women's provincial hockey championship in 1951 (HELEN KENNEDY COLLECTION)

evoke such spontaneous pride and excitement within a community as does an unexpected victory in sport. The Elmsdale Sisters and the O'Leary Maroon Sisters were two such teams. In March of 1950, the Elmsdale team, composed of four Adams sisters and their friends, travelled to Charlottetown to engage the Abbie Sisters for the Island Championship. Ruby Ramsey recalled the apprehension felt by the team as they skated onto the ice at the North River rink against the experienced City team. Nervousness aside, the two teams played an exciting brand of hockey, with Anna Ramsay scoring the winning goal 45 seconds into overtime to give Elmsdale a 3–2 victory, and possession of the Physical Fitness Trophy. It was undoubtedly the first provincial championship captured by a women's team from Western Prince County.

The O'Leary Maroon Sisters duplicated the achievement in 1951 when, led by the scoring heroics of Helen (Jelly) Kennedy, the team won the coveted Physical Fitness Trophy. In 1952-1953, the Borden Nationals Sisters, led by Barbara "Babs" (MacDonald) Blacquiere (formerly of Souris), won both the provincial and Maritime championships.

The postwar era was a step forward for women's involvement in organized sport across the province, one that significantly diminished the gender bias that had persisted in some sectors of Island sport for over half a century.

The sport environment following the Second World War, under the direction of Brigadier General W. W. Bill Reid, was so energized across the Island that it rekindled interest in several areas of sport that had languished during the war years. Men's basketball, softball, and interschool sports were games in point. After forty years as a recreational game at the YMCA, Holy Name Club, and church halls, men's basketball emerged as a full-fledged sport during the late 1940s. A city league was organized in 1946, with teams from St. Dunstan's, Prince of Wales,

Island Senior Intercollegiate Basketball Champions, 1943–1944. Back, l-r: V. Murnaghan (Manager), A. J. MacAdam, J. Murray, W. L. MacDonald, A. McEntee, Rev. W. McGuigan (Coach); Front: F. O'Neil, H. O'Shea (Co-captain), P. Sharkey (Co-captain); M. Hennessey, D. Burge. (MACADAM FAMILY COLLECTION)

City League Basketball Champions, 1948, won over Navy 56–48 in the championship game. L-r: Noel Wilson, Hughie Simpson, Bud Rossiter, Earl Nicholson, Irv MacKinnon, Moe Goodwin, "Windy" LePage, Howard Glover; Missing; Angie MacDonald, Cliff Court. (WALTER "WINDY" LEPAGE COLLECTION)

and two military units, Army (Recce) and Navy. By 1948, the league expanded to a six-team loop with the addition of Ray's Millionaires and the RCAF Flyers. The Flyers were strengthened over several seasons by the addition of Earl Smith and Charlie Linkletter from Summerside. In 1949, the PEI Basketball Association was formed, and, for the first time, provided administrative stability to the game.

The appearance of student athletes from American schools at St. Dunstan's, notably Jack Murray, who was the first basketball player from the US to play for SDU, Jack Reardon, Lenny Sirois, and Fred Ripley, injected a higher level of skill and strategy into the game. The influence of players who had grown up with the sport, combined with a nucleus of talented local athletes, provided the stimulus needed to popularize the game.

Local senior talent included Des Burge, Pat Sharky, Johnny Bradley, and Mike Hennessey at SDU, Don "Funnel" MacLean, Harold "Red" Howatt, and the MacLennan brothers, Don "Sneakers" and George, at Prince of Wales, Joe Cullen and Earl Smith with the Navy team, and Walter "Windy" LePage, Earl Nicholson and Irv MacKinnon of Ray's Millionaires. The Island League was complemented by intercollegiate play and by provincial juvenile playdowns, which heralded such future stars as Jack MacAndrew and Charlie Hine of Charlottetown and Bill Stewart of Summerside. With a core of highly talented players competing in organized leagues, basket-ball attracted a collection of competent coaches (Earl Nicholson and Walter Goss), officials (Wallie Scantlebury), and a growing number of fans that helped establish the game of basketball as a highly competitive, entertaining sport within the sport system of the province.

Men's softball experienced a revival, similar to that of basketball, following the War. After a well-publicized introduction of the game to Island sport fans during the mid-30s, the sport was inactive during the War, with the exception of play by military personnel. However, during the postwar period and into the early 1950s, the game regained its lustre, with players and fans from both urban and rural communities attracted to the fast-paced game. Leagues were organized in Summerside and Charlottetown, with provincial champions declared and Island teams vying for Maritime honours. It was the pitching wizardry of Gordie Drillon in Charlottetown, and Ross Armstrong from the Air Force Base at St. Eleanor's, that changed the complexion of the game in a dramatic way. Drillon was an overpowering, left-handed pitcher, while Armstrong was the first pitcher in the province to use a windmill delivery,

The Sunshine Dairy softball team enjoy an end-of-season banquet hosted by team sponsor Percy Gay. The team was a perennial contender for both provincial and Maritime honours. Back, l-r: Gump Gillis (League representative), Louie Gallant, Charlie Ballem, Art Perry, Angie Carroll, Art Ballem, Ced Ballem; Front: Lennie Arsenault, Joe Gallant, Willie Dunn, Dick Carroll, Percy Gay, Tunie Moore, John Thistle, John Kelly (Coach). (DICK CARROLL COLLECTION)

giving him a repertoire of five pitches. When he combined his talent with that of catcher Layton "Laysh" Schurman, they formed a formidable battery. The calibre of play in Island softball during the period was exceptionally high, as the game attracted such outstanding athletes as Armstrong and Schurman, Angie and Dick Carroll, Willie Dunn, Mike Connolly, Art and Ced Ballem, Henry Hartinger, Duke McCallum, Bert Harvie, Sonny Stull, Wilf Shephard, Earl Smith, and Harold Leard. These players performed for teams such as the Basilica Youth Club, Sunshine Dairy, Summerside Pioneers, Barry's Lions, RCAF Flyers, Bedeque, and the North End Bombers. The widespread interest and competitive achievements of men's softball during the postwar era was a success story for the sport; one that elevated the game to a prominent position within the provincial sport system.

The Provincial Department of Physical Fitness played an important role in promoting sport in the public school system and throughout rural communities during the late 1940s and the 1950s. With the exception of the Provincial Ice Sports that had been organized shortly after the opening of the Forum in 1930, interscholastic sport was pretty much the domain of schools in Charlottetown and Summerside. The achievement of Tignish High School in winning the Provincial Interscholastic Hockey Championship in 1947 changed that perception. Tignish, with a record of six wins and no losses against western schools,

Summerside Academy Hockey Team, 1945–1946. Interscholastic hockey became well-established during the late 1940s with teams representing all major high schools in the province. Back, l-r: Dave Lidstone (Coach), George Walker (Assistant Coach); Middle: Neil MacLeod, Ivan Stright, Stanley Deighan, Don MacNeill, Garth Gay, Howard MacFarlane, Allan Lecky; Front: Gordon MacKay, Layton Schurman, D. R. Morrison, Don Calbeck, Lowel Heustis, Alan Stewart. (CIVIC STADIUM COLLECTION)

travelled to the Charlottetown Forum on March 26 to engage West Kent, victors over Queen Square and Souris. In a well-played game, Tignish outlasted the City School 4–3, with Clifford Bernard scoring the winning goal with less than two minutes to play in the third period. Bernard was an outstanding young hockey talent who later played for St. Dunstan's University, Summerside Aces, and Alberton Regals. Bernard remembers the excitement that prevailed in his hometown following the victory, giving much of the credit to the coaching of Father Emmett McInnis. Bernard remembers fondly the many hours he and his teammates spent shovelling snow off the ice of the open-air rink located behind the Post Office on Church Street, only to have an overnight snowfall cover the surface once again.

During the late 1940s and 1950s there was a groundswell of interest in hockey across Prince Edward Island. The mania was evident at all

West Kent School, PEI Interscholastic Hockey Champions, 1945–1946. Interschool hockey was highly competitive following the Second World War, with strong teams existing at high schools throughout the province. In 1945–1946, West Kent won the provincial championship with NHL star Gordie Drillon as coach, and led by Ralph "Skippy" Carver and Harold "Red" Howatt. Back (l-r): Gordie Drillon (coach), Billie Bevan, Lorne Howatt, Earl Carmody, Skippy Carver, Jack Brown, Ev Cutcliffe (Manager); Front: Elmer MacKenzie, Bloise Carter, "Red" Howatt, Garth Crockett, Billie MacGregor, Jackie Acorn. (HAROLD HOWATT COLLECTION)

West Kent School Girls Hockey Team, Provincial Interscholastic Champions, 1947. Back, l-r: Barbara Rupert, Phyllis Tait, Minnie MacKenzie, Mae MacDonald (coach), Claudette MacMillan, Carol Creelman, Joan Stewart, Phyllis Cutcliffe; Front: Jane Giddings, Shirley Whitlock, Libby Lewis, Elsie MacDonald, Joyce Irvine, Kay MacIntyre. (JOYCE ANDREW COLLECTION)

Tignish High School, Provincial Interscholastic Hockey Champions, 1946–1947. In capturing the Hawley Crockett Trophy, Tignish High School brought home one of the first provincial sport championships to their home town. Back, l-r: Lloyd McLeod, Father McInnis, Coach, Jimmy Baglole, Edward DesRoches, Reggie Arsenault, Kenneth McRae, Freddie Arsenault, Claude Callaghan, Charlie McInnis, Honorable "Joe" A. Bernard; Front: Henry Harper, Jimmy Kinch, Francis Richard, Benny Kinch, Don Pyke, Clifford Bernard, Earl McRae, Jr., Arnold Gavin, Valmore Arsenault. (GERALD KEOUGH COLLECTION)

Queen Square School Hockey Team, 1949–1950, Provincial Interscholastic Champions. Queen Square produced several outstanding hockey prospects from its well-organized sport program; notably Angie Carroll and Junior MacLoed. Back, l-r: Cecil Dowling (Coach), Doc Richard, Bob Kelly, Ralph Trainor, Charlie Ready, Alan "Junior" MacLeod, Cliff Gillis, Charlie MacDonald, Ted Mullins (Manager); Front: Bob Burke, Bob Trainor, Angie Carroll, Dick Carroll, Bill Duffy, Bill LeClair, Cy Burke. (DICK CARROLL COLLECTION)

The 1946–1947 roster of the Moncton Hawks included seven Islanders, Windy Steele, playing coach, Bucko Trainor, Mousie Dowling, Buck Whitlock, Bob Schurman, Cliff Jackson, and George Schurman as manager. The team advanced to the Allan Cup eastern finals before losing to the Hamilton Tigers. The exodus of senior players from the Island was due mainly to the absence of a senior league in the province. The situation contributed to the organization of the Islander Hockey Club in 1950. Back, l-r: George Schurman (Manager), Ian Fraser, George Bell, Roy "Buck" Whitlock, Cail Bastarache, Sammy McManus, — Leadbetter, Maurice Dowling, Frank Taylor, trainer; Front: Clarence Steele (Playing coach), Gene Poirier, Mike Demchuk, Bob Schurman, Hughie McDonald, Donald Charlton, Cliff Jackson, Weston "Bucko" Trainor.

(RON LEGERE COLLECTION)

levels of the sport, with teams/leagues organized in even the most sparsely populated communities of the province. The Grand River Cardinals, Nine Mile Creek Bulldogs, Lennox Island Micmacs, Little Sands, Cape Traverse Rovers, and others spoke to the popularity of the game. As interest in rural hockey continued unabated, there was renewed interest in senior men's competition. Following the highly successful city league format, there was a movement of the best hockey talent in the province to the Maritime Big Four League. Nick Nicolle signed with the Saint John Beavers and no less than six Islanders were on the roster of the 1946–1947 Moncton Hawks. They included Windy Steele as playing coach, Bucko Trainor, Mousie Dowling, Buck Whitlock, Bob Schurman, Cliff Jackson, and George Schurman as manager.

As Island hockey talent performed with excellence in the Big Four League, there was a clamour for the return of senior hockey to Char-

Clarence "Windy" Steele burst unto the hockey scene in 1934 as a member of the Charlottetown Junior Abbies, Memorial Cup Eastern finalist. His outstanding career was highlighted by stints with the Baltimore Orioles, the Boston Bruins farm club, the Hershey Bears, the Providence Reds, and the Pittsburgh Hornets. In 1946–1947 he was the playing coach of the Moncton Hawks and led the team to the Eastern Allan Cup finals. (RON LEGER COLLECTION)

Wes "Bucko" Trainor's hockey career spanned sixteen years, from 1937–1938, with the Charlottetown Junior Abbies, to 1955–1956, with the Grand Falls Andcos. His aggressive style of play caught the attention of the New York Rangers and he was promoted to the NHL Club during the 1948–1949 season. He returned to Charlottetown for the 1950–1951 season where he starred with the newly formed Islanders team in the Maritime Big Five League. (RON LEGER COLLECTION)

lottetown. The response of hockey officials in the city was the formation of the Islanders Hockey Club, headed by Tom Rogers. The club engaged flamboyant Erwin "Murph" Chamberlain as coach, and with great expectations entered the Maritime Big Four League on July 30, 1950. While the team performed well on the ice and proved popular with fans, reminiscent of the Abbies of the early 1930s, the financial viability of the club could not be sustained. The team, after many exciting games in front of loyal fans at the Charlottetown Forum, withdrew its franchise in the Big Five League after the 1954–1955 season. Even as senior men's hockey was once again in limbo, the overall place of the game was firmly implanted in the sport/social culture of the Island.

The role of Brigadier-General W. W. Bill Reid was paramount in restructuring the fragile sport delivery system of the province following the Second World War. While he perpetuated the involvement of the Abegweit Club in the system, and capitalized on the time-honoured name "Abegweits," it was clear that he was committed to the autonomous sport governing system for the governance of amateur sport in the province. In 1947, he oversaw the formation of the Maritime Amateur Athletic Union, and was elected the first president of the new organization. It is notable that S. F. Sammy Doyle, a staunch supporter of the Abegweit Association for many years, was named the Island's representative on the executive, with Major A. W. Rogers appointed secretary-treasurer. In spite of the best intentions of Reid, Doyle, and other sport administrators, the Abegweit AAA, under the presidency of Bill Ledwell, held its last annual meeting in the fall of 1954. While remnants of the venerable sport club remained visible, notably in baseball, rugby, and track and field, the transition of the sport delivery system in the province from multi-sport club to self-governing provincial/ Maritime sport organization was now complete. The immediate consequence was the ever-increasing role of government in the delivery of sport services to the citizens of the province.

With the various components of the sport delivery system firmly entrenched across the province by 1950, factors beyond our shores began exerting major influences with social and political ramifications. It was an era of unprecedented change, featuring a decisive shift in population from rural to urban settings, lifestyle changes, greatly improved technology and communications, especially television, and the realization that the Cold War had projected sport to the unaccustomed place as a political and ideological commodity.

While the local community remained the focal point of the system, where the true value of sport resided, organized sport was becoming a tool for the promotion and profiling of the political systems of major world powers. The decade of the 1950s would witness an escalation of such activity, with elite sport as the main trumpet for political propaganda.

Roy "Buck" Whitlock is considered to be the most prolific goal scorer in Island hockey history. He led the Maritime senior loop in scoring twice, in 1949 and 1950, as a member of the Saint John Beavers, and followed with three scoring titles as a member of the Charlottetown Islanders. The "Old Lamp-lighter" had an adept touch when it came to scoring goals. Whitlock was one of the most popular athletes in the province during the post-World War II era, starring in both hockey and baseball. He overcame serious war injuries to achieve "excellence" in sport in his native province. (*THE GUARDIAN*, MARCH 10, 1953)

Conclusion

When, from the vantage point of 1950, one looks back over a hundred years of sport development on Prince Edward Island, the dominant feeling is one of triumph. On April 9, 1850, twenty-four young men had come together to organize the Charlottetown Cricket Club, the first formally organized sport club in the province. From that moment in our history, sport had evolved across the Island until, one hundred years later, it was the most pervasive social/cultural expression in which Islanders engaged.

During the early years, the system reflected the "British influence," a transfer of culture, with the formation of urban sport clubs, most notably cricket, sleighing, rifle, and lawn tennis. Inherent in the "Club" system was the accommodation of the social and professional elite of the community, a catering to the personal/social needs of the membership. Such a system deprived members of the middle and working classes access to meaningful participation in physical recreation and organized sport. While the system was unbalanced, the leadership and organizational skills of the urban sport clubs were critical in the organization of sport as a distinctive entity within the social/cultural fibre of the community. The emerging sport system found expression during annual visits to the province by the Royal Navy, provincial and inter-provincial competition, and the generation of community pride in the achievement of Island athletes.

During the decades of the 1880s–1890s, there was a groundswell of participation in sport by members of the middle and working classes of society, which fostered new games, new leadership, and an infectious community involvement. Inter-community rivalry, competition, and winning gained importance as trains, ferries, bicycles, and other means of conveyance created a mobile society. By 1900, the citizenry of the province had access to a wide range of sport opportunities that later would constitute the basics of the province's current sport delivery system. Rugby, lawn tennis, cricket, cycling, horse racing, track and field, hockey, baseball, gun club, curling, bowling, boxing, and yachting — their presence reflected a monumental development of organized sport on Prince Edward Island during the late 1880s and the 1890s.

Characteristic of the era was the excitement generated by fans and spectators, who elevated athletes to the status of heroes, and acclaimed fair play and sportsmanship. Leadership was paramount in structuring a sport system that could accommodate the overwhelming response of the populace to physical recreation activities and organized sport. Only the outbreak of the Great War disrupted sports' momentum. In the aftermath of the War, sport was rejuvenated, as athletes and fans returned to sport venues across the province, and achieved outstanding success. The achievement led all the way to the Olympic Games of 1924. The 1930s brought a different set of circumstances, as the debilitating effects of the Great Depression reduced the level of sport activity across the Island. The affluence and optimism of the 1920s was replaced by a sombre mood that only occasionally was brightened by the achievements of Island athletes. During this period, the sport delivery system relied to a considerable extent on semi-private sport clubs and entrepreneurial initiatives to sustain the profile of sport in the community.

When war once again broke out in Europe in 1939, athletes, both men and women, responded to the call to defend freedom and country. In some ways, the conflict altered temporarily the way sport was perceived, with servicemen highly visible in communities across the province. Rather than being a purely competitive experience, other qualities of sport became important to the overall mood of the citizenry. Service personnel played with civilians, leadership skills as opposed to athletic skills were emphasized, and there was an opportunity for respite, a diversion from anxiety, through participation in sport. As soldiers returned home, sport demonstrated its resilience and the postwar era saw a return to its more characteristic competitive expression. The latter years of the 1940s witnessed a massive involvement in physical recreation and competitive sport that permeated every aspect of the sport delivery system.

Over the years, sport has left an indelible impression on the lives of Island people. With its rich history, reflected through athletic excellence, community involvement, and pride of place, we have an inheritance of social and cultural expressions that contribute to our quality of life. It is a legacy that was carefully nurtured by men and women of earlier years, who recognized the true value of sport as an integral part of Island society.

Evelyn Henry, overcoming the Northumberland Strait in 1951.
(EVELYN (HENRY) BROWN COLLECTION)

Barb McNeill, conquering the English Channel in 1989.
(BARBARA McNEILL COLLECTION)

Epilogue

At different times and in different places, during the history of sport of our province, two athletes stood and gazed at a distant headland. What stood between each of them and the achievement of a personal (athletic) goal was the conquest of the body of water that stretched out before them. It was a daunting task, one for which they had diligently prepared. For Evelyn (Henry) Brown, it was the expansive water of the Northumberland Strait that beckoned her, that body of water that gave the Island its distinct identity. Up to July 15, 1951, it had never been conquered and Evelyn Henry felt that, "swimming towards the Island," she could do it. For Barb McNeill, it was the treacherous water of the English Channel that challenged her and her victory came on August 24, 1989 after great persistence and determination.

What our two marathon swimmers symbolize for our Island's athletes is that great moments in sport are not always achieved in front of the "cheering crowd" or for the adoration of loyal fans. Rather, they are as likely to be experienced with family and friends, in the solitude of sport, where achievement and excellence are first nurtured.

References

CHAPTER 1

1. For more information on the early history of Prince Edward Island refer to *Canada's Smallest Province*, Francis W. P. Bolger, Ed. (Charlottetown: PEI Centennial Commission, 1973), Chapters 1, 2, and 3.
2. Finley Martin, *A View From the Bridge* (Montague, PEI: Town of Montague, 1984).
3. S. F. Wise, *Sport and Class Values in Old Ontario and Quebec*, Sports in Canada Historical Readings (Copp Clark Pitman Ltd., 1989).
4. Robert Allan Rankin, *Down at the Shore: A History of Summerside, Prince Edward Island (1752–1945)* (Charlottetown: Prince Edward Island Heritage Foundation, 1980).
5. *Vindicator*, Sept. 21, 1864.
6. Alice Green, *Footprints on the Sands of Time: A History of Alberton* (Summerside: The Alberton Historical Group, 1980).
7. Adele Townshend, *Ten Farms Become a Town: A History of Souris, Prince Edward Island, 1700–1920*.
8. Don Morrow, "Montreal: The Cradle of Organized Sport," in *A Concise History of Sport in Canada* (Toronto: Oxford University Press, 1989).
9. Brian Flood, *Saint John: A Sporting Tradition, 1785-1985* (Neptune Publishing Company Ltd. (Canada), 1961).
10. Don Morrow, *Baseball: A Concise History of Sport in Canada* (Toronto: Oxford University Press, 1989).
11. For more on Henry Oxley, see article by Michael A. O'Grady in *The Island Magazine*, Number 37 (Charlottetown: PEI Museum and Heritage Foundation, 1995).

CHAPTER 2

12. Frank G. Menke, *The Encyclopedia of Sport*, 3rd Edition (A. S. Barnes & Company, Inc., 1963).

13. Leith Brecken, A. A. Bartlett, H. J. Cundall, and Mr. & Mrs. Quirk are names that are associated with the early activity of the Fitzroy Club.

CHAPTER 3

14. John J. Rowan, *The Emigrant and Sportsman in Canada* (London: Edward Stanford, 55, Charing Cross, S.W., 1876).
15. Frank G. Menke, *The Encyclopedia of Sports* (New York: A. S. Barnes and Company, 1963); Arthur Vernon, *The History and Romance of the Horse* (Garden City, New York: Halcyon House, 1941).
16. *Charlottetown Herald*, September 30, 1891. Tracks not mentioned in text that operated prior to the First World War include Cymbria, Upton Park, Montague, Riverside at Vernon, Kinkora, Primrose Park, Tyron Driving Park, Garfield, Hermitage, Pisquid Lake, Johnston's River, and St. Peters.

CHAPTER 4

17. Only during the period of the late 1960s and early 1970s was there a comparable development of sport across the province. During this latter period, with the infusion of human, financial, and physical resources from the federal and provincial governments, the Canada Games, provincial sport federations, and professional staff contributed to a major sport development initiative across Canada.
18. Electric Light meets, with a start time of 8:00 P.M., were popular with athletes and fans in Halifax, Charlottetown, and other major urban centres. The late start for competition was undoubtedly intended to accommodate attendance by members of the working class, both rural and urban.
19. During the period, the Charlottetown Cricket Club, the first sport club to organize in the province (1850) and a major contributor to the development of amateur sport for fifty years, was experiencing a decline.
20. The names of Dr. Edward Blanchard, Rowan Fitzgerald, William Hobkirk, Alexander Warburton, Francis Haszard, George MacLeod, and others reflected the professional and business elite of the community.
21. Don Morrow, *A Concise History of Sport in Canada* (Toronto: Oxford University Press, 1989).
22. Communities with organized teams during the 1890s included Pisquid, Peakes Station, Tracadie, Baldwins Rd., Souris, Roseneath, Mt. Stewart, Georgetown, St. Peters, and Head of Hillsborough. In Charlottetown teams were the Harbour Lights, Diamonds, Excelsiors, Stars, SDC, PWC, Mohawks, and Sundowners. Later the Local Nines, Unions, Abegweits, and Victorias formed in Charlottetown and Stanhope, Darnley, Malpeque, and Kensington in rural Queen's County communities.
23. As quoted in Edwin C. Guillet, *Pioneer Days in Upper Canada* (Toronto: University of Toronto Press, 1970), pp. 208–9.

CHAPTER 5

24. The score of 3½ apparently relates to an incident during the game when the wooden puck hit the goal post and broke in two, half of the puck going into the net. A loud voice from the crowd yelled, "Give them half a goal." It was a logical resolution to the dilemma.

CHAPTER 6

25. McMillan served as deputy minister of public works for the provincial government from 1900 to 1947.
26. The previous year the Wanderers had defeated Ireland to claim the World Football (rugby) Championship.

27. Several months after the Olympics, September 28, 1912, Halpenny defeated H. S. Badcock, the Olympic gold medal winner at Stockholm, in the pole vault event at the Canadian Track and Field Championships at Montreal.
28. A demonstration of the new game of basketball was staged at the Market Hall in Charlottetown on March 22, 1894, when the YMCA defeated Prince of Wales 8–3. Dr. H. D. Johnson and Prof. Shaw refereed the game.
29. Jack Dempsey reigned as heavyweight champion of the world from 1919 to 1926. In July 1919 he won the World Title from Jess Willard.
30. The Ancient Olympic games were held in Olympia, Greece, every four years from at least 776 BC until they were banned by Emperor Theodosicis in 393 AD. Originally there was only one race, a sprint, and the prize for the winner was an olive wreath. Later other races, boxing, and wrestling were held. (David Wallehinsky, *The Complete Book of the Olympics*, Penguin Books, 1988.)
31. On January 6, 1913, a new multi-sport club, the Connaughts, was organized in Charlottetown with Dr. R. J. Ledwell as president. Within a year, the Club had a membership of ninety and were competitive at the provincial level in hockey, rugby, and baseball.

CHAPTER 7

32. James Coyle, *Prince Edward Island Athletes in the Great War* (Charlottetown: Kings Printer, 1918).
33. The name Belvidere, spelt with an i, was used to designate a tract of land to the east of Charlottetown known as The Belvidere Woods. Following the transfer of the land to the Charlottetown Golf Club in 1923 the spelling was changed to "Belvedere."
34. The MacLean Trophy, emblematic of intermediate hockey supremacy in Prince County during the late 1920s, was a much-sought-after piece of silverware. The cup was donated by Alfred E. MacLean, Liberal MP for First Prince.

CHAPTER 8

35. Certain passages of this manuscript were previously published in *Abegweit Dynasty* (Charlottetown: The Prince Edward Island Museum and Heritage Foundation, 1986).

CHAPTER 9

36. Lambros Brothers were the local outlet for the Madison Manufacturing Company, a pool table manufacturer.
37. Refers to Island senior hockey, not the Big Four League of the early 1930s that included Saint John, Moncton, Halifax, and Charlottetown.
38. Charles Duerden, *Sulkies, Silks, Cups and Saucers* (Charlottetown: Ragweed Press, 1988).
39. In 2001, after 63 years as a member of the USTA, the Maritime Provinces' harness racing industry joined Standardbred Canada as the industry's new voice in Canada (*The Guardian*, April 28, 2001).
40. The Montreal Amateur Athletic Association, the first multi-sport club in Canada, was also "out of football" in 1932, a result of the change in governance of amateur sport in Canada.
41. Frank E. Menke, *The Encyclopedia of Sports*, Third Revised Edition (New York: A.S. Barnes and Company, 1963).
42. For a detailed account of the development of clay target shooting in the province, see Ron Atkinson's self-published book *Pull* (1983).

CHAPTER 10

43. "The Denver Connection" has a long-standing family and sport association with Prince Edward Island that originated with the exodus of hockey players from the Island to the Colorado city in 1935.

CHAPTER 11

44. Edward MacDonald, *If You're Stronghearted, Prince Edward Island in the Twentieth Century*. (Charlottetown: Prince Edward Island Museum and Heritage Foundation, 2000).
45. The sport of wrestling had been absent from the Island's entertainment fare for several decades and proved popular for large crowds of fans at the Sporting Club during the War.
46. There were eleven racing days on Prince Edward Island in 1943, six in Charlottetown, including a four-day Old Home Week, three meets in Summerside, and two in Montague. Matinee races were held in Alberton and Riverside.
47. The sport of horseshoe pitching was organized in Charlottetown during the war years on the initiative of Jack McCourt and Nels Whitlock. By 1944, the Brighton Horseshoe Club was formed, with Jack McCourt, Bill Murley, and Len Phillips demonstrating a high level of expertise at the game.
48. Earle Kennedy and Boyde Beck, "Bill Reid's War," in *The Island Magazine*, Volume 38 (Charlottetown:PEI Museum and Heritage Foundation).
49. The total number of Islanders who died in the conflict was unofficially listed at 563.

CHAPTER 12

50. Charlie Ryan played senior ball in the Valley and Dartmouth during the War. He was considered to be an excellent professional prospect. Vern Handrahan played in the H & D League for one season, 1958, when he signed a pro contract with the Milwaukee Braves.
51. Curran & Briggs was a paving, road-building business that established in Summerside in 1941. The company was awarded a lucrative contract for paving during the construction of CFB Summerside. Later the company concentrated on road-building.
52. Donald "Duck" MacLeod began his athletic career in the Charlottetown minor baseball program where he was considered to be one of the most talented athletes of his era. Early in his career he was the recipient of an athletic scholarship from Boston University, where his performance over three years earned him numerous awards for academic achievements, and as an all-star in baseball and hockey.
53. Charles Duerden, *Sulkies, Silks, Cups and Saucers.*(Charlottetown: Ragweed Press, 1988).
54. For an extensive research on the Belvedere Golf Links refer to Ron Atkinson's book, *A Treasure Called Belvedere* (Belvedere Golf Club, 2000).
55. A visit to his home in Charlottetown is an experience, as one witnesses his vast documentation of the history of Island sport. The walls are resplendent with pictures of Island boxers, starting with George "Old Chocolate" Godfrey of the 1880s, and moving through the years to the modern era.
56. During the 1960s and 1970s, a number of new sports were organized across the province due largely to the advent of the provincial and Canada Games. They included table tennis, lawn bowling, synchronized swimming, judo, racquet sports, ringette, cross-country skiing, cycling, gymnastics, field hockey, and cross-country running.

Index

About the Author — CHARLIE BALLEM

Heckbert Studio

Charlie Ballem gained his first experiences in sport/recreation while a student in the the one-room school at Mt. Albion. While organized sport during this period was basically non-existent, there were, nevertheless, opportunities for informal play and recreation activities. After Grade 8, he moved to Charlottetown, where he attended West Kent School and Prince of Wales College. During his high school years he became an active participant in a variety of team sports at PWC and the YMCA, an experience that firmly implanted his love for sport and its related social activities. His sports of choice included basketball, volleyball, softball, rugby, curling, and golf.

In 1957 he began teaching physical education at Summerside High School, a position he held for twelve years. In 1969 he accepted a position as provincial consultant in sport, physical education, and recreation with the Department of Education in Charlottetown. Later he became Executive Director of the PEI School Athletic Association and continued as a consultant in physical education and recreation.

In 1973–74 he completed post-graduate studies for a Master of Science degree at Dalhousie University. In 1978 he accepted a faculty position at Dalhousie as Head of the Recreation Division in the School of Recreation, Physical and Health Education. During his tenure at Dalhousie he was active as a teacher, sport administrator, and researcher. His initial research dealt with the history of sport on Prince Edward Island and in 1986 he published *Abegweit Dynasty: The Story of the Abegweit Amateur Athletic Association, 1899–1954*.

At present he holds the appointment of adjunct professor and continues his research on the history of sport on Prince Edward Island. He lives at Point Prim with his wife, Joyce.